You've Crossed The Borderline

The Correlation Between False Allegations, Parental Alienation & Cluster B

Ibraheem

https://www.youvecrossedtheborderline.com

ibraheem@youvecrossedtheborderline.com

admin@dueprocess.icu

© 2025 Ibraheem All rights reserved.

This book, including any derivative works, is protected under copyright law. No part of this book or its derivative works may be reproduced, distributed, or transmitted in any form or by any means, including photocopying, recording, or other electronic or mechanical methods, without the prior written permission of the copyright owner, except in the case of brief quotations embodied in critical reviews and certain other non-commercial uses permitted by copyright law.

Copyright Protected with www.protectmywork.com.
Reference Number: 27824010425S028
Reference Number: 27824100425S007
Reference Number: 27824290425S075
ISBN: 978-969-8092-30-6 hardcover
ISBN: 978-969-8092-29-0 paperback

For permission requests or inquiries about derivative works, write to the publisher, addressed "Attention: Permissions Coordinator," at the address below.

Copyright © 2025 by Ibraheem
Due Process
MYPUP DARTH VSVKYA
Pleasant's House, Pleasants Ln,
Saint Kevin's
D08 F54N
Dublin 8
Ireland
Copyright and Legal Notice
www.youvecrossedtheborderline.com
© Copyright 2025 - Ibraheem - All Rights Reserved

The contents of this book are protected by copyright law and may not be reproduced, duplicated, or transmitted in any form or by any means—whether electronic, mechanical, photocopying, recording or otherwise—without the express written permission of the author or the publisher.

Under no circumstances shall the author or the publisher be held liable for any damages, losses, or injuries—financial or otherwise—that may arise directly or indirectly from the use of the information contained within this book. By engaging with this material, you acknowledge and agree that you are solely responsible for your own choices, actions, and the outcomes that result from your engagement with the content. The names, characters, companies, locations, events, and situations that bear any similarity to real companies or individuals, whether living or deceased or to actual occurrences are entirely coincidental.

Certain names and identifying information have been altered to safeguard the privacy of individuals.

Important Legal Notice:

This book is strictly copyright-protected and is intended for personal use only. Unauthorized amendment, distribution, sale, quotation, or paraphrasing of any part of this work is strictly prohibited. Any infringement of these terms may result in legal action. Please respect the intellectual property rights of the creators by adhering to these guidelines. Thank you for your understanding and cooperation.

Contents

Introduction...1
Chapter 1
Borderlines don't make friends, they take hostages...............15
Dissociation...30
    Borderline Case Study Anonymous............................... 32
Borderline rage..33
Self-Sabotage...37
Paranoia..40
    Affective Startle...42
    Case Study Anonymous Metropolitan Police-Officer..... 46
Feelings...49
Posttraumatic Stress Disorder (PTSD)..................................53
Anxiety..56
Depression...58
Chapter 2
Rumination, Diagnosis & Treatment................................... 61
Rumination..61
Dr Selby & Thomas Joiner emotional cascade model............64
Diagnosis...71
    Borderline Case Study Anonymous............................... 76
Treatment... 78
    Borderline Case Study Anonymous............................... 85
Chapter 3
Mainstream Allegations & Proceedings................................ 87
Honorable mentions.. 99

Admonition..104
Chapter 4
Defamation & Demonization..107
    Case Study Aisha's Husband...109
    CICA Criminal Injuries Compensation Authority.........118
    The Silver Bullet Technique overview.........................120
    Case Study Anonymous..124
The presumption of guilt..127
    Case Study Glen.. 143
Chapter 5
Enter Narcissistic Personality Disorder..............................155
    Overview.. 156
    Narcissist sub-types.. 161
    Case Study Zhang... 166
Narcissistic supply... 172
Summary & Honorable mentions of
Narcissistic Personality Disorder.. 174
Chapter 6
Cluster B..179
Clusters of Personality Disorders in DSM-5-TR................. 180
Histrionic Personality Disorder...187
    Overview... 189
    Theodore Millon's six types of histrionic...................194
Antisocial Personality Disorder, AKA Sociopath................. 198
    Overview.. 200
    Case Study Anonymous...203
    Principle of pleasure.. 206
Borderline & Narcissistic personality disorders................208
    High conflict personality disorders continued...............209

Chapter 7
Hurt People, Hurt People...215
Codependency...219
    Case Study Aaron... 223
Narcissistic Abuse.. 225
Triangulation AKA Flying-Monkeys.............................. 229
    Case Study Simon...232
Flying Monkeys continued...233
The Lure-Manipulation, Hoovering & Love Bombing........ 240
    Case Study Anonymous...246
Gaslighting.. 249
Get out!... 253

Chapter 8
Inside the Psyche of the Parental Alienator...................... 259
    Case Study Anonymous...269
    More on Alienation..271
Deduction..281
    Case Study Denise... 286
    Parental Alienation continued.. 293
Other possible reasons or outcomes that contribute to Parental Alienation..295

Chapter 9
Defamation & Demonization II.. 301
Imposters.. 303
Ultimatums... 311
No comment!.. 322
    Case Study Anonymous...332

Chapter 10
The Easily-Exploitable, Family Court!............................349
    Case Study Anonymous...352

The Red Flag system..353
Questioning..360
 Case Study Richard... 362
 Court continued.. 375

Chapter 11
Being Innocent Is Not Enough; Don't Be Complacent..........381
Phoney Court Orders & The Culprits...382
 Case Study Chris... 388
 Cafcass New Parental Alienation Policy 2024............... 395
 Tendency for Interpersonal Victimhood........................ 396
 The Exit - More on coercive control............................. 397
 Case Study mother of Sianna...402
 Punishment cycle... 405

Chapter 12
Non-Compos Mentis..411
 Case Study Anonymous..413
 Non-Compos Mentis continued......................................415
 Case Study Dawn..423
 Non-Compos Mentis continued II.................................. 425
 Case Study Anonymous..428
 Forgiveness...430
 Case Study Derek... 433
 Content Creation; speak your truth................................437

Acknowledgements..441
About The Author... 444
 References... 489
 Collaborate with Due Process..504

Introduction

This writing is for the <u>Victims!</u>

Of abuse, harassment, unjust treatment and manipulation.

Who have now discovered that, indeed, the courts, police and even their own children! Can be weaponized against them in a dirty, unfair fight filled with falsehoods furthering coercive control.

The victims are men, women and young children who span from continent to continent. These victims have become broken people, inheriting an insurmountable weight to bear over their shoulders. This weight is precisely placed; the usage of sneaky tactics that everyday citizens cannot comprehend. The victims are left blindsided, bewildered and vilified. They are victims yet perceived in the courtrooms as abusers or criminals.

These are real victims of persecution, lawfare and parental alienation. They are also the victims of coercive controlling behaviour, intimidation and manipulation of all facets and forms.

This writing was initially intended for men as, at first thought, they were the more common target for this type of behaviour.

However, while researching for this book, I heard a plethora of stories from distressed women who have encountered the same fate. This callous behaviour is universal; the case studies used for this book will demonstrate that. Other teachings focus on a specific gender as the abuser in a narcissistic relationship, for example. Beyond, statistics that differ in areas, or a person's own life experience that may cloud the facts; the gender is not important here, the charactor traits and symptoms along with the known tendencies are, as these disorders or traits can be from any gender.

The case studies used in this book are 100% real-life stories, some pending cases currently in court and some historic cases dating back decades. The same elements of behaviour play out to this day.

The book you are about to mentally digest describes situations that are both highly compromising and complicated. Light is rarely, if ever, shed on these complex issues, which is why this reading is also a staple of awareness that needs examination.

To spark debate regarding legal pursuits that are categorically false. Furthermore, the angle of this book delves into the levels of attack used, with a focus and deep analysis of the courts and parental alienation. Coverage of what can be weaponized against a person and how it can be done.

There are plenty of titles in your favourite bookstore that examine the building blocks of Cluster B. These books stem from the perspective of what personality disorders are, reserving patience and how to hopefully validate these people if entangled in a relationship with them. Most books focus on the outlook and tolerance needed in catering to these individuals and respectfully brush over much of the attacking nature attributed to such disorders. The how-tos in terms of displaying validation towards the personality disorder sufferer or even the circumstances and events that may occur given the behaviour.

These titles about borderline or the rest of cluster B are coming from the space of abstract thinking in most regards. They may emphasise that the individual with the personality disorder didn't have their needs met, for example, and the results are excusable under such a context.

The following is a direct quote on the topic entitled Myth 1: people with BPD are manipulative and attention seeking - from the book (The Borderline Personality Disorder Survival Guide) by Alexander Chapman and Kim Gratz.

> "It may simply mean that they are desperately in need of some kind of attention from another human being, and they have not yet learned any other way of getting that need met. In fact, attention and regard from others is a basic human need. Of course, we all would rather get positive attention than negative attention; however, in some cases, that positive attention is not available. In these cases, people are generally willing to accept negative attention rather than no attention at all".
> (Chapman.A, Gratz. K,2007)

Approach such matters carefully to avoid causing offence or being viewed as marginalising. In terms of these disorders, yes, they are manipulative, and they execute it with perfection. There is no dancing around the topic, hoping not to step on an eggshell. In instances where positive attention is not available, and a person resorts to seeking negative attention, do not excuse the extremes these people are willing to go to.

Here's another quote from the same book, speaking of intense emotions regarding borderline personality disorder. Certainly, framing it nice and dandy, but its inaccurate emotional instability and intensity leaves the borderline scattered.

"Now, the downside here is that negative, uncomfortable emotions (such as sadness, guilt, shame) are experienced more strongly; however, the upside is that positive emotions (such as excitement, happiness, joy) are also experienced more intensely. Having intense emotions can be a plus in that it can make our lives feel fuller, richer, and more exciting."(Chapman. A, Gratz. K,2007)

Borderlines are more often than not affected by neuroticism and dysphoria. Framing the emotional intensity symptom as a strength of bliss and joy is not ethical; if this perspective rang true, it would be ideal, but it is not, and that's why it's a disorder. These people need our help, the truth of what they have, and how best to approach these aspects of life. Not thinking about ideals or how we wished it to be, if a borderline was reading that, they would think something is wrong with them even more, especially when a tantrum or rumination kicks in.

This book is more aligned with concrete thinking which has its basis in analysing the facts of what is in front or ahead of us. There is no way to verbalise such matters in a flowery approach when backed up against a wall in fear of what may happen next. This book focuses on these extremes, preparing the reader for the challenge ahead.

The discussions here are not for a person with very mild Cluster B or a few symptoms of borderline for example.

This writing is aimed at the severe sufferers of such disorders, the majority of which do not seek diagnosis. Analysis of the high conflict personality disorders.

Look at it this way: The other titles on the topic of borderline personality disorder address the starting point of a relationship, for example, how to make this better, how to validate feelings, and how to be mindful of the words used. Be calm, patient, and reserved; show resolve; and lastly, try to create boundaries.

This book is mid, end and beyond regarding a relationships, how to survive when one has not validated feelings, was misconstrued or was even clumsy with their words, some of which were taken out of context. Tolerance showing towards behaviours or walking on eggshells did not work. Lastly, boundaries? Boundaries were never an option to begin with; the mere suggestion of boundaries is gaslighting.

Here, this writing emphasises the victims of the outcomes created and manufactured entirely to create friction and drama.

Although some titles about borderline have gaslit ideas such as boundaries, it must be understood that there are elements of different perspectives. In some of these titles, for example, the authors are treating their patients, who they see on and off monthly and aren't relating in terms of a relationship with them. Some have mild symptoms that, although they highlight necessary challenges, are quite manageable. This title will emphasise the negative aspects, such as the correlation between false allegations and parental-alienation.

This work also delves into the legal system and ways in which it can be leveraged against a person through personal vendettas. The outdated and erroneous unfair structure simply does not work and separates loving parents from their children.

Some books on borderline or similar disorders struggle so much to come across as politically correct that their content is not correct. This is half-way psychology, and if we are going to discuss such matters, we tend to take a step backwards with this approach. Furthermore, it will be noted that No-Feelings were validated in the making of this book. These books that adopt this halfway approach are for commercial publications, which is why they need to cater to as much of an audience as possible.

The previous books on the topic of personality disorders focus more on trying to validate or love your partner unconditionally with support for you and them. This book is for the people who failed in that regard. This writing is for when the validation did not work or the patience and love went nowhere fast. This will be the criteria of what ramifications will follow from such situations and conditions highlighting some of the suffering caused.

The better types of psychology books are made with-out regard for an audience, focusing merely on dissecting the disorders to extract results or some understanding. Not every commercial-style book on such matters promotes such a diluted view; some have been inspirational and great reads.

I have read so many of these borderline titles that at least one or two books acted similar to prophecy regarding my own life. I cannot remember the exact titles or authors, but I will undoubtedly come across these books again soon. A borderline book I happened to read two years ago successfully predicted outcomes that would come to pass in my own life, which left me stunned.

Inconceivable at the time, I remember swiping my phone and stumbling upon an old picture or two I took of an informative part of a page from books about BPD. These images showed paragraphs from absorbing parts of chapters dated mid-2023, which began an eerie foreboding as it spoke directly of the court predicament I am currently in. At the time of reading, however, I was just in a chaotic relationship trying desperately to work with the disorders of Borderline and Narcissism, respectively.

This reading you are about to embark on will focus on Cluster B and its correlation with false allegations and parental alienation—it zeros in on the attacks specifically and the victims of these attacks.

The following chapters explore several psychological issues, mainly aspects of personality disorders such as the aforementioned borderline personality disorder (BPD). Not solely but exclusively at times, and that's not to demonise this group in any way, as we should be compassionate and loving unconditionally to all disorders. What is demonised here, however, are behaviours such as abuse or manipulation of not only partners and loved ones but also the courts, and lastly, false allegations and parental alienation. Cluster B will be the focus of debate with analysis on Borderline, Narcissistic, Histrionic and Antisocial personality disorders. Discussions on each-and-every attack method or manipulation strategy. This teaching pivots then into the arena of the exploitable courts. Emphasis is shown towards false allegations and parental alienation.

Whether or not a person has one of these disorders, should they undertake these manipulative actions, they will be spoken about in this writing. Not every person who engages in these behaviours is classed explicitly as Cluster B, but they do share a healthy dose of narcissism at the least.

These attacks exact revenge and ruin onto another; taking everything from their targets, such as possessions, property, life savings and children, among other things. Other honourable mentions are dignity and reputation, coupled with any other possible ways and means to hurt, injure, or destroy their victim.

We know what schizophrenia does to a person; it causes uncontrolled voices and may get a person to listen and act out on these voices. We also see the extent of remorse and empathy, or lack thereof, a psychopath exhibits after doing some deplorable act. We know how out of touch with reality a person can be if they happen to have psychosis.

We know the consequences of self-sabotage a person would demonstrate if they had eating disorders or how obsessive a person can be with obsessive-compulsive disorder. It is hard even to comprehend how in the dumps a person would be if they have all the hallmarks of severe depression or anxiety disorders. Just to name a few, and so on, you get the point. What we don't do too often is dig into personality disorders, specifically cluster B.

If you share an interest in psychology and mental health, this book would be tailored to you.

This writing is full of key information that delves into the psyche of an individual who has inherited such conditions. With a keen interest regarding the outcomes or effects on the target's lives not usually spoken about. Examination of the habitual behaviours and the known aspects of such personality disorders or the character traits involved that lead to such persecution of another.

So, with most of the clarification out of the way, enjoy the following chapters, whether you're looking for a casual read, a change in genre, or even research purposes.

If you're here for any other reason however? An educated guess would spring to mind;

You've <u>Crossed The Borderline</u>

Coming Soon

Due Process Exonerations Project title TBA

Narcissistic Abuse Recovery Project title TBA

You've Crossed the Borderline The Second Edition TBA

Children's Book Series title TBA projected 2025/2026

Have you or a loved one faced the exploitable-family-court ?

Via false allegations and parental alienation,

Tell us about your losses. Register your story at www.youvecrossedtheborderline.com

"its sufferers despised and even feared. Perhaps leprosy or, syphilis or AIDS fits this category. Borderline personality disorder (BPD) is such an illness.

In fact, it has been called the "leprosy of mental-illnesses" and the disorder with "surplus stigma." It may actually be the most misunderstood psychiatric disorder of our age."

(Gundeson, J, G.Hoffman, P, D.2016)

Chapter 1

Borderlines don't make friends; They take hostages

Borderline Personality Disorder (BPD) is grouped within Cluster B, along with histrionic, antisocial and narcissistic personality disorders. These are the different personality types within this cluster, which will be discussed at times, referring to each and or multiple disorders using the term personality-types. One of the hallmark symptoms of Borderline Personality Disorder is relationship difficulties; the symptoms, however, reinforce this aspect. This creates tumultuous and unstable relationships. Everything is in terms of extremes; emotions, mood swings, etc, all stem from extreme highs and lows.

They may idealise their partners one moment and devalue them the next. Quite similar to narcissistic personalities, supply and discard abuse cycles. This reaction is termed devaluing and idealisation. Or an aspect of splitting; polarizing views and feelings about others, for example-I hate you' don't leave me; is a book, amply titled regarding borderline splitting. This behaviour erodes relationships, leading to frequent conflicts and misunderstandings. This pattern of intense and unstable relationships contributes immensely to feelings of loneliness and rejection.

Harbouring inadequate feelings or fears of abandonment as a result. The sudden shift of opinions about others demonstrates all good or all bad thinking. In the mind of the borderline, these people may be decent and loving one minute but could switch abruptly to vile or putrid.

Their clinginess can confuse or drive others away, and when left alone, they can become irritable and lonely. They are impacted heavily through relationships and tend to ruin relations. They destroy their relationships; even with their significant other, whom they don't want to leave in the first place.

> "Borderlines create the vicious circles they fear most. They become angry and drive the relationship to the breaking point, then switch to a posture of helplessness and contrition, begging for reconciliation. If both parties are equally enmeshed, chaos and conflict become the soul of the relationship." (Millon, T, Grossman, S, Meagh, S, et al.l,2004)

A borderline personality disorder is shaped by factors such as heredity, strict parenting styles, environment or circumstances and possible trauma early-on. The majority of BPD statistics have reported experiencing traumatic life events; these usually are an abandonment at some point, abuse or a tough childhood.

Cluster B personality disorders, including BPD, can be comorbid with other personality disorders or mental disorders. Borderline personality disorder is the title more commonly used diagnostically. However, it is also known under the lesser-known title of emotionally unstable personality disorder (EUPD).

Borderline personality disorder symptoms or character traits are as follows;

- Self-sabotage, self-destructive or harming-behaviours
- Splitting / Idealization and Devaluation
- Intense feelings of emptiness & despair
- Suspicion or paranoia
- Disturbed patterns of perception and thinking
- Emotion overload or immaturity
- Irritable mood swings, explosive outbursts, anger
- Intense or unstable relationships
- Lack of empathy or inability to access empathy
- Motivated by a sense of real or imagined abandonment
- Extremely Impulsive and irrational behaviour
- Identity issues

Hyperemotional is the tendency to have dramatic or intense emotions. This will cause disruption and can bring about a false or artificial crisis. This symptom can result in an exaggerated response or contribute to impulsivity. Cluster B is known as a dramatic or erratic disorder.

Dramatization is a common thread within Cluster B. All of these personality disorders will emit drama in a variety of ways.

Drama is used to dismantle a person, breaking them apart. It can distract from inner feelings or be a boost to self-esteem; if you feel bad now, I feel good. This could start as I love you now, I hate you dynamic and then back again. It ends up as a trauma bond, a relationship with someone who causes great harm. Abuse is then repeated throughout the relationship, along with the tolerance reinforcing bad behaviour.

> "To live a life analogous to a soap opera is to live the life of a borderline personality.
>
> **Wrought with emotional ups and downs, these individuals are known to be unstable and especially angry."** (Millon, T, Grossman, S, Meagh, S, et al.,2004)

This identity disturbance is an unstable self-image. It ties into affective instability and abrupt shifts in moods. Identity disturbance or the lack of a mature sense of self-identity is common among Borderline Personality Disorder. Individuals with the disorder struggle to establish a stable sense of self. This then leads to feelings of emptiness and despair. They ruminate and even become confused about who they are in life. They may adopt different personas or roles regarding interactions or situations. Identity disturbance takes over, leading to a sense of fragmentation within the self. The lack of a cohesive self makes everything they pursue or their functionality with life issues seem more and more scattered.

Paranoia and dissociation are overlooked symptoms of Borderline Personality Disorder. Paranoid thoughts will foster a sense of suspicion in those close to them. Believing that others are out to get them or that they are the topic of conversation in a negative light, persecuted in some way. They may also experience dissociative thoughts or feelings that interfere with life's everyday challenges, inflating the intensity of the other symptoms.

Borderline Personality Disorder is complex, challenging and still, to this day, a very misunderstood mental health condition. Diagnosis issues plague this disorder, with the majority undiagnosed or unaware they have it.

"The answer to this paradox is to never let any relationship become too stable. Here, chaos is not just a pathological outcome but also an instrumental strategy.

When relationships become too normal or things are going too well, stability must be sabotaged.

By keeping others frustrated and exasperated, the borderline creates a soap opera that keeps each side of the dilemma just barely tolerable." (Millon, T, Grossman, S, Meagh, S, et al., 2004)

By increasing awareness of some of the symptoms and character traits of Borderline Personality Disorder, we can aim to interact with the disorder more efficiently. We can also suggest treatment options for those affected.

Impulsivity is the cornerstone of BPD, along with emotional disruption, such as explosive anger, jealousy, or insecurities about abandonment, which then usually lead to conflicts and misunderstandings that ultimately doom the future of a relationship. BPD categorically couples all of these strong emotional feelings, which if one of these feelings were isolated, it could easily be mistaken for normalcy as everybody in their life has felt these feelings somewhat.

Looking at some behavioural aspects alone cannot determine an accurate diagnosis of any personality disorder; it's when all the pieces are put together or when there's a clear repetition of delusion in the mix that can lead to a telltale sign. At least five symptoms out of the nine shown on the DSM-5 would give a clear inclination; also checking for any comorbidities if more symptoms not present on the list are evident.

Identity disturbance is another key symptom, which involves a heavy need for validation. Individuals with BPD may struggle with a sense of self and have difficulty establishing a stable and coherent identity. Feelings of despair coupled with dissociation can lead to a lack of clarity about the life situation. This can result in difficulties concerning making decisions and maintaining a consistent sense of self over time.

If the sense of self is misunderstood or even unknown at times, the person with a personality disorder may try to do whatever is necessary to feel something! No matter how negative it could be, at least it establishes a story of self that they then can identify with.

Identity determines how you see yourself, along with how other people in your life experience perceive you. It is all based on perception.

It is intertwined within the personality, constituting the characteristics and behaviour of a person's unique adjustment to life. A person who has a personality disorder has a perception overload, if you will; they are scattered in terms of self-identity. They have destructive behaviours innately that emerge from the personality disorder and try to make sense of it by creating the turmoil their identity can bond with and perhaps even reason out.

There is a systematic need or outcry to make things end up with the worst possible outcome, even if it's unlikely to end in such an outcome, demonstrating the delusions of the disorder.

Furthermore, emotional instability plays a key factor; if, for example, the borderline does not take mood medication, which is all too common, then situations that arise that would make any other person absent of the disorder feel bad; the borderline in that same situation would feel bad but multiplied immensely. It's unimaginable for them to see others not as bothered either going through similar situations or worse and maintaining composure through it, as maintaining composure is not an ability for the borderline.

Erratic behaviour is not thoroughly thought out, and there is no comprehension of what may occur regarding the consequences of their actions. Remember, the borderline is stunted from emotionally maturing. Trivial matters that would not require much thought, never mind much feelings, have the ability to deeply distress the borderline. "Borderlines are interpersonal tornadoes. Some men are even romantically drawn—at least for a while—to the drama such women create around them and the helplessness they often display. For decades, however, it has been an open secret that psychiatrists dislike dealing with borderline patients." (E Svoboda, 2013)

In no way should a person take anything on a personal level; we should understand this is a condition and these people need help, awareness and support throughout society. On the other hand, it is not an immoral notion to want to protect oneself from the dangerous attacks that can and do happen and will continue to occur because of this disorder or other similar conditions. Any person who trains you to tolerate abuse is wrong, whether they have a disorder or not.

Worst-case scenarios are a frequent commonality among this condition, and anybody who has had a life experience or relationship with an individual with BPD knows that there is no negotiating with these people. This is incredibly frustrating in predicaments where full cooperation between both parties is needed to better the situation. The lack of negotiation typically manifests through the legal system in one way or another.

These include but are not limited to family/home life or family court cases, as well as raising children. Also, acceptable behaviour is how people should and should not be treated. Coercive control is prevalent among BPD; coercive behaviour is not an acceptable treatment coming from any person. Control, manipulation and abuse should not be recognised as acceptable regardless of whether you have a condition or not.

Borderlines don't make friends; they take hostages. This saying encapsulates their coercive control and is a common way of life for a loved one trying to continue a relationship with a borderline in some manner.

Coercive behaviour is a honed skill that is fully utilised by abusers. It includes humiliation and intimidation, either assault or threats. Any form of abuse that encapsulates harm is used to punish or frighten the victim. Furthermore, this behaviour is done covertly in darkness and at an innate level; the abuser knows it is wrong.

Borderlines do have conscience up until the point of devaluation or when they discard. It's ingrained in us to have a sense of conscience, which is a moral sense of right and wrong. If a person lacks a conscience, then they lack healthy guilt and are willing to do bad things to us as long as nobody is watching.

> "If an NPD/BPD spouse can still manipulate you into submission, they may not seek to destroy you, provided you remain a reliable source of narcissistic supply.
>
> Conversely, if you're no longer easily manipulated, new supply is available, or the narcissist fears you will expose them, they'll escalate their aggression with the intent to annihilate."
>
> (Dr. T.J. Palmatier, 2024)

"BPD is often grouped with other mental health disorders such as depression or PTSD, for example. BPD is a construct that can account for the co-occurrence of a wide range of affective, impulsive, and cognitive symptoms in the same patient".(Paris, J.2007) There are four subtypes of Borderline personality disorder. The discouraged borderline is considered Avoidant, Dependent and Depressive. This is the more submissive type and can be humble or even loyal. They are easily influenced and marred by constant feelings of vulnerability. Hopelessness and depression will be the focal point of this type of borderline. Ruminating on worries and fears.

They feel powerless, which brings about certain anxiety. The Impulsive Borderline is considered more on the spectrum of Antisocial or Histrionic. This type is considered more fake and superficial, like the histrionic, with behaviours such as flirtatiousness or seduction. Their attitude can be distractible and frenetic, or they may display sudden mood changes like anger and irritability. They are also very depressive, fearing loss or showing signs of worry over the worst-case scenario in any given situation. This depression can lead to self-harm or even suicide.

The Petulant borderline feels unworthy or unloved one minute, and then the next can erupt into uncontrollable anger. This is the entitled borderline- very possessive, highly manipulative, and controlling. This behaviour then ends relationships prematurely. Their attitude is negativistic, and they can be easily slighted in social settings. They show signs of being disillusioned, stubbornly defiant and bitter. They are bad-tempered and sulky, motivated by pessimism.

The self-destructive Borderline is depressive and self-depleting. They display anger and often direct it inwards, tending to blame themselves.

All the signs of self-sabotage, such as self-harm, substance use, eating disorders, etc. Increasingly moody or agitated but are known to conform or be deferential. They want people to like them, trying to mask some of the default behaviours of the disorder. Easily upset, nervous, and display possible suicidal or self-harming tendencies.

This lack of conscience is among psychopaths, and it's definitely a grey area among borderlines and some of these other conditions. Psychology needs defining and would benefit further if adequately utilised. Mental health conditions are not getting addressed in this day and age. People in need of help are going undiscovered.

This is important for everyone involved—the children or partners in the relationship and especially the individuals who bear these mental health conditions. Exemplary care and recognition of these disorders would lower the numbers of abuse, suicide, marital problems or false incarceration. These are major issues that destroy lives and wreak havoc on society.

The news cycle will prove that every time, with the depravity of content regarding regular people's lives, the deaths, abuse and tragedies.

People with BPD target relationships specifically to create unsurmountable distress. If you are unsure if your loved one has BPD, some of the following symptoms will summarise the main key points that you can liken to their behavioural characteristics and may help you prevent or plan for future issues. Link any of the following symptoms with borderline impulsiveness: The tendency of acting without thinking; and life complications are promised.

DISSOCIATION

Dissociation is a defence mechanism that the brain uses to nullify or become numb to circumstances or surroundings. This could be recurring negative emotions or an effect of traumatic events. The person becomes disconnected from self, almost like they are observing themselves live life. Recollection issues will become a trait with the often gaps in memory or a selective memory. This is also the beginning of foggy or even delusional memories. In a study examining dissociation in 290 subjects with BPD, it was found that 75% in this group reported experiencing 23 out of 28 dissociative events up to 20% of the time, compared to 5% in the control group (Zanarini, R, Frankenburg, & Hennen, 2000)

Dissociation usually results in depersonalisation, which is the deep-seated perspective or feelings of unreal or lifeless surroundings. The person who encounters this frightening symptom remains in a state of confusion, deprived of sensation or self-awareness.

Another form is derealization, which is similar to a sort of dream-like state. Encompassed by feeling like the world around them is altered. Almost as if their surroundings and existence are distorted or multi-dimensional in some way.

These experiences are disorienting and quite intense and may be a motivator for a diagnosis. Dissociation is the disruption of consciousness or the normal aspects of it, this impedes the ability to function in daily life.

Dissociation is a way to escape or cope with stress, but it leaves the recipient feeling numb, like life is happening and they have no say in it. This dissociation could originate from unaddressed trauma that revisits through emotions or memories. This is where the person will ruminate and overly picture things in their mind, leading to dissociation. It can and often does lead to feelings of despair. There is a disconnection that occurs socially leading to more problems such as acceptance or validation.

Treatment involves therapy such as dialectical behaviour therapy (DBT) or trauma-focused therapy. Indeed, people with BPD sometimes careen through life as if they're driving a 350-horsepower car with no breaks; they often act on the spur of the moment. (A, Chapman, K, L, Gradz 2021)

Borderline Case Study Anonymous

I experience psychotic episodes from my bipolar disorder. I often become paranoid and think people are out to get me or have done horrible things to me. In those cases, yes, I've falsely accused people of these things. It's not an intentional thing, though.

I fully believe it's all real. I've even called the police on people multiple times because I think they're doing things to me, like poisoning my food and such. Also, when we split because of our BPD, we often wind up enraged because of our black-and-white thinking, so we may also accuse people of being a bad person or not caring because of being triggered by even just one minor transgression, which sometimes is just perceived but not true. Again, though, that's not intentional.

BORDERLINE RAGE

Intense anger is a common symptom of borderline personality disorder. Borderline rage, as it is referred to lately, is not normal anger. This anger engulfs any minor or normal interaction, resulting in the amply described walking on eggshells. This will be the most noticeable symptom, likely the first symptom that will be recognised. This and splitting will probably be one of the first recognisable symptoms.

This eruption of anger can be challenging to manage and understand. Like clockwork, the borderline often experiences overwhelming feelings of anger or rage. This then escalates quickly with outcomes of outbursts or aggressive behaviour. This intense anger can be triggered by various factors quite easily. including perceived rejection or the most common factor, which is feelings of abandonment. This anger comes sporadically, lasting for long periods without any great cause for such aggressive outbursts. Cooldown periods or a sense of calm will be nullified by the compulsion to erupt emotionally.

Frequent tantrums over trivial matters cause any company present to feel like they are walking on eggshells. The anger and the response to the anger can trigger more anger. Borderline Rage typically includes screaming, physical aggression, verbal threats, or even self-harming behaviours. This intensity of the emotional rage is unnerving and can be immature at times.

Borderlines have an inability to self-soothe following the experience of a negative emotion. It may seem as if you can do nothing right, and the borderline just targets you.

However, this could be the borderline trying to throw you off balance in life because they can't bear to see you leave or see you have things work out in your life. The deep triggers of borderline personality disorder are usually in the relationships department, possibly adopted through childhood.

Therefore, any delusional stimuli that they receive that make them question or envision unwanted circumstances can make them lash out. There is no stopping this behaviour; once it is triggered, the borderline is zoned out, and a tantrum ensues. This can be over trivial matters that don't make any sense, but to the person with BPD, it's an outlet to release some built-up aggression or anger that they have been fostering.

This behaviour is most noticeable when splitting occurs, which is the thinking of the borderline, which ultimately shifts their patterns of behaviour from one extreme to another. They could be joyous and bubbly one minute, unleashing turmoil on the unwitting victim the next. This splitting is the mismanagement or conflicting emotions that the borderline harbours.

It could be the person on the receiving end of the tantrum is difficult to manage or, all of a sudden, intolerable due to the splitting. Splitting is a term to describe the borderline's excessive behavioural shift due to their unique perception. It's thinking in terms of extremes, more commonly mentioned as black and white or all-or-nothing thinking.

> "Individuals with Borderline Personality Disorder have even been shown to interpret social acceptance as subterfuge or deception." (Whitbourne, S K,2018)

Intense anger; its duration and the build up to the anger can be reduced through dialectical behaviour therapy. This therapy can teach how to regulate emotions or destructive moods appropriately.

Through DBT, such benefits would be mindfulness, distress tolerance, emotion regulation, and interpersonal skills. For more on the treatment options, see the following chapter.

Therapy and anger management are not the only sources of treatment. Medication may also be prescribed to help on this journey. Antidepressants, mood stabilisers, and antipsychotic medications are often used to treat symptoms of Borderline personality disorder.

Borderlines want to make sense of this anger. They will attempt to observe their surroundings and create a narrative to fit the reasoning for the anger or tantrums. Forgetting that the behaviour itself is the cause, this displays a lack of accountability, but fundamentally, this is down to the borderline's lack of insight. This anger is a challenging symptom that requires immense patience and understanding.

This symptom, coupled with impulsivity, can be carnage. We should try wholeheartedly to demonstrate compassion and support to our loved ones with BPD. It can be easier if there is a diagnosis, hopefully, the discussions lead to seeking therapy or medication to mitigate the emotional outbursts.

SELF-SABOTAGE

Self-sabotaging behaviours are one of the most direct and serious of traits. The impulsive symptom, by default, ignores any consequences from actions. This sabotage can be directed inward on to themselves, outward towards another or both. These behaviours are anything destructive, such as engaging in risky sexual behaviours, self-harm and substance abuse.

People with borderline personality disorder are relentlessly complusive and emotionally withered. Once control is lost, either within their feelings, outer circumstances or over others, it is not uncommon for them to self-sabotage as a way to cope or to seek refuge from feelings of emptiness and loneliness.

Borderlines have a wound of abandonment, and this aspect systematically plays out throughout their relationships. Self-destructive behaviours are also a way to express to others their inner pain and turmoil. This behaviour could be a cry for help, a way to seek attention or to force validation from others. Or perhaps even a way to punish themselves for perceived failures; possibly caused by the behaviour that they cannot account for.

It can be a way of demanding immediate attention by any means. It is not uncommon for the borderline to manipulate in extremes, for example, to threaten to self-harm or commit suicide if a partner tries to leave the relationship. Maintaining control and a cycle of emotional abuse. Self-sabotage comes in many forms and is undefeatable once momentum is gained. This fundamental aspect of the condition is likely driven by impulsivity.

The life situation of the borderline can, at times, feel like a tug of war. These self-destructive behaviours can lead to extremes such as cutting or other forms of self-injury in some cases.

Life is complex, and the mismanagement of emotions or the inability to regulate them is what drives the individual to self-sabotage. It can be challenging to witness a loved one engaging in harmful behaviours, possibly even blaming others for the behaviour.

Any self-sabotaging behaviours should be addressed professionally, and the person should receive medical care immediately. There are high suicide rates with disorders like borderline personality disorder.

Medication is an expeditious fix and can prevent any impulsive negative behaviours that can cause harm.

PARANOIA

Frequent Paranoia or suspicious thinking can plague the borderline. This paranoia is a motivator for much of their reckless behaviour. It is characterised by intense feelings of mistrust and suspicion of others. This can then lead to an irrational fear towards other people in their life experience. If you are on their bad side, you will become a target. "However, it is of note that the quality of the cognitions thought to underlie the borderline's distortions may be particularly interpersonal in nature. Dysphoric cognitions uniquely associated with BPD compared to other personality disorders reflect themes of paranoia and being tortured or abused, among others."
(Zanarini,M.C,Frankenburg,F.R,DeLuca,C.J,1998)

People with BPD have unrealistic expectations and can over-exaggerate meanings and sentiments displayed by others. Also, they have difficulty distinguishing between reality and demonstrate distorted perceptions.

They might even jump to conclusions either in terms of allegations or perceptions; such as to believe that others are out to betray them. They do this without ever examining their erroneous perceptions to avoid being wrong about them. This can cause significant distress and impact their functionality in relationships or life choices.

"It has been hypothesized that the dysregulated emotional symptoms in BPD are a result of greater reactivity to emotional stimuli, and/or poorer regulation of these reactions" (Linehan, 1993)

The following chart and study are from the work of Antonia New, Larry Siever, Erin A Hazlett, Marianne Goodman and Harold W Koenigsberg. They conducted a study involving a group of borderline patients and a controlled healthy group. The study consists of measuring startle-eyeblink and fMRI (measurement of brain activity) while observing photographic images that vary in affective valence and are categorised as unpleasant, neutral, and pleasant. The BPD patients used in this study have no PTSD (post-traumatic stress disorder), but their reactions are noteworthy.

This study reflects on and delves into the defensive versus appetitive motivational systems, helping to display the stark differences between the two controlled groups. It also examines in-the-moment information intake and the activation of the fight-or-flight response. "Our view is that fundamental appetitive and defensive motivation systems evolved to mediate a complex array of adaptive behaviours that support the organism's drive to survive—defending against threat and securing resources." (Lang, P, Bradley, MM 2013)

Borderline patients also have an exaggerated startle response during scripts that have a theme of rejection and abandonment.

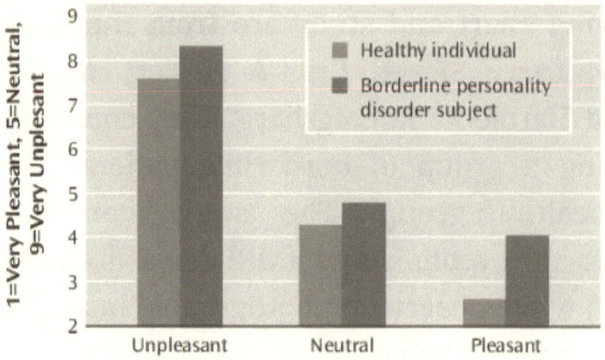

Quieting the Affective Storm of Borderline Personality Disorder – Scientific Figure on Research Gate 2009

The results of the study from the BPD patients found psychophysiological evidence of both affective startle and amygdala activity of highly exaggerated processing. Borderline patients rated unpleasant pictures as being more pleasant and pleasant pictures as being more unpleasant compared to the healthy control group.

The high sensitivity to emotional stimuli plays off with the impulsive nature of the borderline, which can lead to suspicion or paranoia. This research offers insight into the aversion to positive outcomes and the fixation of the negative ones—the innate attention allocation with an almost predictable negative response from the stimuli or outer perceived events.

Borderlines show an exaggerated startle response with feelings of unpleasantness over good pictures that could be good relations and positive life choices.

Affective startle can denote feelings and key motivators from a vision, which could be a life event or even imagined. This can cause a disturbance in impulsive control, exacerbating the paranoia in the borderline. This will result in the individual with the said condition targeting their perceived opponent with the assumption that they are out to get them.

Affective startle targets the amygdala, and these responses are much higher among BPD people, causing outbursts and unpleasant disgruntled behaviours. This then denotes a common tendency to misinterpret the intentions of others. For example, if the borderline can misinterpret a comment made or an innocent action as a deliberate attempt to undermine them in some way. They then react defensively, or harbour negative feelings as a result of the perceived comment or action. Paranoia can lead to behavior aggressive in nature in response to perceived-threats. Paranoia can also manifest as constant vigilance and hypervigilance (the-elevated state of constantly assessing potential threats around you).

This paranoia then keeps the recipient on edge, combing or scanning the environment for potential threats or dangers. This heightened state of arousal can be exhausting. It manifests the individual's struggles with their emotions and relationships. This shared quality with other disorders is difficult to treat and is anything but temporary.

Couple this with the lack of empathy or remorse, and they could target a person for their entire life span. Paranoia is one of the most overlooked and challenging symptoms of borderline personality disorder. A relatively innocent interaction can be misconstrued and can significantly impact the outcome of relations. This may seem mindless or silly, but to the individual with BPD, this is an indication of their false perception and worst-case scenario, which they like to indulge in.

If the borderline misinterprets something simple and non-related, they will vehemently believe their own perceptions over evidence or truth. It is challenging to relate or get the point across to the individual with BPD; matters such as making jokes or displaying a sense of humour are pretty costly.

Paranoia or diluted thoughts can bring out the impulsive nature of the borderline, followed up by personal vendettas, court cases or parental alienation. This can lead to dangerous forebodings driven entirely by speculation.

Irrationality is the borderline's friend; this toxic behaviour can have drastic effects on the person with BPD. Any close relative, relationship, or friend can be next, which is why maintaining these relations for long periods of time, they find quite challenging.

Case Study Anonymous

Metropolitan Police-Officer

I'm a partner of a police officer falsely accused by an ex-girlfriend. This happened at the time that he dumped her for cheating on him. She claimed domestic abuse at the time, and after that, he was immediately suspended. After an extensive 2-year long investigation, nothing has proceeded further and now they are using her as a witness for the claims she is making rather than a victim.

She's continuing to pervert the course of justice and engaging in systemic abuse by taking advantage of the failures in the system. Meanwhile, he's completely tanking his otherwise untarnished career of 11 years. He has not ever had a single complaint from anyone whatsoever during his time on the force. The whole thing is absolutely outrageous and stressful. His charge was made public even though it's only an accusation and not proven in a court of law.

I think the state of policing by The Met is in quite a state across the board, and they are using heavy-handedness against their own officers as a publicity stunt, in my view, to buy public opinion. It has only further highlighted systemic issues within the organisation.

In due course, this may be proven otherwise if they look at the lack of evidence outside of her "claims" that she saw what she did. Her motive is clear as she has changed her story repeatedly. She is using the justice system to continue to abuse him. She had no contention with him prior to being dumped for being caught cheating (red-handed).

She has had him arrested multiple times (and he has since successfully sued the force for wrongful arrest), so they have admitted to wrongdoing in the same case. It's an academically interesting case and an entertaining read that highlights how broken the very system that's meant to protect the public is.

How can she be a reliable witness if she has been an unreliable victim? His devices will also disprove many of her false claims, which have been seized and have still not been released, so why aren't the police using that?

It seems odd that they would have anything to gain from this; his life has already been destroyed for 2 years now. It's likely to affect his employment opportunities indefinitely going forward. The only time she had made a complaint was during their breakup when she was caught cheating, which then she had a clear motive. I am not from the UK, but he is a citizen, and he is based there. None of this makes any sense to me. It would not fly in the United States.

I'm on multiple forums now that are UK-based and it seems that just an accusation is enough for an arrest, and that is a very different standard of policing then what exists in the rest of the world. There needs to be evidence to corroborate those claims? And there is evidence directly contradicting her claims.

What is hard to understand and deal with is the perversion of facts of what has happened based on evidence versus just her point of view. That is a unique UK issue. What I'm trying to ascertain is the recourse available to address this.

A woman's accusation alone does not go far with corroborating evidence in the US system. I have friends here who are lawyers and judges and who will confirm this. An accusation will be investigated, but there is no arrest without evidence.

An arrest warrant has to be signed by a judge to be issued in the first place. However, in the UK, an arrest is not the same standard since an accusation is an arrest. A charge also does not need to have evidentiary material to proceed. Evidence in the UK is assessed in court, and by this point, it has already gone too far, especially with false accusations.

Perhaps the argument is that real victims are not believed at their word easily in the US since not all crime that is sexual in nature are able to be evidenced. However, the reverse of this is what we're seeing in the UK, where no evidence is needed at all to proceed. Looking really far into our legal system, you see a lot of people continuing domestic abuse through systemic structures that allow for easy manipulation.

It is shocking in the UK that a woman's word alone can cause a man to lose his job as well as his reputation with an arrest on record. The fact that the public is not upset about this or doing enough to change this is also shocking to me. The US system that is based on evidence is far superior. Now the argument can be made that evidence standards across different crimes need to be addressed, so I would agree it is not perfect.

However, someone's accusation and allegation does not result in a trial by public opinion. The police in the UK use mob mentality to effectively convict an innocent person in the media before they get evidence. That is a perversion by any standard. So how does one get justice when all the police are concerned about is not the evidence but rather looking like they're doing something about it which is a farce.

FEELINGS

Chronic feelings of emptiness are caused by the constant rumination of life's problems. Real or fictitious makes no difference to the borderline. It could be what's to come or how things went. It's dwelling on the lowest possible feelings; A focus or deep concentrating on that despair. It is being consumed by this repetition of negative emotion. This ubiquitous feeling of an inner void is debilitating while also triggering or compounding the negative behaviours, thoughts and emotions. The root cause of this despair is the focused attention on the negativity itself or the rumination; without any ability to function with it or process these feelings adequately. Coupled with some of the other comorbidities or symptoms such as impulsivity for example, only creates further problems. Life moves fast for every person, and we are all faced with specific dilemmas time and time again. This impulsivity impairs discernment, increasing the anxiety followed by feelings of emptiness.

> "A borderline personality disorder is essentially a dysregulated limbic system. Feelings are so big that they cannot be contained, and everything spills over, creating emotional messes that other people end up being victims too." (Jordan, K, 2023)

Individuals with borderline personality disorder report feeling like they give up, unworthy or in a hollow depressive state. This unceasing onslaught of emotion is present regardless of the results, achievements or how well things may be going. The difficulty explaining chronic emptiness can be frustrating for both the individual experiencing it and their loved ones. These feelings are linked to identity disturbance; and exist as uncontrollable experiences.

They are present not by choice but rather as a symptom of the underlying psychological struggles inherent with borderline personality disorder. Enduring these perpetual depressive states results in persistent dysfunctional relationships.

When people face difficulties forming connections with others; stages of isolation and detachment increase. Rumination and bouts of depressive episodes soon follow. This then exacerbates the feelings of despair, furthering the challenges that arise from the condition. Borderlines are known to be needy and dramatic, which can invoke or create trouble; this ultimately reflects how they feel.

Effective management of this severe depression requires a multifaceted approach. A combination of either therapy and medication maybe even some lifestyle changes.

Cognitive behavioural therapy serves as a tool to help negative thought patterns that contribute to depression. Medications such as antidepressants or mood stabilisers may also be prescribed to improve emotional symptoms.

The despair will remain even if the external life conditions are beneficial and good. By understanding that this is the catalyst for the outbursts or behaviour, we can concentrate on treatment options such as medication.

Medication can help if they voluntarily seek that path; Although the individual with BPD may discontinue use. Depending on the person, some can find treatments or medication an asset, and others see it as a loss of who they are. This factors in with their identity distortion or their idea of who they are. BPD is a complicated disorder; even the notion that they have a personality disorder is abhorrent to them. Depression lasts long periods with no glimpse of happiness; this can be difficult to process for any person. The person with borderline mismanages emotions or finds it impossible to accept or regulate them. It can be much harder for them concerning chronic feelings of despair.

This leads to anxiety, confusion and poor life choices. A sound support system and depression medication are crucial for dealing with negative feelings and unwarranted emotions. Mindfulness would also be a key practice as this could alleviate the heightened negativity these feelings create. This practice takes you out of the rumination of negativity and focuses your attention on the present moment. All worries and thoughts are trained to subside and become less significant. It acts as a shift in how we perceive what our conscious awareness is faced with, such as judgments.

We can go about life mentally labelling every aspect of it or attaching great expectations to it. Practicing mindfulness allows us to detach ourselves from the cycle of becoming trapped in fault-finding and worry.

It costs nothing and has numerous advantages, such as stress reduction. It acts as a brief meditation, if you will, bringing all of your attention into the present moment.

Meditation is another technique that could immensely help with calmness and clarity. There are so many different types of meditations, all unique and helpful. This doesn't have to be hours of meditating under a tree; it could be as brief as 15 or 20 minutes with instant results.

Post-Traumatic Stress Disorder (PTSD)

(PTSD) Post-traumatic stress disorder is a mental health condition developed through a traumatic life event or past incident. PTSD; alongside any given personality disorder, the symptoms become exacerbated, multiplying in strength. The co-existence of these disorders can cancel out any chance of treatment. Complications in life can be much more difficult to overcome, or the person may be unable to navigate through life's pressures.

The comorbidity between PTSD and BPD and how they can intersect throughout life complications is another challenge as the person is always posturing at a defensive-stance; At times they both share origins such as childhood trauma or a traumatic event.

Unfortunately for BPD, the cycle of pain or additional trauma can be a running theme due to the symptoms, such as emotional dysregulation and impulsivity, which are hallmarks of the disorder.

Unwanted flashbacks can haunt a person, ultimately aggravating symptoms or leading to depressive episodes. These Intrusive memories create a heightened emotional state or a reactivity in response to a trigger. These triggers then, are related to a traumatic event or any unwanted or unconscious trauma experienced. Visual (images), auditory (sounds), kinesthetic (touch and internal feelings), and olfactory (smells) all can create a trigger.

A trigger can represent that same threat from the past or repressed emotion in real-time. This can cause profound implications for anyone who has been through a traumatic event, bringing the event to the surface once more.

We then struggle to cope with these chaotic feelings as they don't seem to go away. This is all stored information in our subconscious mind, leading us to feel isolated with unwanted memories or emotions. Bottling up or suppressing emotions is detrimental as the emotion then gains more power and control.

This then brings difficulty in distinguishing between the past trauma and present reality, becoming disassociated in the process. These triggering events usually result in a heightened state of fear, panic and hypervigilance.

This can make it challenging for individuals to engage in therapy and other forms of treatment. They may struggle to trust others and fear re-experiencing trauma during the therapeutic process.

> "**PTSD is one of the most common co-occurring disorders among individuals with BPD, with comorbidity rates ranging from approximately 30% in community samples to 50% in clinical samples**" (Harned, M.S., Korslund, K.E. 2015)

The DSM-5 defines Borderline personality disorder as a "pattern of instability in interpersonal relationships, self-image, and affects, and marked impulsivity". Attention-deficit-hyperactivity-disorder-(ADHD), according to the DSM-5, is a neurodevelopmental disorder characterised by "a persistent-pattern of inattention and or hyperactivity impulsivity that interferes with functioning or-development" (APA, American Psychological Association 2013)

Anxiety

Anxiety is common amongst people in general; this reaction or symptom is also experienced by people with Borderline Personality Disorder. Anxiety is often described as an uneasiness or pervading worry. An ingrained fear demonstrated through panic overwhelms the person's ability to function. This anxiety has a strong emotional effect and happens in spontaneous times and situations. Situations such as social interactions or being in public settings. Social and societal pressures, childhood trauma, social exclusion or isolation and adverse life events can all lead to anxiety.

The stressors of life can be complicated to manage for anyone. These stressors result in exacerbating emotional dysregulation, which can be fierce and involve intense fluctuating emotions.

Additionally, the fear of abandonment, which is a core component of BPD, can heavily trigger the state of anxiety. The constant fear of being rejected, abandoned or discarded by loved ones is what devastates the borderline.

Even if it's improbable to occur, they almost go out of their way to make it happen before it happens to them. Borderlines are prone to rejection hypersensitivity, which engulfs their anxiety. It is characterised by the severe anxiety or negative emotions they feel before an anticipated rejection.

The emotion dysregulation model (Mennin DS,2004) posits that generalised anxiety disorder (GAD) is marked by experiencing emotions at quick succession, easily and with high intensity. There is also an inability to self-soothe following a negative experience or emotion.

Depression

Depression and Borderline Personality Disorder often go hand in hand, creating a harsh combination. People with BPD are inundated with extreme mood swings, impulsivity and feelings of emptiness, which contribute significantly to depressive symptoms. The constant fear of abandonment and unstable sense of self are significant factors that bother the borderline. One root cause of depression is rumination, which will be discussed thoroughly in the next section. Rumination is the continuous lingering or emotional revisiting of loss or failure that causes you to feel much worse about yourself.

This process stirs the pot of negative emotions and can come in many forms, from self-talk or dwelling on drama. The depressed person ruminates on one's downfalls and feels guilty about past events.

Adolf Stern felt that Borderline patients evidenced 10 major characteristics: narcissism, psychic bleeding, inordinate hypersensitivity, psychic rigidity, negative therapeutic reactions, deeply embedded feelings of inferiority, masochism, somatic anxiety or insecurity, the use of projective mechanisms, and the tendency to experience difficulty in reality testing, especially in interpersonal settings. (Stern, A., 1938)

Adolf Stern was a psychiatrist and psychoanalyst; he coined the term Borderline and is credited with the first formal account of borderline personality. The cycle created by intense emotional distress and feelings of worthlessness can be overwhelming and difficult to break away from; especially with an inability to regulate emotions once they arise.

Medication can help improve emotional instability and address underlying issues that lead to levels of despair. Support and a routine of activity can help manage some of the depressive symptoms of BPD.

Rumination contributes heavily to depression, which will be discussed in detail next. The misinterpretation of how their behaviour affects those close to them will cause relationship problems. They believe they are being abandoned again and that there is something significantly wrong with them. Without adequately addressing the behaviour that drives people away. Regarding relations with significant people they want around them; when these relations are no more, depression settles in.

Levine, Hood and Marziali found that borderlines differed from normal subjects on four measures of processing emotional information, suggesting that borderlines have more limited capacities for processing emotional information related to self and others, recognizing facial expressions of emotion, and integrating conflicting or ambiguous emotional states.

In addition, tasks that require effortful processing of stimuli may present a unique challenge to individuals with borderline personality disorder.

(Levine,D,Marziali,E,Hood,J.1997) (Lenzenweger,M.F,Clarkin,J.F,Fertuck,E.A,Et,AL2004)

Chapter 2
Rumination, Diagnosis & Treatment

Rumination

Rumination is the behaviour of passively thinking about one's mood or situation with an intentional inward examination of the feelings. It is deliberately thinking about a situation to understand it from every angle, creating uncontrollable thoughts. This is the root cause for some of the preceding criteria, such as despair, anger, anxiety or self-destructive behaviour. Rumination is a major aspect of depression and helps reinforce and prolong it. The repetitive thinking worsens existing conditions, focusing primarily on pessimism and cognitive distortions. This negative indulgence is a cycle that can become fixated on for long periods of a person's life.

Rumination is a term used to describe the engagement of consistent negative thought patterns preceding the feelings.

A habitual construct loops these destructive thoughts without any end or completion. This act of stirring up unwanted negative emotions would cause the participant to become drained and depressed.

It doesn't have to be factual. It could be perceived; it's the focus of all your attention directed upon distress. This act of rumination can happen to anybody at certain times in life when there are valid worries and issues to confront.

To actively do this, however, almost as a hobby or as a way of living, that's where we stumble upon disagreeable emotions like guilt, shame, anxiety and depression. When this cycle builds enough momentum, it diminishes our chances to find an escape from it. Rumination is a symptom of several relatively common mental disorders, such as anxiety disorders, obsessive-compulsive disorder and depression.

Usually, the topics that are recurring for people are about being worthless or inadequate. The person would dwell on consequences or future failings rather than solutions, practicality, or even reason. There is cause and effect; something happens here; therefore, something must happen in response to that thing. These people are dwelling on the causes of each and every bad decision or life result. This rumination process is a cornerstone of anxiety disorders and depressive disorders. Recurring problems arise in every person's life experience. There is no escaping some form of disagreement or unwanted emotional pain.

Becoming adaptable to the changes that come from this shift or suffering is what can be difficult. As not every person has the same resilience to withstand adversity. Stress tolerance during life difficulties differs from person to person. How are life complications handled by a healthy controlled group and a group that has borderline personality disorder?

That's exactly what Dr Selby and Thomas Joiner Jr did in this study. They named their work after a series of steep waterfalls joining up in successive stages, all connected from the primary source which is known as a cascade.

They put together these controlled tasks to monitor the before-and-after effects of the experiments on the two groups in their work, which is amply titled Emotional Cascades.

In this work, Dr Selby points out that the act of rumination increases the intensity of emotional discourse for the subjects, creating more problems and sorrow for the unwitting person and resulting in more frustration.

The charts show the results from the groups involved in the rumination induction experiment.

This involved a five-minute task in which they thought of personally driven, upsetting situations. As you can see, the borderline group was much more upset even before the experiment took place; their baseline was already significantly high. The baseline is before the experiment, and the post is following the experiment of each group.

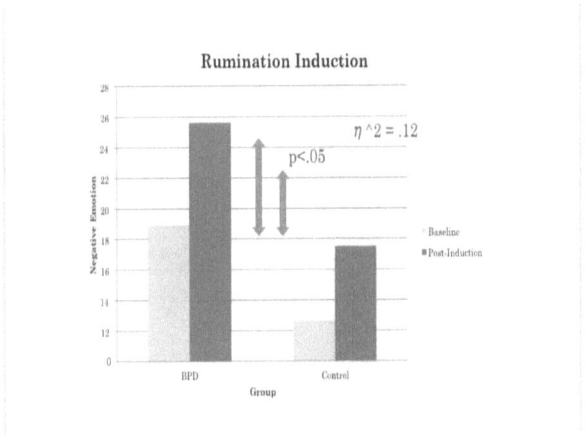

Selby et al. (2009)

There is a significant change from the before and after sections on the charts; the BPD group is in much more anguish than the others. The BPD group were much more upset after the five-minute task than the group without BPD.

The groups did the same tasks, which were not real negative life events, but they didn't even need to be real to elicit such strong responses. The BPD group's reactivity to these perceived feelings and thoughts drastically dwarfs the controlled group. This shows the borderline's nature of simply thinking about problems, getting enraged and intensely reacting.

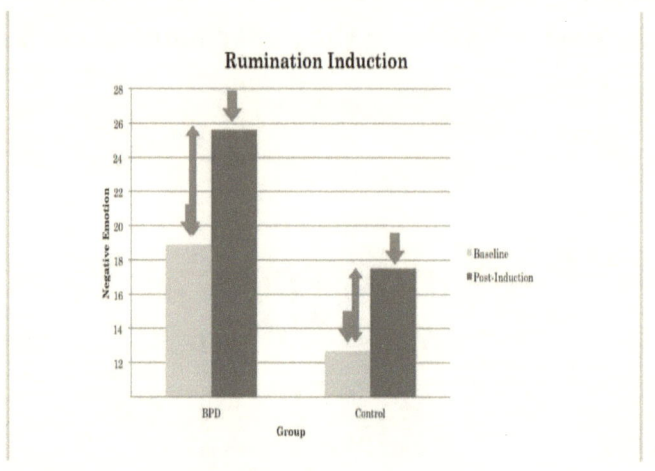

Selby et al. (2009)

This compounding of emotions or perceived problems leads to behavioural dysregulation. Consequently, actions that lead to negative outcomes such as binge eating, self-injury, tantrums or overspending.

All of these destructive behaviours act like a pacifier to the borderline. These reactionary acts, and many like them, alleviate some of the emotional pain or emotional cascade.

This highlights how much more upset people with borderline personality disorder are when experiencing the same life event.

Let's say an interaction involving despair or loss would hit them emotionally harder than others inflicted with the same pain.

Depersonalization/Derealization (DEP-DER) is a dissociative experience which is related to psychopathology and distress. Yet, the aetiological factors leading to DEP-DER are not sufficiently clear, but what is clear is that rumination is one possible antecedent.(Miriam Vannikov-Lugassi, Hadar Shalev, Nirit Soffer-Dudek 2021)

Furthermore, in terms of constantly dwelling on worst-case scenarios amid this rumination process, Dr Selby and Joiner postulated that the end result would likely be in the form of destructive behaviours.

This is where the outbursts of rage and splitting originate; in fact, Dr Selby went on to say that the borderline is a staggering 90% more likely after rumination to engage in these self-destructive behaviours. (Selby, E. A, Anestis, M.D, Joiner, T. E. 2008)

Instability of Rumination

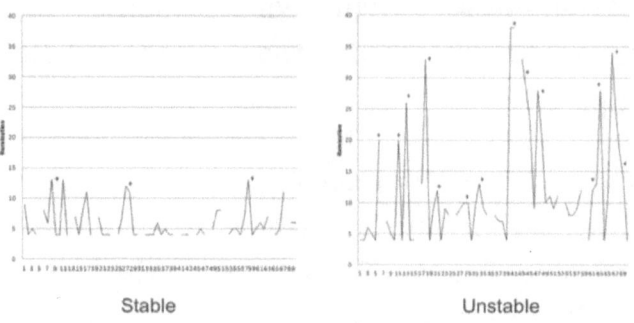

Selby et al., (2013) J clin Psychol

The instability chart shows that the borderline's result tends to spike at a really high rate. It peaks and then fluctuates at irregular levels, demonstrating the effects of the rumination. They appear to be completely scattered and unstable. Compare the chart to the person who is under the same process of the rumination task, which is visibly much lower and far more stable. Every little plus sign on the instability of rumination chart highlights dysregulatory behaviour.

After a series of ruminations, the borderline will likely create some destructive behaviour or engage in something of like nature to self-soothe, and then it's back to dwelling and ruminating.

Anger rumination, in which individuals focus on angry moods and prior provocations, is particularly associated with BPD features. (Peters, JR, Eisenlohr-Moul, TA, Upton, BT, Et Al. 2017) (Baer, RA, SauerSE, 2011)

This highlights so much in terms of reactivity, along with hasty life choices a person with borderline personality disorder will tend to lean into. It also highlights the predictability of such people, as the emotional cascades can be a precise prediction for self-harm, for example. If a person were cutting with a blade or smashing their head against a wall, inflicting bodily harm on themselves, this would release some of the emotional build-up which has occurred while ruminating.

There is a clear pattern of dwelling over and over again and then demonstrating the behaviour that coincides with the extremity of the feelings.

The more they ruminate, the more they engage in these problematic behaviours. One insignificant moment, misunderstanding, perhaps an innocent thing said, or anything inconsequential whatsoever, the borderline would answer that, with extreme outcomes. All the negative thoughts and feelings compound together and put forth a scenic view to habitually dwell on.

This mainly includes feelings of intense Invalidation or criticism from others. Some criticism is legitimate, such as constructive criticism, but not to the borderline.

This will tail-spin the person, and invalidation, whether real or perceived, would be a likely cause for the rumination process.

The rumination and instability charts demonstrate quite a low distress-tolerance.

When they get in this whirlwind of negative reactivity, they are prone to more invalidation and criticism. Then, they develop more distorted thoughts and perceptions about people and events in their lives.

Now, we will move on to the diagnosis and treatment options and some of the recurring issues associated with them. Diagnosing Borderline is challenging due to the regular overlap of symptoms with other mental health disorders.

Diagnosis

In the DSM 5 diagnostic criteria for BPD; the pattern of unstable-interpersonal relationships are one noticeable symptom that can garner a diagnosis. It can be almost impossible for a person with borderline personality disorder to maintain a stable long term relationship. That is because the symptoms are chaotic and repulsive to a loving relationship, these codependent relationships vacillate between Idealization and Devaluation. These relationships are abusive and manipulative; diagnosis is the only answer for some stability. Borderline patterns of behaviour; by default foster frequent conflicts and misunderstandings in relationships.

Personality disorders are still misunderstood to this day; borderline is stigmatised with a lack of awareness of the complexities of the condition. Understanding the unique needs and behaviours of each disorder and distinguishing between them can be a challenge.

Some mentions of personality types are Borderline, Antisocial, Avoidant, Dependent, Histrionic, Narcissistic, Obsessive-compulsive Paranoid personality-disorders.

Personality disorders are grouped into clusters; this book focuses primarily on Cluster B. Understanding these disorders or even just the character traits is crucial if we are going to be in a relationship with a person who has one of these disorders. Also, educating ourselves can help develop more effective treatment plans and more accessible, low-cost, findable consultants who specialise in these areas.

Borderline Personality Disorder affects a large portion of the population, primarily women. However, men do get the disorder, but it is not as noticeable among men. Some men are terrified of abandonment, for example, and display clear signs of Borderline.

Men with mental health disorders are often pushed into the criminal justice system more quickly and develop drug habits.

This then leads to the symptoms of BPD or other common disorders to go unnoticed. They would likely be perceived as displaying drug-related tendencies or side effects rather than having a precise diagnosis of what could be under the surface.

The narcissist would never want a diagnosis; they would typically visit a health professional for something else, such as drug use, life problems or depression, for example. They would never seek it out as they don't think anything about their behaviour is wrong in any sense. If the therapist does not agree with their perspectives, they will more than likely drop out of the therapy.

A misdiagnosis of an antisocial disorder or psychopathy could be the result for the male. About 80% of patients receiving therapy for BPD are women, but sex differences are less striking in community samples. (Skodol 2002 et al) As is the case for personality disorders in general, BPD is associated with lower social class and lower levels of education.(Samuels, J ,Et al, 2002) (Torgersen, S, Kringlen, E, Cramer, V, 2001)

Furthermore, men don't have the same attraction qualities as women. If a man constantly displayed characteristics in a relationship even remotely similar to a BPD sufferer, they would be considered creepy and weird, and the relationship could abruptly end. They could be perceived as an angry, paranoid man displaying toxic masculinity.

Displaying signs of aggression, jealousy or even wife-beater characteristics. It wouldn't raise the same red flags as it would if the roles were reversed. Men, to their detriment, may be inclined to look past visible red flags in a woman, such as chaotic mental health.

Women, on the other hand, are more inclined to visit doctors or psychiatrists than their male counterparts, as they are more connected to feelings and intuition.

The DSM-5, for example, indicated that approximately 75% of individuals diagnosed with BPD are females. That's the females who are recorded as diagnosed; the figure is much, much higher regarding both sexes. For instance, not every person has an affordable income to pay the psychiatrist's fees, even if they accept the behavioural issues and want to seek help.

There are so many people without an accurate diagnosis. They either live with symptoms while blaming other for their reactions etc, or they are not aware of the disorder or destructive traits. Psychology has taken a back seat in recent years; there is no point in knowing what we know in terms of psychiatry if there are no facilities for people to readily use; regarding affordability or to even have any treatment centres available in their area.

The average person wouldn't dream of wasting money, especially if their disorder would rather squander the funds; it's not practical. Average DBT therapy can range between 80€ to 100€ per session, causing the individual with borderline personality disorder little hope of easing the volatile condition. There is an important phenomenological distinction between temporal patterns of depressive symptoms in depression and BPD.(Gunderson, JG, Philips, K. 1991)

Therefore, not only are there people refusing help, or there are also those who are offended by the mere notion that there may be something odd about who they are as a person. But there are vast numbers of people who wouldn't be able to ever get the help even if they desired it. Both men and women get the same disorders; it only varies on commonalities and subtle nuances that frequently remain undetected. BPD is associated with chronic lowering of mood, particularly dysthymia with an early onset. (Pepper, CM, Anderson, RL, et al. 1995) Dysthymia is a long-lasting form of depression, which is also known as persistent depressive disorder.

Borderline Case Study Anonymous

I was diagnosed with bipolar disorder at a very young age, which I do also have. I am 54 now and would actually consider myself in remission. That happened before diagnosis. My daughter finally diagnosed me in her junior year of a psychology degree. She suggested DBT about three years ago, and my life has changed since then. I was sexually abused as a small child, 4-9. They should automatically warn people of the risk of developing personality disorders when they find out about abuse like mine.

I was sent to therapy from age 17, and no one even gave me any kind of testing. If you get depressed and have mania, you must have Bipolar. Before I got treatment, I was so mean to my son's dad that I accused him of being mentally abusive and a REALLY bad person. I talked with others about him and pointed him out to be a devil. But he wasn't any of it; he was such a wonderful person with a really kind heart, but I was too broken to deal with my own emotions, so I let it all out on him. Because in my mind, he was this abusive man, and he was always so mean to me. But I didn't realise I was the one who broke him down.

Even now, over 10 years later, he is not 100% healed yet. He is having a hard time even talking about his son to anyone, because they never got the chance to get to know each other. I have so many other stories of what I have done before I got any treatment. But when I got treatment and now, over 9 years later, with hard work (of course, I am not totally fine yet), I can finally say I've learned how to control my emotions. When I get a bad thought, I can now stop it before it becomes a feeling. And that I'm sooo thankful for.

These co-occurring disorders can make a difficult diagnosis. The overlap between one another cancels out a clear diagnosis at times. Also, the sufferer of a personality disorder may not be willing to get diagnosed in the first place. Other likely comorbidities would include NPD, ADHD, ASD, psychosis and the common association of bipolar.

"This is to some extent understandable as some of the features of DID (dissociative identity disorder) appear superficially to mimic those of schizophrenia and/or Borderline Personality Disorder" (Coleman, J, 2002)

That's not even mentioning mood disorders, anxiety disorders or substance abuse, so we can see why this is extremely hard to diagnose with the lack of common symptoms. The diagnosis is taken on an individual basis; for example, let's just say the person had five out of the total nine listed for the criteria for BPD on DSM-5; what would be looked at here is the frequency and duration of the symptoms. This can look different from person to person, and often, the BPD diagnosis gets overlooked by the professional. Structured interviews pick up many cases of BPD missed in ordinary practice. (Zimmerman, M, 1999) Personality disorders often lack precise symptomatic criteria; several attributes describe problems in interpersonal functioning. Resistance to diagnosing patients with a personality disorder may be based on the idea that these conditions are untreatable. (Lewis, L, Appleby, L, 1988)

TREATMENT

The Diagnosis of Personality Disorders and the treatment options are pivotal topics that must be addressed. Providing full understanding and support to people with these conditions is essential should they volunteer to seek help. Borderline and similar personality disorders are very misunderstood, even to this day. The compulsion to act out at loved ones makes it hard for people to tolerate behaviours or suggest help. It's easy to feed into the vendetta politics that these personality types wage, but understand that these people do require help. People need to be aware of the diagnostic criteria for each disorder to recognise the subtle signs demonstrated within the behaviour.

The diagnosis of personality disorders is made by a psychiatrist or psychologist. A thorough evaluation deciphering the symptoms and behaviours follows. The Diagnostic and Statistical Manual of Mental Disorders (DSM-5) outlines specific criteria depending on the disorder or cluster that results in a formal diagnosis. Symptoms do overlap between personality disorders, making it hard to diagnose at times. So many health care professionals refuse to diagnose borderline personality disorder regardless if the person has 9/9 of the symptoms.

The problem with the diagnosis is the complexity of the clusters, possible multiple disorders or the attitudes of these personality disorders. They remain either too stubborn or deflect any abusive behaviour, completely unable to take accountability for it. Perhaps it is easier to get a diagnosis early on as once adulthood hits, the person's personality is already well established; avoiding any change at all costs would be the default stance. They are more likely to avoid taking the steps to get into treatment or to get that diagnosis.

Borderline personality disorder often receives a bipolar disorder diagnosis as it is more well-known and exhibits most of the same direct qualities and criteria. Individuals with Borderline or Cluster B tend to avoid seeking professional help. This is due to their unacceptance of the fact that something is wrong with their behaviour. When they do get diagnosed, they are usually originally there for depression or anxiety. The identity disturbance aspects of personality disorders are a motivator for the unwillingness to seek help. Their behaviour is visible to others, but to the person with the disorder, the behaviour is justified. There is a limited ability for self-reflection on such behaviours and a disregard for how other people feel. There is also an inability to negotiate the behaviour as they will not accept anything about their sense of self as being wrong or may need adjusting.

The importance of early diagnosis, however, can improve outcomes and prevent the escalation of the symptoms. Treatment options would typically involve a combination of therapy and medication. Schema therapy can help alleviate some symptoms of borderline addressing unmet needs. Schema helps break negative patterns of thinking, feeling and behaving. The major downside of schema therapy is that it's quite scarce to source out.

Dialectical Behavior Therapy (DBT) is the most widely used form of therapy. It is the most effective thus far in teaching individuals coping skills to manage intense emotions or how to relate to others. Medication is also an option to help alleviate symptoms such as depression and anxiety. A mental health provider can find the right treatment plan tailored just for the patient. For a high-conflict personality type, diagnosis and treatment are crucial topics for consideration, but again, many people who have this disorder simply don't want the help.

Furthermore, they don't even want to admit that there is a problem. So, if a person were to think these treatments could be the answer to everything, unfortunately, they are not. If suggested; to your partner with a personality disorder, the suggestion may get stonewalled, and you could be punished severely.

Trying to converse and highlight such behaviour can lead to a tantrum, exacerbating the situation. This adds to the chaotic situations routinely brought about by the borderline, for example.

Borderline personality disorder, left untreated, creates higher chances of unstable living dynamics such as keeping a job and can also lead to legal or financial difficulties. There is no single medication that is solely for Cluster B or borderline personality disorder. Every medication prescribed is from other areas of mental health, such as depression, anxiety, etc, which can be helpful to ease specific symptoms. Health professionals are even trying out different types of drugs, such as Memantine, a drug used for Alzheimer's patients, targeting the areas of cognitive disturbances involved with them.

There is no one pill or even one therapy; the best outcome for the person who has the diagnosis would be having fewer of the symptoms associated with the disorder. For borderline, if a person has only some symptoms out of the nine symptoms on the DSM 5, then they might be able to live without the need for medication or therapy. However, others who have BPD can only get help when they know why they need the help.

The majority of people with cluster B don't understand what they are being treated for; they can't comprehend that there is anything wrong with their behaviour. They would avoid the treatment or even the thoughts that something is wrong with them to begin with, maintaining a defensive stance. This causes issues in their personal lives and those of their loved ones.

Mental health professionals are presented with an array of unique challenges from Cluster B personality disorders. Mainly the manipulative and harmful behaviours associated with individuals with Borderline Personality Disorder and Narcissistic Personality Disorder. There may be attempts to manipulate the health professional, for example.

The woman who developed Dialectical Behavior Therapy (DBT) is Marsha Linehan, and she mentions, "People with BPD are like people with third-degree burns over 90% of their bodies. Lacking emotional skin, they feel agony at the slightest touch or movement"
(Linehan, M, 2021)

Dialectical Behavior Therapy (DBT) is a known treatment for both disorders. Borderline is anchored with emotion-dysregulation, and DBT is best known for this therapeutic approach.

It focuses on teaching individuals how to regulate their emotions which is one main cause for several of the symptoms. It also improves interpersonal relationships and helps develop coping skills. Dialectical Behavior Therapy can help manage two major aspects of BPD, intense emotions and impulsivity.

Another beneficial approach regarding NPD is Cognitive Behavioral Therapy (CBT). CBT helps the person focus on how to challenge the distorted thought patterns or the beliefs held that contribute to their narcissistic behaviours.

Cognitive behavioural therapy, attempts to change these maladaptive beliefs; the person then can develop a more realistic sense of self. Therapy can help process and cope with trauma or attachment issues.

Therapies such as Eye Movement Desensitization and Reprocessing (EMDR) and therapies with a focus on unhealthy attachment styles and behaviours-these are the most effective for regulating past traumas. These therapies treat mental health conditions that happen because of memories stemming from traumatic events that emerged in the past.

We need to approach these relationships with empathy and understanding. Remember the causation of such behavioural issues or disorders. Also, to try encourage help or treatment if the person is willing to go ahead and is self aware.

Shame, inadequacy, moods and the fear of been left behind or abandoned will be the borderlines stance. Cluster B personality types tend to gravitate towards adopting manipulative and controlling behaviours. Once this manipulation has snowballed and the devaluation or discard phase begins, salvaging the relationship is unlikely. If there is no sign of treatment and the relationship is too abusive, a break from the situation or ending of the relationship is an option. If children are involved, it gets quite difficult to navigate, especially when under scrutiny or attack. If treatment options or a diagnosis is out of the question, more information on the manipulation tactics will be further ahead, see the chapter (Hurt People Hurt People)

Borderline Case Study Anonymous

I was misdiagnosed with Bipolar II for 20 years. I took treatment into my own hands when I realised the doctors weren't right and started putting me on medication to counteract side effects. I was on seven pills at once and given ECTs at 17 years old. I was misdiagnosed for so many years. I was given medication like Lithium and Seroquel and a million different cocktails of drugs to treat Bipolar Disorder. I didn't get my BPD diagnosis till I was 21.

It definitely did not make life easy, but I am super self-aware and fairly stable. It was easy to accept a diagnosis because a name made it something tangible for me to manage. My Mother had untreated BPD, so she was my gold standard for how not to live or treat people. I have 8 out of the nine symptoms of borderline personality disorder from the DSM-5. I have CPTSD(Complex post-traumatic stress disorder) and Major Depression, so I can get depressive episodes that last months; my longest was a year-long episode. My CPTSD mostly stems from medical procedures and abuse from childhood. My mother was very verbally abusive to my father and me; she was either loving or a monster. I never knew how she would be from day to day, and my father didn't either. If she didn't like something my father did, "like vacuum the wrong direction", she would destroy his stuff.

She would threaten us as well. If I wanted comfort, she would withhold it because she was hurt. It didn't matter how loving we were or how good; if she thought otherwise, she'd be horrible. My mother does have trauma that she didn't get help for until most of the damage had been done. That is just the tip of how she was. My best treatment was CBT/DBT, taught in the correct way, along with ACT and having a kind therapist who taught me how to use my self-awareness to simply stop before reacting. I microdose fungi, and that has changed who I am for the better, and I use THC under my Psych's care. I have found no benefits from pharma. Many of my symptoms occur under stress, but it's all still there because I can't process my trauma.

I felt that someone was actually listening to me and seeing me. BPD diagnosis made it easy for me to find information, do the research and find people who can relate to it. DBT (dialectical behaviour therapy) has helped so much; it's beyond words. I had state insurance when I did it. So, it was approved. It is way cheaper than 2 weeks in IN patient psych facility. That's one of the reasons I started looking for out-of-office therapy. Much easier to get on a video call than having to go to an office once a week. I also found a few good companies that did extensive outpatient therapy. My office therapy was called Charlie Health, and they were amazing. (Charlie Health specialises in virtual intensive outpatient (IOP) programming across many US states. Charlie Health treats those with anxiety, depression, dissociative disorders, mood disorders, OCD, and more.)

Chapter 3
Mainstream Allegations & Proceedings

"They said we're going to take you to the precinct. They said most likely, we're going to let you go home. But then I never went home." Kalief Browder

Kalief Browder was only 16 years old when he was arrested. He was identified and kept in prison until trial. All the while, the witness did not make appearances, delaying the case and the time Kalief spent in jail. The allegation was that he stole a backpack. Kalief spent over 1,000 days in New York's largest prison, Rikers Island.

He was placed in solitary confinement for about 2 years, more than 700 days. He attempted suicide several times in despair at this point in his life. He tried to use the sheets and a ceiling light to achieve this.

Meanwhile, the corrections officers would encourage him to commit suicide. Kalief had over 30 court dates that all led nowhere; his ridiculous case dragged on and on.

After the onslaught of delays, the end of his case approached, and the case was ultimately dismissed. The amount of time that this teenager spent in solitary confinement was beyond egregious.

Also, Kalief was subject to starvation and beatings by the guards and the other inmates. He was released from Rikers Island in 2013. The charges were finally dropped. In 2015, plagued by what he said was the mental anguish and trauma from his time in jail, he hanged himself in his mother's home. Kalief was just 22 years old.

Today, we are thriving in the areas of entertainment and technology. We take for granted the tech we've inherited. Not realising it wasn't too long ago that life used to be vastly different. Look around, and you will see incredible feats of AI, virtual reality, and numerous concepts brought into existence by this species. Living in the future compared to the previous generations. The court system, however, let's just say we like to have that one bit of nostalgia with. For the family courts, let's just keep it dated all the way back a century, at least.

Society tries to upgrade and improve on the previous generations. Benefiting from being able to learn from mistakes and flaws. We can see the previous results of what has worked in the past and what has not. Generationally speaking, we have not advanced to our highest potential; instead, we have downgraded.

There is a complete disconnect as we advance in some major areas, all the while alongside unethical just law parameters. The structure of the legal system is witnessed generationally and passed down. Hopefully, soon, there will be a possible turning point that will add to history, potentially shifting some of the outdated and very primitive variables of law.

Issues that get brought up for debate in the court of public opinion do fundamentally change perception for the most part. Court proceedings still demonstrate bias and unfair rulings, such as libel, slander, or even the alienation of children. We have people working within the legal system today who see sham cases clearly and remember back to their childhood when they were alienated children, for example. Matters like these seem to be universal; the same issues exist all across the world.

This accusation-phenomenon is reaching its peak. The statistics tell us that the majority of the victims of these false allegations and parental alienation are men. But once more, women can be unfortunate enough to get roped into this predicament. For this brief section, we will focus on the former.

The accusation of harassment alone can be a manoeuvre used to cause a detrimental impact on the targeted man. The #MeToo era arrived in full force. The movement showed us the impact of areas once hidden; our favorite actors and producers were now on the chopping block. Prominent men were crumbling in front of the masses, and rightfully so. This movement eradicated some foul, high-profile, very powerful men in Hollywood. It is a much-needed movement which focuses on real abuse and harassment. This movement did great things, highlighting real abuse and situations such as sexual propositions to get movie roles etc. This movement has made waves, and it is fully supported in this writing, protecting women's rights and highlighting the harassment of real victims. This writing focuses on the imposters of these real victims.

The pretend made-up stories, just for the sole purpose of ruining a person's life, is what we are aiming to discuss here.

There is no movement for being the target of falsified allegations and the abuse that it incurs as of yet. Men are increasingly finding themselves as the prey of false accusations. These accusations not only damage a man's career but also his personal relationships and so on.

Tina Greenland, a nanny, falsely accused her boss Nicholas Mouna of rape after he made it clear that he did not want a relationship with her (Telegraph Reporters, 2012), while Welsh woman Leanne Black was jailed for multiple false rape allegations made over an eight-year period against five ex-partners. (Duffin, 2013)

An online poll was conducted from February 22-March 1, 2019, two years after the height of the #MeToo movement. A national sample of 5,182 employed adults in the U.S. all of which were over eighteen years old. Data for all surveys have been categorised with regard to age, race, sex, education, and geography using the Census Bureau's American Community Survey to reflect the demographic composition of the United States aged eighteen or over. One finding of the data showed;

> "60% of managers who are men are uncomfortable participating in a common work activity with a woman, such as mentoring, working alone, or socialising together, That's a 32% Jump from the previous year"(LeanIn/SurveyMonkey, Online Poll, 2019)

A narcissist or borderline may feel "abused" or "unsafe" when, in reality, no abuse has occurred. (Zepezauer, 1994) For example, a borderline wife fears her husband might reveal her numerous affairs to their pastor, exposing her true nature. Rather than admit her fear of exposure, she fabricates vague claims of "feeling unsafe" or outright lies of abuse to manipulate the situation and protect her image. This kind of fear should not be grounds for a restraining order. (Palmatier, T. J, 2024)

In recent years, the issue of false allegations has entered the limelight. Vindictive people have made some; others have been made out of the hopes of a cash settlement. An honourable mention would be that of Jussie Smollett, who would garner sympathy for his incredible story only to be convicted of the hate crime hoax. His story had all the bells and whistles for public support; it had racism, homophobic insults and political hate. At a very divisive time in America, he went as far as he did with inventing a timeline, props such as a noose, and going on national TV with his expert acting skills, crying crocodile tears. This guy is a high-profile actor, and in his mind, it must have been worth the risk. Perhaps he thought people would buy into it; why wouldn't they? He tried to capitalise on the negative Trump press and become a martyr for his politics, maybe even receive a boost in his career as he became more notable.

Another case which was a central talking point and highlighted Borderline Personality Disorder, gaining significant attention in legal circles, was the Amber Heard and Johnny Depp case. Amber Heard used the MeToo# movement as a catalyst to extort her ex for financial gain and notoriety of her own.

The psychiatric evaluation given of Heard had the results concluding both borderline and histrionic personality disorders. A histrionic personality disorder is filled with drama seeking; see chapter (Cluster B). The person begins to feel extreme discomfort with not being the centre of attention. They make up stories to be the centre of attention, taking on the victim role and becoming the princess that needs saving. So here we see a comorbidity of two very chaotic disorders which explains so much regarding this case.

She lied under oath about domestic abuse, and it was later revealed that she was the aggressor. For example, she claimed he hit her so many times in the face that she couldn't remember. She faked a police call out the night she invited Depp to her apartment. As they were talking metres apart she simultaneously had her friend on the phone.

She then begins acting erratic, making it seem like there is some sort of dangerous situation occurring; the friend on the phone can just hear screaming and commotion on the other line. No situation was happening but the police were called by the friend, which would be considered quite normal.

Depp's fashion is distinct and always has been; he is likened to the maximalist style, with multiple rings on each hand and almost every finger. This means the style of rings worn is chunky, pointy, and awkward. If they made contact with facial skin, there would undoubtedly be some visible signs. She testified that it felt as if her lip went through her teeth, and there was blood spatter on the wall.

She was cross-examined about having no photos of that incident, among others, and she put it down to a blunder on the court's part. Police testified to the call-out in question, denying any marks or visible bruising. That night, the police were equipped with body cams, which did not include one cut or mark.

In the days following, she shows up with a bruise on her arm in front of the paparazzi. The photos they take show a clear face and one bruise visible on her arm. Heard was also in hot water over claims of carrying makeup, which she used to hide bruises for the span of the two years of an abusive marriage. Trying to make a viral moment in the courtroom, her attorney held up the product, claiming that Heard had become very adept at mixing colours to conceal and hide bruises.

During the marriage, she would carry this particular makeup product in her purse and cover up any bruise or cut should a beating occur. Depp and Heard were married from 2015/2016, and the brand of makeup was Milani Cosmetics. Milani Cosmetics came out almost immediately to verify the claims and insisted the palette in question didn't exist till the year 2017. Amber Heard filed for divorce in 2016; her statement was factually incorrect.

All in all, the lack of photographic evidence and medical records tripped Heard up. There were so many different incidents, such as the broken nose claim, which shortly thereafter, on the timeline of suffering a supposed fractured nose, she was in multiple pictures at the Met-Gala with a perfect-symmetric nose.

This case was a hot topic and went viral multiple times on social media, with analysts and critics alike following every step of this real-life soap opera in real-time. If you go back and watch the case, the psychiatrist takes the stand and explains the complications Amber Heard has emotionally involving her (BPD) borderline personality disorder. As I recall, the entire courtroom couldn't grasp the concept of borderline personality disorder. Also, nobody really spoke about or reported on the subject as it's such a complex issue; it's hard to digest or understand, especially to the casual viewer.

Unfortunately, men can be viewed as perpetrators straight away in a legal setting. The courts can't fathom a male being the victim of abuse or coercive control. If something is alleged, the man is usually not heard, believed or considered due to gender bias. One person can abuse another person just with words bundled together. In story-form, with a protagonist and a villain, and if you're a man, you are rarely the former.

Most people would be ashamed or embarrassed to admit they were falsely accused. Men would be ashamed to admit being a victim of an abusive relationship. However, speaking out brings some much needed awareness, highlights the issues and prevents others from going through the same experience. By sharing our stories, we can help bring to the forefront the awareness of false accusations and parental alienation, a result of coercive control. False accusations are a devastating punishment.

The result of being accused in-the wrong, can lead to such extremes as suicide. If suicide ideation occurs, immediately take precautionary measures. Seek help and prevent suicide from becoming a possibility. There are options, such as counselling or even your doctor, which would help with prescribing some serotonin boosters or antidepressants. This, then, should help alleviate the psychological trauma that you've become exposed to. A person who uses tactics this dirty would salivate at the idea of making a person kill themself; unfortunately, that's just how deceitful and hateful people can be.

If you have friends and family members who stick by you, it can be a blessing. Benefitting from advice and being heard on the matter. If suicidal ideation occurs and you are struggling, immediately seek out professional help. Arrange an appointment with a counsellor who can help you process the shock-laden despair and develop coping strategies to help deal with the burden of this ineffable situation. There are some organisations and support groups out there but they lack any merit; their hands are tied with what they can do.

Try finding the groups dedicated to advising those who have been falsely accused. Connecting with other people who have experienced false allegations can provide closure and validation. Seek sound legal help, and don't pick too hastily, as you could get stuck with an incompetent legal representative. Always check reviews and do some research of the legal team that you choose for representation.

Honorable mentions

19-year-old Nikki Yovino was at an off-campus party in Connecticut. She claimed that she was raped by two football players at the party; this rape took place in the bathroom. One of the men lost his scholarship, and the other was forced to drop out of college. The men's dreams of football, scholarships and even their reputations were ruined. They admitted to having sex with Ms Yovino, but it was consensual.

Others at the party claimed they witnessed Ms Yovino willingly go into the bathroom and heard her say that she wanted to have sex, enticing the guys. Ms Yovino then changed her story and admitted in her sworn statement that it was consensual sex and that she made up the story. The reason she decided to falsely accuse was a spur-the-moment move on her part.

She claimed that there was another male student in her college whom she liked. This allegation would help to garner sympathy from the guy she liked and others, but it would also secure the idea of a potential future relationship with this guy.

"It was the first thing that came to mind" she mentioned in her sworn testimony; as she was explaining why she falsely accused the two men of rape.

The men claim they have anxiety and PTSD after these allegations and don't feel safe around people. Nikki Yovino was smirking in court and rolling her eyes as she heard the court proceedings play out.

"She admitted that she made up the allegation of sexual assault against (the football players) because it was the first thing that came to mind and she didn't want to lose (another male student) as a friend and potential boyfriend.

She stated that she believed when (the other male student) heard the allegation, it would make him angry and sympathetic to her," the affidavit states. (Live5news 2021)

In 2017, Jemma Beale was sentenced for her allegations. She was a serial liar or a serial false alleger. She made several false abuse and rape allegations. Between 2010 and 2013 she claimed that she was sexually assaulted by six men. Also during this same period, she claimed nine other men had raped her.

This is fifteen men she has accused within three years. One of the men Ms Beale accused of rape in 2010, Mahad Cassim, was tried twice and jailed for seven years.

His conviction was quashed by the Court of Appeal in 2015 after his defence team and the Crown Prosecution Service were alerted to serious doubts over Beale's allegations.

She had been awarded £11,000 by the Criminal Injuries Compensation Authority and had told a former girlfriend she had lied to get the money, the court heard. (BBC 2019)

We can't forget about the fifty-year-old man known only as Nick for legal reasons.

The head of special crime at the Crown Prosecution Service (CPS), said: "The police investigation provided evidence that the man had made several false allegations alleging multiple homicides and sexual abuse said to have been carried out in the 1970s and 1980s. (Chris Baynes, The Independent 2018)

Nick's fraud charge was for £22,000 from the Criminal Injuries Compensation Authority.

He was seeking damages as he was supposedly abused by a paedophile ring. Nick was believed at the time he made all of these accusations.

The commander of the Met Police called Nick a victim. This made High-ranking officials in the MET Police described Nick's claims as "credible and true". (J Halliday, B Quinn, J Elgot The Guardian 2015) (Chris Baynes, The Independent 2018)

Calling Nick a "Victim"; keep in mind this is before the investigation concluded. By doing so they publicly created a presumption of guilt for all of the accused.

This is how the police and the courts treat false allegations. They hear the allegation and think it must be true, why else would they allege this? They had to apologise for this blunder publicly.

This is the police force thinking out loud. They should take the allegations and let the trial take place. Innocent until proven otherwise should be the stance of the courts and the police.

Presuming a person's guilt while turning a blind eye to the possibility of a false statement plagues our justice system.

ADMONITION

The methods described in this book do have severe adverse rebound effects on the recipient. We need to understand the vulnerabilities of our mental health. Manipulation and abuse at extreme levels will cause suicidal ideation or suicidal thoughts. This ideation may formulate an automatic desire or mental imagery of the self-inflicted death route.

Most people who have these thoughts don't go on to actually commit suicide, but this needs to be mentioned as a cautionary statement and crutch for those who have experienced this act of despair. If you are facing suicidal ideation, remain centred, speak to a health professional or try to detach from the situation. Go non-contact for a while, focus on yourself and talk to loved ones or friends. If you have nobody in your life at present, Be your life coach and remain in the fight.

These self-centred tactics and methods of attack are purposely manoeuvred in such a way that chaos in life will be the inevitable outcome. Understand that this will pass, but a heavy burden of depression will be present, and unfortunately, that is the goal that they aimed for.

Police harassment may result in an innocent encounter or visual of sirens or what looks similar to a siren, causing severe anxiety. Things like police uniforms or walking by a police officer could make you reflect or act as a trigger, feeling terrible, accompanied by distrust and feeling unsafe. Stimuli will indeed happen in the external world; This does pass, remain focused on the false allegations, prepare solely for the easily exploitable courts, and watch out for future traps that could be laid out for you.

Expect to adopt PTSD, Depression and or other mental health problems; systematic abuse for prolonged periods of time creates that. Talking about the situation with someone who understands and empathises can help alleviate feelings of isolation and helplessness.

One of the first steps in rebuilding our clarity is acknowledging the damage done and trying to mitigate any further repercussions. It will never be easy; it will involve learning to live with the hurt and betrayal caused to you and those around you.

Get beyond the falsehoods, Being innocent is not enough. Get your life back, and try not to dwell on the outcomes or the unjustified treatment. Take your mind away from it as much as possible, and don't let it defeat you. We must garner control especially in the courtroom setting. Hurtful things will be said, controlling our reactions is vital. We will get pushed and tested; remain composed. It is easier said than done; But remember it is natural to feel angry and frustrated. Don't allow this reaction to be the cause of another charge; Or worse be a pointer of erratic behaviour that seemingly solidifies the false allegations. Stand up against the smear campaigns and false accusations, advocate for justice and fairness and speak your truth. If researched, one would find that this false allegation method or using courts as punishment is getting spoken about more frequently with each passing day. Form the group or be a part of one, write, speak or make content regarding this unjust dilemma. Too many people deal with it by bottling it up and never speaking of it again. If we counteract an abusive relationship or a situation filled with coercive control in this manner, we multiply the effects it has on us. Bring a sense of empowerment back into your life; this is what was under attack in the first place. Overcome the stigma; you are not defined by any false accusations. We need a societal awakening that this behaviour is occurring, as most people don't understand it. Speak your truth and control how you respond to these challenges.

Chapter 4

Defamation

&

Demonization

Moving forward, the discussion will focus on the faults within the court system. A family court case can and may escalate to the criminal courts depending on the nature of the case or allegations. The narratives created don't seem challenged whatsoever and merely account to that of hearsay. False allegations are prevalent in the justice system and contribute to a large portion of false convictions.

> "The majority of false reports appear to be filed by people experiencing substantial psychological and emotional challenges for whom accusing another person satisfies a personal motive" (Lonsway, Archambault, Berkowitz, 2018)

In the book 'Perceptions False Accusations of rape-journal of gender studies', there were interviews involving 40 police officers. All of these interviews were questioning perpetrators that have been involved in rape cases the previous year. They believed anywhere from 5% to 90% of assaults were actually false allegations, with an average rate of perceived false reports of 53% across the sample. (McMillan, L.2018)

Whatever the false accusations are, they could be of harassment, abuse or other; the implications of the allegation alone! Can ruin a life. Even if the story is recanted or there is some form of admission to the fabrication, in no way does that help the real victim legally or socially. Often the victim is assumed guilty until proven innocent, facing severe consequences as a result.

False allegations and parental alienation are a universal occurrence and happen to any gender. One of the most damaging types of false accusations is that of abuse. Usually domestic, but this allegation can be in a public or work setting, which is quite difficult to disprove and contributes to lost reputation and serious legal repercussions, among other things.

The Discard or Devaluation phase, is the reason for many of these false-allegations, and parental alienation situations.

Case Study Aisha's Husband

Aisha's husband went through quite an ordeal and was recently behind bars. He was convicted based on no evidence for a historic offence. He was found guilty of one count-rape in the retrial in March 2020 whilst Aisha was heavily pregnant with their 3rd child. Their ordeal started in 2017, involving two individuals who happen to be close school friends, both with accusations. I will refer to them in this case study as girl#1 and girl#2. He was questioned for girl#1 in August 2017 and questioned for girl#2 in February 2018.

There were three trials, with a number of men in each trial that had already been convicted. The trials were separated into three parts, and her husband was in the third trial. There were three men in her husband's trial for the same victim. One of the men proved this girl had lied in court by bringing in an expert witness who undermined her version of events. Girl#2 said Aisha's husband was the first person she ever had any sexual relations with.

She remembered him in 2018 after taking part in two trials in which she never mentioned him at all. It was only after the first two trials she remembered who the first person was and claimed it was him. This didn't make any sense, keeping in mind she had already convicted several men before that. The amount was in the ball-park of around fifteen men all in all from the previous trials.

The grooming gang trial involving Aisha's husband took place in late 2019, but just before the trial, some shocking evidence was revealed, and girl#1 was severed from the trial.

This was due to audio recordings coming to light of a conversation in which she was saying that she "didn't even have the right person to begin with", referring to him and the case.

The recordings were played in court and she vehemently denied that it was her voice. They conducted a voice analysis test and later confirmed that it was in fact her voice, all three charges were dropped as a result.

The girl was caught lying due to this discovery of evidence that was eventually playing in the courtroom. The fact that she lied under oath and wasn't even prosecuted is worrisome; there was no penalty or fine, and there was no justice.

Had Aisha's husband been found guilty, he would have been looking at a term of 17 years of incarceration solely based on false allegations with the intent to ruin his life.

There was no apology from the police or no special treatment to the victim of such a heinous false allegation. The girl had admitted to lying about the whole story and placing him in it. The police were told on multiple occasions by other key witnesses that she had told them her truth, that she didn't even know him.

This briefly stifled the case leading to confusion, he was then only tried for girl#2 which resulted in a hung jury followed by a retrial. The court dates were set in place falling over the Covid peak pushed his case forward from June to March.

In that trial one of the defendants brought in an expert that analysed his mobile phone and had proven that girl#2 had also lied. The other defendants' charges were then dropped at this point.

She had lost all her credibility as a believable victim as she was caught lying under oath. Following this was a hung jury or a deadlocked jury in the 2020 trial. A decision was made from the CPS to retrial that same year.

In that trial they were not allowed to discuss the first trial or what happened leading up to the deadlocked jury, also important details such as the fact that one accused man proved her to be a liar and was found not guilty because of it.

Now, this girl said the offences dated all the way back to 2005. It's worth noting she got the colour of his skin and his overall description wrong, including his age, and she couldn't remember the time, date, or even the location. In her first statement, she created the narrative that the attacker was a random man. Then, all of a sudden, she changed her story, claiming she now remembers his name, which happened to be an incorrect name. Another thing she mentioned that did not corroborate with the time-line was that she claimed the man was in his 30s, but in 2005, the accused was a teenager, only 15/16 years old at the time.

She picked him out in a line up and said 100% his brother was also in the line up, another inconsistency as when this was double checked there was no brother in the line up. The retrial was a very aching process, even with no concrete evidence against Aisha's husband, nevertheless the trial took its toll.

During the cross-examination, a question was asked about his background, and her husband answered that he "was a hard-working young lad who would work at a family business, and his friends were also very hardworking". They followed up with a rebuttal to that answer, implying at the age of 15, he had been in trouble with the police here and there, trying to refute the hard-working description he had of himself back then, which was quite irrelevant to the case.

The prosecution took this and ran with it claiming that he was creating a false impression of himself by stating he was a hard working man. Clearly pressed for real evidence they followed up with permission from the judge to use some aspects of his previous trial as evidence.

It was made clear to the jury that this girl was abused by others and was the real victim here, even though 70 per cent of the trial was based on her other experiences of abuse. This form of evidence had nothing to do with Aisha's husband whatsoever. As her cross-examination began, she started to add more details which she never mentioned before and even accidentally referred to Aisha's husband as a "victim".

She had to be corrected on the term she used by the attorney cross examining. Also when asked what made her remember him after all of the trials, she had told this story of remembering a police officer who came to visit her at her psychiatric ward as she has bi-polar disorder, that's when she had the aha moment and remembered it was in fact him.

She was hushed on this by her attorney during the trial, as there were no records of this visit on the disclosure. The lacklustre memory didn't help things make sense as it wasn't in her evidence, so she couldn't speak about it in court. Even though it was important to highlight, it begs the question, did she even have the mental capacity at the time to identify a person while she was institutionalised?

Aisha and her husband had one of the investigating officers visiting their home on a regular basis. He gave them information in regards to the victim (Girl1#) going through things with her children. He also said that he knew in his heart that Aisha's husband hadn't done this and then spoke about the defendants as being weird.

Girl#2 had previously had several men sent to prison and, in some cases, had friends corroborating the story. Time and time again, she kept coming back, saying she remembered her abuse with different men. This should be acknowledged in the courtroom and looked upon as a serious matter to avoid putting the wrong people behind bars.

There were so many inconsistencies that should have been considered in the trial. There was an instance in which she described him as being very light-skinned, but he is and always has been of dark complexion. A blurred black and white mugshot from police records was displayed during court, which revealed he looked very Caucasian even though they had legal documentation with pictures of him back in 2005 of him having a very dark-skinned complexion. He was found guilty based on hearsay with no real captivating evidence shown in court.

He was offered a plea deal during the trial but refused it as the CPS was seeking to pervert the course of justice and force him to admit to an offence, which he didn't do but was of a lesser stature. This would have resulted in a lesser sentence, an offence with which the victim nor the police had alleged to have happened. The prosecution's plea deal would mean if her husband pleaded guilty, he would only do a one-year sentence.

There was no solid evidence and it all came down to her word against his. Even with the pressure of the case and the plea deal exit route he could have taken, he still wanted to remain in the fight for the truth to clear his name; ultimately not bargaining with the plea deal.

He ended up receiving four and a half years (based on the 15-17 year old guidelines). Days before Aisha went into labour, there was a press release from Dailymail, which was highly inaccurate; in the article, they mentioned that Aisha's husband pleaded guilty in court when he did not. Aisha mentioned that they are trying to set up an appeal but are wondering what else can be done about the failings of the police and the CPS. Also, she brought up the fact that this case and many others like it end up in the courts of law with just hearsay and no evidence, an injustice faced from false allegations.

Aisha's husband was underage at the time and was sentenced as being underage but then was made to appear in the media as if he were an adult man. Her husband didn't even know the girl and denied any involvement.

There were some instances in court where this girl swore at the judge in trial 2, and the judge refused to have her produce her evidence in court and ruled it would be done by video link going forward. Since the trial, girl#1 has recently made a memoir and the events that she has written about are not factual when compared to her statements for the case. The girl's aunt was and is a serving police officer on the case with an all white jury which could have reinforced some bias.

It was made clear in the earlier trials by the prosecution that he wasn't part of any grooming gang leading up to Aisha's husband's fight for a lone case on the retrial. She had him convicted of one count of rape, and he was sentenced to 4 years, 6 months and served 2 years, 3 months.

He hopes to appeal but has been quoted upwards of 40k for a solicitor to take it on. Legal aid doesn't take on many appeals as they only receive a few hundred, so going private is his only route. Also, with an appeal, you have to have new evidence to contribute to the trial.

Because of the evidence produced at court for girl#1, another 18 men's charges were dropped. In the United Kingdom, cases like these are handled by CICA (Criminal Injuries Compensation Authority). With CICA, there are some handsome payouts on conviction that entice a person to bring an instance to court or falsely accuse.

This compensation could reward you with $1000 to $500,000, depending on the severity of the conviction. They range from Assault (including ABH and GBH), actual bodily harm / grievous bodily harm, Sexual abuse (including historical childhood abuse), Domestic abuse, Threats of violence that have caused psychological injuries, A loved one that has been murdered, Human trafficking and acts of terrorism. In some cases, a full conviction isn't even necessary to get compensation through CICA, but the crime needs to be reported to the police. In fact, This offender does not need to be convicted under the CICA scheme! The compensation payouts are made on a balance of probabilities. (GOV.UK 2014)

To make a claim if found untrue or false, resulting in the dismissal of the case, will result in no repercussions, penalties or fines for the false accuser.

Even if CICA tries to get the compensation back from the accuser which later was found that the accusation was false, the money would likely be spent leading to reimbursement problems for CICA as there isn't much else they can do at that point.

It is crucial to be aware of the nature of some people, in other words, to know who is capable of what. It can be quite a shock when, out of a mere squabble or disagreement, pretty soon you're getting served a stack of court-papers.

These falsifying accusation-situations can also occur over nothing. Maybe your partner wasn't validated enough or wants to inflict punishment to keep you in line. False allegations of abuse are typically used against a dad or husband to get an emergency protection order to gain possessions or the home. The most important gain here would be that of the children. They use this method in courts quite often, and it is a clear winner when implemented.

THE SILVER BULLET

The name for this method is the silver bullet and likened to the name, it's a one-shot kill to the opposition. Attorneys and legal teams know about this method and at times even encourage it by seeking payouts and unconstitutional court punishment without double checking the accusation. There is a lack of care in these cases. A person can deliberately make a false order exploiting the court, the judge and the police. No effort from the court when it comes to truth-seeking. This technique is widely known throughout the courtrooms, without being challenged. This case will lead then; to the assumption of guilt, with the false accuser free of any repercussions for falsely accusing.

Bogus false allegations of abuse or fear of the other parent, resulting in a restraining order or a protection order. This is then used as leverage in the divorce or custody case. This is the silver bullet technique, which is a well-known tactic in the courtroom. Parental Alienation is inevitable following the silver bullet. This can also be used to blackmail; The offer of dropping criminal charges for full custody. The following chapters primarily focus on this technique.

Other allegations would be False accusations of substance use that can sway opinion quite quickly. Making it look as if the person is under the influence damages their credibility as a stable person or parent. Making any other alternative version of events less likely to be heard. Substance abuse or alcoholism can be used as a smear in the build-up to a family court dispute.

Serious consequences are afoot from allegations, such as possible loss of the job role if its a colleague, Just the rumour of professional misconduct can be a death sentence to the given career. Opportunists use false accusations to damage reputations and end any future endeavours. It takes its toll when involved in a constant battle to protect a career or livelihood. Falsely allegations of abuse would find a person ostracised from their communities, labelled as perpetrators without any evidence to support the claims.

These false accusations can lead to the breakdown of familial relationships, loss of custody or access to children and even criminal charges. These highly negative circumstances and the duration of time a person is put through them can haunt them for the rest of their lives.

The emotional toll of being falsely accused and or put through parental alienation can be unbearable, leading to depression and suicidal ideation.

Furthermore, be cognizant of future allegations even if everything is okay now. Maybe it's not you but a friend or loved one that this could happen to. The thoughts of future fake allegations can bring worry and stress in times to come, which can cause some justified paranoia. This fear of what could potentially unfold breaks any sane person. If you were a level-headed person before, prepare for bouts of depression and angst. It is sickening the fact that people can freely label others through disagreement or punishment.

A false allegation changes a person's trust in others, and the simple action of being yourself will be no more. Know who you get with; do not fall for love-bombing. Unfortunately, people are vulnerable and care for others and even wish to help them. They believe in being a good person, so much so that they tolerate any abuse. If a relationship started, ok, but now there is non-stop abuse? There is always the possibility of it reverting back, right?

If we are in a relationship with a high-conflict individual, we need to recognise it early. Do they have any symptoms of a personality disorder, or are they just a high conflict-jerk? Are they constantly causing drama and ruining situations in other people's lives if given the chance? Are they causing hurt and seem to enjoy dishing out punishment? If so, this punishment will soon become your punishment. Think in terms of becoming preventive of a loved one's mental state that can and will use any of the above narratives to their advantage. If the ultimate goal is to hurt and destroy a person for whatever reason, would they pull the trigger?

In truth, there doesn't have to be a reason; people who have borderline personality disorder, for example, use these elements as a strategy against a person. Munchausen syndrome has shown likely characteristics of this behaviour along with the aforementioned histrionic and narcissistic personality disorders. It is almost a way of playing god, seeking and destroying a life and then on to the next one.

Case Study Anonymous

My wife's sister passed away unexpectedly and suspiciously in May of 2020 in Monroe County, Tennessee; she left behind an 11-month-old and an almost 18-year-old son and a recent ex-husband, along with two sisters and both parents. Also in this aftermath was her unemployed, drug-dealing, car-part-stealing boyfriend! Who was the father of the 11-month-old; Knowing this man was in no way fit to raise a child, we consulted with attorneys about our options and did not have much to go on to launch a case to remove the child until 1/21 when dad attempted to take his and the child's life, we quickly went in for emergency custody, being that we lived out of state I flew to Tennessee and retrieved the child and brought him to our home out west.

During this time, we paid out of pocket for medical evaluations for the child who was so malnourished and below every benchmark that the attending nurse (who was reduced to tears at the site and situation of the child had no other choice but to refer us to our states CPS for a home visit, when the CPS caseworker visited our house she had the same reactions, we were ordered to take the child for a hair follicle test, those results showed exposure and/or ingestion to several prescription drugs, the same ones that the father was prescribed.

Unfortunately, we would be ordered to return the child to his father by Monroe Co child/family court before we had the drug results; when these results were provided to the father's attorney and my attorney, they were never presented to the court as they were waiting for a hearing date to present them.

Then again, suddenly and somewhat unexpectedly, on 11/21, the father passed away somewhat mysteriously, and that was when a former stepdaughter of the father stepped in and took (kidnapped) the child. She was only supposed to have the child for the weekend as the father died on a Friday night, and she was supposed to help DCS identify a family to place the child with. We had been interacting with this person ever since the child's mother died, and she knew we had a case open for custody but never called DCS back to tell them the responding case worker said a paperwork "mistake" resulted in them never following up on the child's whereabouts or well being, so the "stepsister" without any legal standing went and filed for custody and competed with our filing, and did everything in her power to keep the case from going to court for as long as possible when we finally go our day in court (April 2022) they allowed her to file for adoption and froze the custody case.

Since the judge was too lazy, he just allowed this to happen and said he didn't want to decide on anything because either side would appeal, and it would be a waste of court resources, so we could just fight for adoption. How does that apply to case history and legal proceedings for family members? We were allowed to take the child for 7-12 days visits in our home and told we should be lucky that it was allowed; even though we were the only biological family members that were seeking custody of the child, we were treated like criminals by this court with not ever committing any crimes in our entire life.

Sadly, after this much time and money, we have had to give in and allow for the adoption of our nephew by non-family members and now will have very limited contact with him for the rest of his life; it is a shame how the system has treated us including collusion by the court-appointed guardians, attorneys, judges and DCS, and we don't even know where to go to voice this or take other legal action. Thank you for allowing us to speak about this. I am sure I have left out many other details, but it is difficult to recall this story in its entirety. We believe there is some level of profiting and child trafficking taking place in Monroe County, Tennessee; these non-relatives have done nothing but live off the system and profit through the child's dead mother, who, at a point before her downward spiral, had a somewhat productive and successful life.

THE PRESUMPTION OF GUILT

The presumption of innocence does not apply anymore? Why is this overlooked? No course of action is taken to clear an innocent name. False allegations and parental alienation simply aren't tackled within the justice system. The accused faces insurmountable challenges trying to restore credibility and does so alone. Being on the receiving end of an allegation is disastrous, resulting in side effects such as anxiety and depressive episodes. Suicidal ideation will be gifted to the victim as a result of running them through the mud.

The only aim for a person who attacks a victim with said methods is to destroy them completely. These extreme side effects can happen to anybody, regardless of whether the person has a healthy mental state. The stress and fear of being falsely accused will end up contributing to severe depression and insomnia, among other things.

Also, false accusations create unpredictability creating fear of the unknown; what is this person going to say next? This constant worry of being labelled leads to distrust among other people, making it difficult to move on and repair your life, which is the goal here.

The presumption of guilt is often attributed concerning allegations; under the circumstances of no evidence and hearsay. We should impartially approach cases, get the truth and serve justice. There are too many false allegation cases to speak of, and we have to look at our approach to these cases.

What about the real cases? The real cases will be looked upon with a higher degree of competence if the false cases are weeded out. We can address false allegations through measures like fines and penalties, listed on a register, alongside weekly station sign-ons. If we keep presuming that people aren't inclined to lie and make phoney allegations we will keep seeing innocent people go to prison, tarnished and suicidal.

We need to set up a system where allegations are not believed right away. The presumption of guilt is given to innocent people without any case concluding. At times straight away after the allegation.

There are too many people who are exonerated of false allegations and spent decades in prison for nothing. We are not preventing this but rather adding to it by believing every bit of hearsay evidence.

For sexual crimes, you're looked upon as the worst of the worst in prison. If a person is exonerated they get no help from the state or the system. If they have no family to go to; they will come out of prison homeless. Some come out and they are afraid to drive because of police stops. Some don't even use bins to rubbish their bottles or cups etc; In case their DNA is ever used to convict them of something.

Mental issues such as PTSD and severe depression will haunt a person wrongfully convicted. These are life-long issues; These are people! We assume they are all criminals and deserve every bit of punishment. False convictions come in many forms; hearsay, slander, mistaken identity, wrong forensic evidence even false confessions; it's not just allegations that wrongfully convict, but there is a staggering amount from this area. Allegations need to be addressed fully to protect the livelihoods of innocent people who get caught up in severe drama for no valid reason. With false allegations there should never be an assumption of belief from the very beginning. The allegation should be taken seriously but the alternative viewpoint should also be present; People do lie. The presumption of guilt from the start is counter-productive to the case.

Drug use allegations are aimed at bringing about unfair child access issues. This is one immediate accusation that makes you appear as dysfunctional and incompetent as possible. It is often done if the accuser just wants a good enough reason for you to lose your custody rights. The wasted court time is another contributor to the parental alienation epidemic: Family-court drama resulting in adjournment after adjournment.

Cases are constantly getting pushed back for one thing or another. This is all in a parental alienator playbook; this is the objective of the accuser: to waste as much time as humanly possible. The recanting or even the inventing of stories, no matter how fictitious or ridiculous, is still a win for the accuser. Mountains of court paperwork and delays in the legal system not only benefit the false accuser but are a major part of why they are accused. The clamouring of punishment filled with sheer suspense; portrays the victim-role with zest, the high, the importance, the new-found audience.

There could be much more of a focus on the encouragement of co-parenting for the children's sake. There could be measures to mediate or agree on terms and there simply isn't. These cases can be petty or even stem from mild disagreements blown way out of proportion or typically revenge from a broken relationship.

These court orders and false allegations only serve to put misery on the significant other's life. The personality disorders that embellish this route or scheme enjoy this as it brings about heightened significance. It is all done to destroy a person by having the system do it on behalf of them, courts, jail or homelessness; it's shifting the opposition's environment against them.

They use parental alienation to affect the emotions while the accusations fog the senses. So many of these false cases can be boiled down to the accuser displaying symptoms of a psychiatric disorder. Personality disorders are insufficient, with one everyday communicational function that is the basis for the majority of these cases.

That one act or function is; Negotiation. These disorders are non-negotiable and seek outrageous and unfair practices. They don't relate well to others, and they want everything while seeking the mistreatment of the other. There is no common ground here or even a slight chance to try to relate, even if just for the children's sake. That's why courts need to be the decision-makers for these types of relationships, but it shouldn't have to take a judge and a court to do so. These matters should be under a mandatory mediation system, avoiding any court process leaving only high-risk cases to enter the courtroom.

Hearsay shouldn't be substantial enough, nor should a tit-for-tat relationship fill up court dates with children not being addressed. Parental alienation is becoming a big enough societal issue, and we need to find ways to implement change going forward to free up court time for real cases.

Resources from the courts are being squandered, children are being left with manipulators who use them as mere-weapons. If we can weed out the suspicious cases we can pay full attention to the real cases that need a hearing. Sifting through endless paperwork, hiring attorneys or solicitors? all for; well nothing, just to test wills, hurt feelings and break well established bonds.

Get good legal representation, build a case and prepare for the next hurdle, as every step is either one step closer to exoneration or ruination. When introduced with characteristics that point towards a person's destructive nature, as outlined here; caution and knowledge of the traits are important. Document interactions with the partner or spouse; try to establish if they do indeed fit the criteria for such mental disorders. As the most dangerous people are not medically diagnosed, they refuse to seek help and would be offended if the topic was brought up in conversation.

Study up on personality disorders and mental health conditions if you believe your relationship is somewhat odd. One must self-diagnose, carefully observing the traits and behaviour patterns of loved ones. This self diagnosis would preferably be executed without the partner known as this, can trigger various personality disorders resulting in vendettas and reactions made out of spite.

So many people either live the remainder of their lives with the knowledge that they have something or are completely unaware of mental health conditions, never considering getting an assessment done.

These days, the court systems are outdated. Anyone can go in and make a protective order, for example, with non-sense written on it. No proof and no cross-examination considered. In fact, not even a simple questioning is performed, people don't lie, right? They are incapable of lying under oath, the courts believe. It's just filed, printed and ready to be posted to your address or even hand-delivered by the policeman on duty.

Legislation must be reviewed and improved within the context of false reporting or bearing false witness; someday in our lifetime, it may just happen if it is pushed forward.

Think about the strenuous court system we have with the understaffed, overpopulated and unimaginable amounts of cases that aren't actually real cases. If eradicated, how much court time would be saved? Real cases would see the light of day, and the police would have their attention on matters that need attention.

In turn, that would impact the community greatly, rather than wasting the time of solicitors, judges, and every member who works within the legal system. Furthermore, it would not only bring light to the shameful actions of the false accusers, but it would also be an unimaginable gift for the real victims of such abuse and crimes, more time focused on the real cases that have merit.

There are women out there who have unfortunate life experiences relating to aggressive psychopathic men and need help immediately. It does not only help in terms of policing and court, but we also need to see to it that they are not impersonated. They need stability and direct attention, and by eliminating fake cases, these women would indeed be provided with better assistance and faster justice.

These courts attempt to minimise abuse or friction among families. The courts need some education on abuse, as it comes in many different forms. Abuse can come as coercive control with the usage of court orders against a person to distort the truth and punish. Abuse can come in the form of alienation of children, ultimately forcing children into the hands of actual abusers. Addressing false accusations head on will create a much needed requirement to process court punishments fairly. A simple review or meeting with a person after they've made allegations could be enough to deter any motive they have to harass someone. It shouldn't be too difficult to detect false accusations before the court date. The point here is there is no attempt to weed them out.

There should be a review of such cases and the allegations scrutinised in terms of legitimacy and credibility. Cases or behavioural actions that stick out are cases with word against word with no merit, a clear malicious attitude towards another or the refusal to try mediation services. With how easily manipulated the courts are today, ideally, we need to blow the dust off the lie-detector tests.

Even a meeting or questioning regarding the allegations or a cross-examination, if you will. Staff trained with proven abilities, perhaps body language experts trained to look between the lines. Nothing is done now; court staff are accepting anything and everything with no filter, causing massive stagnation throughout the court system. If something, anything, was done to decrease the abounding caseload, we would, in turn, have much more man-power to tackle these areas efficiently and competently. Motions need to be set into place, such as penalties or fines if proven to be giving false statements.

The need for deterrents would minimise a person looking to flex their lying abilities. If some measure were put into place, it would deter most people, either simply wicked or who suffer from mental conditions, from utilising the legal system as a weapon.

The weaponization of court usage is a real thing that affects millions of people worldwide. Furthermore, the deliberate act of alienating the children from the other parent is commonly adapted for use as a weapon. This needs to stop, and there needs to be updated laws highlighting this as it's extremely damaging to the children involved.

The police can also be used as a form of harassment which can lead to them paying visits to the accused over bogus calls and accusations. The police can be constantly phoning the target or seeking arrest all because they cannot simply refute claims and suspect personal vendettas. It is not in the job description of the police to use discernment in cases even when they know the real situation just by intuition alone.

Domestic calls are a must for the police, and they definitely should call to the premises and take it completely seriously. In saying that, there are requirements that are not met in terms of policing. The police should document their patrols more efficiently, detailing perceptions and opinions. They should have an updated system, and it is compulsory to update it after each task or patrol is handled, including domestics, searches, traffic stops, etc. This information could be used for future court cases and behavioural displays from individuals. The active police should have to document each callout, including what happened, what was said, and the conclusion. If they are called for a domestic call, they simply believe it and will arrive again and again without documenting that it's a fake call-out.

They might write a few details down on a notepad, nothing substantial, and it's simply not logged with any details other than it being a domestic call. It doesn't matter how many times they are called with no evidence, no neighbours with similar calls, no bruises or marks on the victim or even a reason for what happened at times, simply because they are looking at the abuser and not the victim, the real victim is being vilified. Watch out for fake police-call-outs; this could be signs of a future court battle in its infancy. That's how these people think; they think well in advance and plan a case. These fake police call-outs could corroborate their future false allegations.

On file, all it will say is yes, the police called out here, here and here with no other details. These people believe they are smarter than everyone else and proceed to manipulate others in their lives easily. Pay close attention if you are a victim of false police callouts, as it could be a precursor to future events. Policing can be a tough job, and yes, they should respond in all seriousness to every crime, but equally, they should flag calls if it's a constant prank-like call. People with psychiatric disorders think they can outsmart the policing system and leverage police time over mere disputes.

In a relationship, some of the instances that could trigger this behaviour could be a feeling of trust being broken or feeling unvalidated; perhaps they feel their partner is leaving them, and they think police usage is a good revenge. These petty incidents and others like them are a precursor of extreme revenge. The knowledge of such disorders, even in basic terms, is not known to police either, nor are they aware of dynamics that foster false allegations or punishments of loved ones.

Our courts, police and children are being exploited for superficial purposes for the most part. False accusations are unfortunately all too common. How to navigate through them is the hard part especially when the topic is rarely spoken of. The court system administers criminal law, resolves civil disputes, and upholds the rights of citizens; in no way should it be used as a tool for revenge regarding petty disputes or a hurt feeling of not being validated.

There are no repercussions for making such claims, and if there are, they are never exercised and cannot be unless legislation is altered in a way to find out if a person is being truthful or not. Ideally, every single case should be categorised and independently worked upon by a team of mediators trained to resolve disputes. We could create a new branch set up for these cases. In particular, they could act as a conduit for the courts.

A review of family court cases before any trial commences, which could potentially transfer over to trial depending on the variables from case to case. If deemed a possible legitimate case, it would be sent to trial, but if it's not a real case, it would be settled out of court with the parties involved required to participate. Taking the stage of court away from potential false accusers would diminish their motivations to lie and bear false witness.

Most of these cases can be settled easily if the right approach is set. The court is currently not designed to settle cases or protect children from being alienated. Ideally, there should be forced mediation between couples, and the mediation services could then funnel results to the court or be given the ability to make decisions on behalf of a judge. Keeping cases that are a waste of time or lack any merit out of court completely.

Likewise, training staff on the subtle nuances of these types of cases and the cases that previously occurred would be quite beneficial. What to expect, what's possible and how the system can be weaponized should be trained thoroughly. Parental alienation is a highly depressing subject and we need workers skilled and updated on the ways in which this all works, along with key indicators to look out for. Obviously there is too much money to be made right now in the legal industry and these ideas are just ideal thinking. Money from judges to attorneys or solicitors, that racket will never end and dragging cases out deem extremely profitable for the few.

That being said we as a society need to start perfecting some aspects of these legalities and how these matters are processed. We need to bring these key points into the public domain so as a whole we can make suggestions upon best courses of action. We need suggestions and solution orientated ideas, the system is broken. People should have their data stored digitally on police records, for active duty police men and women to visually see if it is assumed a person makes regular unfounded calls or claims.

When speaking of false allegations of rape Sandra Newman listed four key motivations. This is in the area of deliberate deception regarding falsifying reports. Newman listed four: revenge, producing an alibi, personal gain, and mental illness. (S Newman 2017) and Eugene J Kanin listed three: revenge, producing an alibi, and getting sympathy or attention. (E, J Kanin1994)

We need to work on minimising the overcrowding that is prevalent in our court systems. It is imperative to free up court time especially if it's being wasted on hearsay, slander and non-sense. The persumption of guilt right away is the wrong approach considering what we know about false allegations.

Case Study Glen

This next case study is from Glen, an alias name as requested for his anonymity.

He has three children (16) (6) (2) with his ex-partner and an 18-year-old nonbiological son. They stayed together for 16 years and were married 10 of those years. Glen recalls back when they first met, she would mention some hardships such as her mother and father's break up, which really affected her.

Another hardship she would beat the drum off is her ex, who she made out to be a horrible person. She claimed throughout her life, men had taken advantage of her, and this sentiment inspired Glen somewhat to actively be there for her and protect her.

He bought flowers and fell in love with her and thought it was going to be "a forever thing". It turned into an on-and-off relationship with them living apart.

As he was living apart, peculiar behaviour started to unfold regarding who this woman was. For example, as they were living apart, his friend's housemate received a missed phone call from her. The strange thing about this is Glen's friend doesn't actually know her; calls came through with her having sex in the background. After verifying the number on his phone, Glen thought this was weird. His friend mentioned not to ever get back with her, which is not how things unfolded. He eventually got back together with her, looking beyond odd behaviour as they were broken up at the time.

She soon was kicked out of her parent's house for throwing parties; her mother chose her stepfather's side and kicked her out. They ended up moving in together, and things seemed normal.

She would constantly say negative things about other people. Glen was into the cleaning/restoration business and would work many hours a day, sometimes 6 days a week. He then got into the sales and marketing firm down south after the second baby, as there was money to be made. With the amount of work Glen did week in and week out, he became a bit more distant from his then-wife. She had what she needed financially and was well looked after, but he began to feel like he wanted to be there more and had ideas of starting his own thing, his own business.

It felt like the more he made, the more she spent; excessive spending continued throughout the relationship and with demand, there came supply, so Glen had to keep making more money. So, with the money he had aside, he ventured out to start his own business. Originally, the business was going to be glass, but it soon led to everything, such as front drives, landscaping, and, eventually, a turnkey development business.

While waiting for the next baby, Glen started to hear unsettling rumours about whether the baby would be his. Rumours about his then-wife and her friend were with multiple other men. When confronted on this, she claimed it was rape and became angered.

In six weeks, her baby was due, so Glen thought he would stay together with the kids. As time went on, she never pursued any charges for this supposed rape, and this action told Glen it was consensual. The relationship was toxic and abusive, and Glen mentions he was broken. He worked and worked, and with the business niche he had, the house was done up to perfection, but they lived almost separate lives.

His business evolved into the property business while rumours continued to circulate about his wife. They had another baby, and she mentioned to him, do you see, "It's yours" after having the child. Alcohol was in their life quite a bit at this point, and the relationship went into a downward spiral. Glen remembers the first time she attacked him, punched his glasses off and threw pint glasses at him. She called him a coward and tried to hit him with a broken glass repeatedly, which Glen feared for the children and did not defend himself. After being on and off again, the back-and-forth relationship continued; Glen wanted to remain in the children's lives and gave it a chance.

Not long after, that would be the second time she would attack him. From the kitchen to the living room, he's just taken it; she was drunk and hitting him. He eventually grabbed her wrists and tried to calm her down, but then she bit him in the chest. She swung a few times and then ran into neighbours. Soon, the police would be called.

This would be Glen's first offence, never being in a police station, never being in jail, never in trouble with the law. While he was in the station, she was brought to hospital. She alleged that he raped her that morning. However, their daughter's transcript conflicted with that entire argument.

The police came to Glen and said we are rearresting you for sexual offences. and were placed into a Dry-cell which is a prison cell that does not have a toilet or running water. She claimed in the hospital that he'd raped her that morning, and when asked can they do an examination on her, she refused. The charges that Glen was giving were ABH (Actual Bodily Harm), coercive control and battery.

There were no sexual charges, which he quizzed the police as he was read out the charges. "Where's the sexual stuff?" he said, to which the police replied, "There is none". Back to the cell and then court soon followed, to which Glen pleaded to his solicitor that his clients need paying, he's got a business, please help. The judge decided to put him on remand. Meanwhile, the rape squad would pay a visit to his wife. They interviewed her on a Monday for a couple of hours, then on the Wednesday, which they had to bring her back in for.

In the first interview she did, there was nothing sexual whatsoever. In week two, in the prison cell, Glen wrote her a really nice letter, stating that things went wrong, keep the house and everything else trying to make some sort of progress or amends.

The 5th week, he was in there when someone who knew Glen mentioned to her at a school run, "Did you know he was planning on leaving you?". The letter should have never left the prison, but Glen was none the wiser as there were no restrictions or nothing was ever mentioned. The indictments were ABH, coercive control and battery. Now added to the indictments was another ABH from 2 years prior. The letter that he sent her resulted in him being charged with witness intimidation. He asked one of the lead builders at his design studio for the business to go around and get some personal possessions out there, which led to a charge of stalking.

Then, at week 7, she decided to go with the sexual allegations. The charge was a campaign of rape from 2018 to 2022. By this time, he is two months in prison and has 13 indictments against him. He is looking at a life sentence, the campaign of rape he believes would have been 25 years minimum. The ABH is five years for one charge; he had two, then the stalking and witness intimidation all add up to a considerable amount of time to live behind bars.

This was Wakefield prison with a possible move to Belmarsh prison. Glen began to lose hope and expected to be in prison for life. He became a Wing Listener while locked up before he was even a sentenced prisoner.

A wing listener is a volunteer scheme within prisons which aims to reduce suicide. Listeners are prisoners who provide confidential emotional support to their fellow inmates who are struggling to cope and want to commit suicide.

Glen prevented two suicides while incarcerated. The main wings were okay, but as soon as they put Glen into Papa's wing, he encountered horrible inmates. What hurt Glen the most was being on the wing with some of these vile people; there was a guy next door who raped his own 14-year-old daughter because he bought her some trainers and said she had to start paying her way. The guy opposite them had kicked his own baby to death. Glen tried to get on with his life behind bars and became a wing chef and kept active doing some prison courses.

During the prison sentence, the police would set up interviews in which Glen usually said no comment to any of the questions asked. Three prosecutors looked at his case and wouldn't take it. An incident happened with his wife while this was going on. She attacked her own son, and she attacked a neighbour and also her friend.

As the commotion was going on, there was a pile-on with people present grabbing and trying to restrain her, and she accidentally hit a child (2 & a half years old) in the face. This was an incident from a transcript from her son. In the same transcript, the son talks about her promiscuity, having different guys over and openly displaying flirtatious behaviour. They argued, and he said to his mother, reminding her that she said she was going to concentrate just on the children.

She eventually made an argument to deflect the narrative and made out that her son attacked her, but the transcripts and reports are pretty damning and paint her in a negative light highlighting her toxic behaviour. She was arrested for multiple assaults, and the police decided Not to let the CPS know what their 'witness had done or about the incident at all, as Glen was still in prison for these ongoing false allegations.

Meanwhile, the mention-hearing was on with Glen's case, and a prosecutor was supposed to look into his case. He never turned up, so they had a different prosecutor on standby.

The mention hearing begins via video link, Glen in prison observing, and the prosecutor mentions, "With the limited information I've read, we won't be taking this case". The prosecutor went on, "What I can see is there are protracted delays by the police and the CPS as a whole, which is very alarming about the case". The police let CPS know about Glen's wife's arrest a couple of months later. There were reports, internet search results, statements that night and the following day and bodycam footage.

So much from the moment she was arrested was redacted, but this information was available to both parties in the case. The next mention-hearing arrived via video link again.

When Glen found out what had happened with the escalation to CPS and his wife's behaviour and arrest, he broke down in tears; he said something along the lines of "I can't believe you're still doing this; I'm in here for all the things you said I've done wrong, and you're just proving what your like, why can't you just be there for them children".

Unbeknownst to Glen, the prosecutor was still on the screen watching and could hear his exasperation. In the mention-hearing, the prosecutor claimed, "With the new evidence that has come to light, there will be dynamic changes within the case as a whole".

They organised a quick crisis meeting with the CPS, social services, and the police. The next few days, Glen received a call from his legal team, to his disbelief, he was "getting out".

They wanted to do a plea deal, but Glen was not interested; he was the victim in all of this; in fact, his wife admitted she attacked him. The solicitor mentioned he could remain in prison and that there is a concern for care around your children. They wanted to give him the charge of ABH, but there was no way Glen would accept that either. Then, he was offered excessive self-defence, which he accepted. Then, a few days later, Glen was hauled away in the police van to court. The court began at 10 o'clock that morning, and it took them just 12 minutes to find Glen not guilty on all charges, although he did take the excessive self-defence plea. This was not guilty on 12 indictments.

While he was waiting to be released, there was a delay. The charges were so serious that the judge had to get in touch with the governor, who was on holiday because the prison wouldn't release him. Assuming that there was some sort of mistake, eventually, the information came to the prison, and Glen was finally released. He began to suspect his wife of having either narcissistic or histrionic personality disorder.

Now, as he's out, the doctor diagnosed him with PTSD, Anxiety and Indefinite Depression due to his stint in prison. He was also type 2 diabetic, and shortly after the diagnosis, he began to get his life back together.

The depression was also caused by not being allowed to see his children or his wife not allowing him to. He sold his business to investors and works with and contributes to men's mental health and suicide groups.

His wife ended up with the home. He stayed to try to protect the children, and he regrets it to this day. Completely turned off any future relationships due to the malicious nature he encountered with his wife. Glen was abused as a child, and his wife used it against him; he is completely against domestic violence; he was manipulated for finances and was targeted to have his heart broken repeatedly in every which way.

"In case you needed a reminder, your narcissistic partner is not going to change.

There is virtually no evidence of good treatment outcomes in the literature on narcissism."

(Dr Ramani Durvasula, 2015)

Chapter 5
Enter Narcissistic Personality Disorder

Narcissism is a term that originated from the story of Narcissus in Greek mythology. The story goes that Narcissus couldn't stop gazing at his reflection. He fell in love with himself, or rather his image, which appeared out of a pool of water.

Fascinated with how good he looked, he remained in the gaze, completely self-absorbed. This one-way relationship went nowhere fast and ultimately came to his demise as he died of thirst and starvation or, in some versions, killed himself with a dagger or drowned in that same pool of water.

Narcissism itself can be viewed as a personality trait; those who display self-importance or grandiosity. There can be a healthy form of narcissism with actions such as taking care of yourself or showing confidence in life tasks, potentially even reaching goals.

Narcissism exists on a spectrum, meaning a person who has some traits of narcissism; This doesn't precisely conclude they have a narcissistic personality disorder. For example, having some personality traits without the inability to take accountability for one's own actions or having a sadistic streak within them, delighting in the suffering of another for a gain of some sort.

Narcissistic personality disorder symptoms or character traits are as follows;

- Complete lack of empathy
- Expect to be recognized as superior
- Grandiosity
- Unreasonably high sense of self-importance
- Preoccupation with power, beauty, or success
- Entitled and arrogant
- Exploitative for personal gain
- Thinking others are Envious; while Envious of others
- Need for excessive admiration
- Narcissistic supply
- Narcissistic rage
- Fantasies about deserving or having the best of things

Narcissistic personality disorder (NPD) is one of the most complex and dangerous personality disorders. The individual with NPD will form an ideal egoic image, often referred to as an inflated image of themselves.

This image is grandiose and superficial, at times, even delusional. The unhealthy attachment to this self-image acts as a distraction from the deep-seated insecurities the narcissist truly feels inside. They don't care to show this part to the outside world; to others, the narcissist puts on the front of the unstoppable inflated self.

Narcissistic personality disorder involves a path of self-centeredness with no consideration for other people. They ooze arrogance and are patronizing and highly demanding. It's the narcissist's way or the highway, and in case you're thinking of taking the highway, they have that route all planned out for you, too. They have a craving for excessive admiration. The individual with NPD will shamelessly show their skills of lacking empathy for another person as if it's a desirable characteristic.

The narcissist is stuck in their thought-forms with the need to reinforce their egos. Therefore, they are susceptible to any or every act of criticism. They can't bear to think that an opposing viewpoint exists of who they are. The mere act of handling criticism, even if it is constructive, is a daunting task.

The narcissist is ingrained with the inability to self-reflect, limiting any learning experiences. You will notice if you're involved in a relationship with a narcissist that lying and gaslighting are perfected by them. Another possibility is they may not do chores as they feel it's beneath them. Money is spent quicker than it comes in as they are pretty careless; they want the best. They might go out of their way to impress you at the beginning of the relationship, possibly love bombing, but pretty soon, their true form appears, and it's adoration to everyone else except you. They have honed skills such as manipulation and doing whatever it takes to get what they want.

> **"The borderline personality is peppered with many aspects of other personality disorders"** (Millon, T, Grossman, S, Meagh, S, et al., 2004)

The narcissist is emotionally immature, a well-known similarity with the borderline. When looking into personality disorders, you'll find symptoms or behaviours that overlap with other personality disorders. The criteria can be lengthy, but the more studies on these disorders or the more time spent with, say, a narcissist, the symptoms are blatantly obvious.

The behaviour of NPD is centred around disparaging others, reacting strongly with rage or bullying others to feel some superiority. They have difficulty managing emotions and can be agitated when not receiving the recognition or treatment they feel entitled to.

They can be offended quite easily, leading to difficulties in social interaction. Stress or adapting to any form of change can also be a challenge, and if a predictable failure is afoot, they may exit the situation entirely. The narcissist is cunning, thinking ahead of all the different possibilities a situation might lead to and preparing for each probable outcome.

If they wish to do battle in a court setting, they could bait a victim into doing or saying something incriminating well in advance of the court case even coming to fruition. If they exhibit any abuse or chaotic behaviours, leaving traces of evidence through text, video or other means, they will erase it well in advance.

Cluster B can be quite cunning in this regard to prep for a case while their partner gets hit with the element of surprise. One thing that impedes a Cluster B type personality in the courtroom is that with every question asked involving their partner, it's over-dramatized, or they take the opportunity to regurgitate-up some extreme accusations one after another.

Narcissists are motivated by the fear of being exposed, either to their systematic abuse or as a failure. Feelings of insecurity, humiliation or shame may plague them, which could result in a spiral of rage or depression.

They would stop at nothing to derail a person's life and even derive pleasure from causing harm to others. They indulge in feeling entitled and superior and would feel threatened or challenged quite easily. With the empathy deficiency surrounding cluster B, they all have an egoic tendency to dehumanize the other.

Narcissists are skilled at manipulating others by playing off their emotions, so it is vital to put yourself first. At least try to negotiate any form of boundary-setting or workable solutions that can protect your self-esteem and livelihood. Don't be swayed off-course by fearing the narcissist, and love yourself enough to leave the relationship if it contains too much abuse and manipulation.

This requires a combination of assertiveness, self-awareness and education. By having an understanding of these disorders, you can recognize some of the traits and systematic abuse patterns that these disorders are known for. If possible, establish clear boundaries as soon as you can, if you can at all, as setting boundaries can be next to impossible. Addressing your feelings and concerns can seem futile; Nothing is about you. It is all about the narcissist. Throughout a relationship with a narcissist, you will constantly find some pushback to test personal limits of what's tolerated. Yielding control in any relationship is an impossibility for the narcissist.

Stress will trigger the narcissist, causing some uncomfortable anxiety within. Noticeable anger can be visible through their words or facial expressions. When anger is built up, the narcissist explodes with what's termed as narcissistic rage. This rage brings unsettling, onward drama throughout the situation or relationship. This would be intense explosions, screaming, and shouting, incredibly disproportionate to the situation.

After the coercive-controlling, abusive relationship is all said and done, what can usually erupt within the emotional stability or even deflate the narcissist's ego is their victim getting by pretty well after the fact. Specific triggers would be an outcome of success such as in housing, relationships or other areas of life, even just happiness. Beneath it all, narcissists lack any cohesive ability to sustain any self-esteem and need support from others for their sense of self. Their ego appears strong, but with a mere feeling of inferiority, they may crumble right in front of your eyes. Try to promote your lifestyle and upload that video or picture; the narcissist is watching and feels your esteem and mood. If the narcissist did not obliterate you, then this visual of getting your life back will hurt the narcissist for once.

When researching narcissistic personality disorder, you will be introduced to many different types of narcissism categorized with variances. Depending on where you look, some teachings reckon there are five and some as many as 14 different types of NPD. For this section, we will briefly go through some relevant types.

The Overt or Grandiose Narcissist is the typical type, unveiling grandiosity and trying to impress others in their life. They can charm people and be well-liked socially. They are the type to lie about or completely exaggerate instances to impress and have people think highly of them.

They are quick to point out flaws and cannot accept any flaw within their own behaviour. They can be pretty outgoing, gain attention, and be comfortable socially, boasting and charming. Like the rest of the categories in NPD, they have feigned relationships and an inability to feel empathy. Believing so firmly in their abilities, they would dismiss any expert, disregarding opinions, including a mental health professional's analysis. Their central theme, like all narcissists, is to believe in the hype about their importance or exaggerated view of themselves, also known as delusions of grandeur.

Covert or Vulnerable narcissists are a bit more reserved and fragile. They have a difficult time with criticism and tend to be envious of others. Often leaning into a state of judgment, either judging others or their shortcomings.

They would likely be a loner due to all the reflecting regarding themselves and others, deep thoughts on possessions, relationships and social standing. Passive-aggressive and lacking self-esteem, they are engulfed in shame. This makes them more prone to depression, rumination or even suicide.

Hypervigilant Narcissism is centred around paranoia, constantly scanning around for possible threats. Rejection is a deep-seated fear for them, and they are very attentive to their surroundings.

They tend to search out for subtle disrespect from others or possible insults. Socializing doesn't come easy, and because of this, the ability to handle abandonment or rejection is tough for them.

Malignant Narcissism is often associated with the traits of antisocial personality disorder. Harming others for attention purposes and using manipulation for control like the rest of the types of narcissistic personality disorder.

Showing areas of behaviour such as sadism and aggression towards others in their life, lacking remorse and exhibiting more of the extreme symptoms of narcissism.

There is a likelihood of having other co-occurring personality disorders to accompany malignant narcissism. The tendency to exploit others, gaining pleasure from the mistreatment they give to their loved ones, often displaying behaviours of abuse and remaining vindictive and paranoid.

Case study Zhang

This case study is from a woman, and it highlights so many NPD characteristics that are probably motivated by narcissistic injury, in which the individual with NPD will stop at nothing to destroy their partner. This woman is frightened and can't sleep due to anxiety. She also doesn't trust anyone and remains a recluse and unsocial from her experiences with her ex-husband. She married this guy back in 2010. He is 15 years her senior and has a long history of substance abuse and alcohol. He had been lying to her since the beginning regarding his addiction.

She was pretty naive because he was the first guy she ever dated. After they got married and moved to California, he stopped working for two full years, claiming he couldn't find a job, and he was very depressed. He would say he felt very withdrawn by leaving behind his friends and family as it was her who decided to move states. She felt guilty, so she didn't push him to get a job or continue any dispute.

Things changed when she became pregnant; his demeanour was different; her parents visited and noted the husband didn't do anything helpful for her but would rather lay on the couch every day eating chips while his 8-month pregnant wife had to work overtime.

There were several arguments between the husband and her parents, but eventually, he found a job. He worked for a few years and became unemployed in 2020 due to a coronavirus outbreak. She was okay with that in the beginning as she thought it would be a temporary thing. Then, when the restrictions were lifted, the husband showed no intention of going back to work.

This time, he used kids and housework as an excuse, but she knew it was just a lie, as she had been working from home during the pandemic. Last spring, she noted his lifestyle changed significantly overnight (he worked out crazily, changed the password on his cell phone, etc.). She suspected he had an affair with another lady, but he refused to explain.

Then, in July 2023, he turned around and started consulting a family law attorney. He withdrew his Roth IRA account in August and September for a retainer. She accidentally found out about his early withdrawal in November. Three days later, she questioned this action out of curiosity, moving so much money without any communication.

He filed for divorce secretly and started to collect "evidence" to prove she was mentally unstable. Her father, who lived with them and was the primary caregiver, was terminally ill at this point, so she was pretty busy taking care of him.

The husband not only refused to provide any emotional support but also started creating conflicts during that period. Harassing and calling her at 2 am on Xmas Eve from upstairs when she left her cell phone on in fear of her father's life as he was in ICU. He also kept asking when the parents were moving out, with explicit knowledge that her father only had a few months left to live. He would callously ask why she cried for her father and why she expected him to live forever.

Insulting her in front of her kids and saying degrading things caused so much drama during this period. She was busy with work and taking care of the other family members, and she ignored this behaviour. He couldn't get any solid evidence to prove she was crazy. So he wrote this lengthy request for a restraining order (14 pages) claiming she was physically, verbally and emotionally abusive. Also, he made allegations of a sexual nature of abuse and financial abuse of himself and the kids. He was not able to provide any solid information, but the judge was overwhelmed by this lengthy dossier of accusations, so he got a temporary restraining order against her.

Then, she was served with the divorce papers and a restraining order at the same time and was removed from the house where she had lived for 12 years. This restraining order took away her custody of the kids and also prevented her from seeing her father, who was not mobile due to illness.

After she was removed from the house, he started physically and emotionally abusing her parents as he planned to remove them from the property. He pushed her mother to the ground, causing a big bruise on her nose and fracturing two of her ribs. He constantly showed the middle finger to her mother and smirked at her.

He dumped compost outside of their windows, and he broke into their dwelling in the backyard. He then filed a restraining order against her mother 5 days after her father passed away, claiming she was crazy and that she hit her head against the staircase as an alternative to the abuse he inflicted. He then dropped the case a couple of days later after realizing her mother had been hospitalized and wouldn't be home anytime soon.

He boasted to all their common friends that the persona they had witnessed up until this time was all an act. She suspected he may have narcissistic personality disorder or that he is a psychopath, considering the constant lies and manipulation. One aspect that affected relations is his inability to take any constructive criticism, his extreme lack of empathy, and the numerous false accusations.

There were two protection orders against her and one for her mother. He dismissed the two fake court orders directed towards her as his primary purpose was to occupy the property by himself during the divorce process. Since both the ex-wife and mother had already moved out, his goal was achieved.

He dropped his case so the judge would never find out his lies. Her attorney advised her not to move back in because of the high-conflict situation.

It is a typical tactic divorce attorneys use in the United States, especially when their clients are housewives or house-husbands married to affluent people and want to stay in the house for as long as possible. Once the other party moves out, the judge will likely not support them returning even when the false accusations are dismissed because the other party claims he or she is scared!

It is common in California for both parties to split the property evenly and get joint custody (50/50 shares).

She had $8k in her safe, and he took most of it. He has a history of stealing money and lying; he also stole the credit cards and maxed them out, only getting $500, but still had the intent of taking over, along with everything in his path.

He built new fences between the property and neighbours. He used the credit cards for materials for that fencing while the neighbour reimbursed her for the materials purchased, feeling sorry and aware of the lies and deceit occurring.

He miscalculated during the divorce process and was manipulated by his greedy attorney. His attorney thought we were big fish, just like her other wealthy housewives. So they thought that by removing her from the property, they could keep the main residence using the alimony money, as the mortgage is quite low.

But they underestimated the debt, as she's been borrowing money from family for years, and her sole income can barely offset the expenditures.

He currently still resides in the property that's up for sale and is manipulating the children without any consequences. He initially thought he could keep the property with his narcissistic tactics.

He greatly overestimated the net wealth and dragged the process of the property from being sold for as long as he could. Police called on him many times during this whole time frame with no outcome or evidence.

NARCISSISTIC SUPPLY

Narcissistic supply operates on a basis of attention; This could be good or bad, as long as it is attention. This could come in the form of admiration or recognition, which would supply a dose of positive energy to the narcissist. Alternatively, attention such as repulsion, hate, or fear, as there is no differentiation concerning the energetic supply, positive or negative, makes no difference.

It's the attention that they are getting that is all that matters to the narcissist. They can project to the outside world that they are living a good life or in a loving relationship while annihilating their partner's self-esteem. The supply towards the narcissist is an essential aspect to them.

If the supply ceases to come in, they may drop the relationship and seek out another. This energy preoccupation that the narcissist has is why methods such as grey rocking were created. These people are focused on draining energy from others and will stop at nothing to make a person feel something.

The observation of others hurt, confused and angry feeds their supply. Validation is sought after intensely; any attention, good or bad, will give them their much-needed narcissistic supply.

The narcissist divides all people into two primary groups: Those who can provide them with narcissistic supply regularly, this being the high-grade, unmitigated source of supply—full of criticism, drama, disagreement and conflict for example.

Those who can not or do not usher in this supply are abruptly devalued and discarded. Those who can are nurtured or groomed and maintained until they can no longer provide the narcissistic supply. Then it is rinse and repeat; every person is considered an object of sorts.

Summary & Honorable Mentions of Narcissistic Personality Disorder

Triggering a partner to the point of hysteria in an attempt to bait them into a situation or gain a reaction or meltdown from them. This triggering could be recorded as a way to discredit and prove the partner's instability in evidence form, with the end result being the narcissist is the poor, innocent victim.

This is reactive abuse and works through the partners' ignorance of the manipulation tactics being deployed. The victim has a hard time realizing they are getting set up. The narcissist keeps people separated from each other, feeding different information to each of them or no information to others. Then, they sit back and watch all of the drama unfold.

The narcissist doesn't love you; they love the idea of controlling you.

They play the victim and use DARVO - deny attack reverse victim and offender. Darvo is an acronym that describes the narcissistic manipulation-repertoire used to abuse and shift blame, bearing no chance of accountability. The narcissist will hide who they truly are and have a deep-seated fear of exposure to who they truly are. This encourages some of their behaviour, such as smear campaigns and accusations.

When the narcissist speaks, it's almost like they are speaking to themselves or to a mirror. When the mirror does not reflect what they desire to hear back, this triggers them powerfully, as it's not what they idealized it to be. Their personality is malleable or changeable depending on what is necessary for their wants, and they can play whatever character is appropriate for the situation.

Such as the victim or past victim, the darling who love-bombs at the beginning of a relationship or the person who creates rumours, turning others against one another and playing both sides. Like many others aforementioned, psychopathy and narcissism can overlap, with very few differences. Almost half of borderlines have narcissistic personality disorder (Grant BF, Chou SP, Goldstein RB, et al. 2008)

For more on the inner workings of an individual who exhibits narcissistic traits and how they are likely to manoeuvre, see chapter (Hurt People, Hurt People)

Narcissists will usually accuse their victims of being a narcissist. They will become accusatory of the behaviour of another that they themselves demonstrate. For example, they could accuse of gaslighting with no basis, almost like knowledge of the tools that they themselves use, but projecting it onto others, bringing about confusion. This works in some areas where the victim is baited into an angry confrontation or argument, which would then become the fault of the victim rather than the instigator. The narcissistic person is performative in multiple facets of life, having many different double lives at one time, in terms of a new supply, flying monkeys, or just manipulating others. They don't change for new people or even a new supply; this chaotic behaviour is hardwired within them.

It is traumatizing to finally come to the realization and to see the narcissistic abuse for what it is. How evil a person can be, the annihilation, destruction and callous attempts to destroy a so-called loved one. The narcissistic-abuse coaching niche is booming now because of it. Once a person becomes aware of this cycle of abuse and is heading for the exit, so to speak, this will bring about shock and shame and trigger narcissistic injury. The shame and injury to their ego will infuriate them, motivating them to pursue the revenge cycle.

No matter how low they go with this revenge, they will be absent from any accountability. This is where they use the children as a way to manipulate and cause significant distress, furthering the abuse and or coercive control.

They expect you to tolerate devaluing, insulting, humiliating behaviour, cutting off contact or cheating, smear campaigns and much more.

Only a close partner or person will see these aspects of the narcissist. The narcissist will be more likeable to everybody else in life; they will show everyone an ideal image of what they want to appear as. This aspect is part of the multifaceted personality disorder; it is almost like their sole focus is on living as many double lives as possible.

Their reasoning could be to get the most out of life. They are the lovely neighbour, the darling pedestrian, the darling victim even. All the while being a tyrant in their relationships with others, demonstrating evil tactics with the sole intention of ruining another person's life.

This mask flips almost instantaneously. The neighbour they just said cheerio to would never suspect that this person would be incapable of empathy or compassion. We don't know what goes on when the doors close and this covert, abusive nature rears its ugly head.

Chapter 6
Cluster B

The grouping of clusters within DSM-5 is a categorisation varied by similarities and shared character traits. For example, there is overly dramatic or emotional immaturity, an inability to maintain relationships, odd behaviour regarding how they are viewed, or a combative nature that will be followed by impulsive reactions or calculated manipulation.

There is a distress level among the group and a tendency to find it quite a challenge to manage emotions to the point of instability and unpredictability concerning their life choices and outcomes.

Some aspects of personality disorders differ, and some people with the disorders can range differently than others with duration of the symptoms or severity.

Clusters of Personality Disorders in DSM-5-TR

The DSM-5-TR divides personality disorders into clusters, each being in the category A, B, and C, each with a distinct set of personality disorders with commonalities regarding symptoms, behaviours, and underlying psychological patterns. (Novais F,Araujo, Godinho P 2015) (Crocq MA 2013)

Cluster A:

Personality disorders displaying characteristics of an odd or eccentric nature, including paranoid, schizoid, and schizotypal personality disorders. Individuals within this cluster group have difficulties forming close relationships and experience social withdrawal, mistrust, paranoia and a lack of emotional responses. This group can be suspicious of their surroundings and remain cold and distant, lacking empathy. (Esterberg ML, Goulding, SM Walker EF 2010)

Cluster B:

Cluster B encompasses personality disorders with dramatic, emotional, or erratic behaviours. This cluster includes Histrionic along with Antisocial, Borderline, and Narcissistic personality disorders. Individuals within this cluster typically display impulsive actions, emotional instability or, turbulent, dysregulated emotions and challenges in maintaining stable relationships.(Turner D,Sebastian A,Tüscher O, 2017)

Cluster C:

Cluster C encompasses personality disorders with anxious and fearful characteristics. These include avoidant, dependent, and obsessive-compulsive personality disorders. Individuals within this cluster tend to experience significant anxiety, fear of abandonment, and an excessive need for control or perfectionism. Despite the historical context of using the "cluster" system, limitations exist when approaching personality disorders. While the diagnosis of HPD provides a framework for understanding and studying these behaviours, ongoing debates in psychology and psychiatry revolve around the nature and validity of personality disorders, including HPD. Our understanding of histrionic traits and behaviours continues to evolve.
(Massaal-van der Ree LY, Eikelenboom M, Hoogendoorn AW,et al,2022) (Tackett JL, Silberschmidt AL, Krueger RF, Sponheim SR,2008) (Monaghan C, Bizumic B.2023)

"Impulsivity has a negative relationship with academic success, and impulsivity, emotional instability, and irresponsible lifestyle are observed in cluster B personality disorders, especially borderline disorder"
(Mateus, C, Campis, R, Aguaded, I, et al.,2021)

Cluster B personality types are skilled in telling people what they want to hear, or Superficial charm as it is known. This is the social act of saying things well received by others. They don't typically want to do it or say it, but in the context of the situation, they will oblige and play the role. This could be done before they discard you, for example, to lovebomb or manipulate a situation to cause you great distress.

Superficial charm could also be used to establish triangulation through flattery or adulation. This is one big game to these personality types, ably using these attack-methods to entrap and swindle, before they checkmate. Besides the court obstacles they are known to throw at their opposition, they all share qualities or intertwine with one another in different ways.

They all share an emotional or dramatic side, and they are completely dysfunctional in relationships. They cause drama; in fact, they can be reluctant to live a life without drama. They also display erratic, nonsensical behaviours. This chapter will discuss the destructive tendencies of these personalities and some common attack methods they have become accustomed to.

"Most people with whom I spoke said that their lives were never the same again after a relationship with a narcissist. It was years before the self-doubt began to fade, and they felt whole again.

They had spent years walking on eggshells and feeling unheard. Self Doubt continued to characterise their lives"
(Dr.Ramani Durvasula 2015)

Methods Cluster B inherently use or even the tendencies and character traits; all seem to weave manipulation within their arsenal, disregarding any victim, causing significant distress. Remember, these personality disorders can overlap and be comorbid with one another. These personality disorders can also share a comorbidity with other mental health conditions. This chapter will highlight areas of behaviour and the symptoms of each personality disorder.

Some of the causes of these disorders are believed to be #1 genetic, which dictates the person's likelihood to adopt the disorder given the circumstances presented to them early on. #2 Environmental challenges and life experiences could develop a personality disorder.

For example, if a person was exposed to hostile conflict settings or early parental loss. Anything that damages a person early on, such as emotional abuse, child abuse or severe neglect.

Moreover, the individual with the personality disorder seems to be, by default, living in an attack-stance.

Perhaps as they experienced the unwanted abuse or neglect, they dissociated and lived life, ultimately becoming the abuser. Taking on the abuser role, in turn, would limit their probability of falling victim once again.

The combination of circumstances and genetics is the precursor to the mental health issues they've developed in life. It is said that these disorders remit with age, and there are conflicting arguments that they don't. Not everything is fully known about these personality disorders or mental health issues.

The constant need for validation acts as an enemy radar that will pick apart others, demonstrating unhealthy attachment responses. Constantly scheming against a loved one to be ten steps ahead in a perceived future confrontation displays the untrustworthiness of any and everybody.

The attitudes and manipulative abilities set by each personality disorder are ingrained and adopted into the experiences they've endured. The tendency to cause trauma somehow initiates a response within them that seems to justify the trauma they once felt in the past.

The scattered consciousness on display is the refusal to conform to social norms or the inability to adjust to life's issues. The rejection of ownership within situations and behaviours is common among these disorders.

A diagnosis of something may seem like an attack on them personally or who they have become, so they aren't interested in voluntary treatment. Discover Cluster B; The Cluster of manipulation, entitlement and disruption. They are known for making false allegations, partly hardwired to cover ground through battle. This cluster is attack ready, nothing is off limits, the psychological manipulation will commence, whatever hurts you they will uncover that aspect and exploit it, fake police reports, parental alienation; nothing is off limits.

HISTRIONIC PERSONALITY DISORDER

The word Histrionic derives from the Latin-word histrionicus and histrio, which means theatrical, dramatical or actor. The main function of this disorder is attention; all eyes must be on them. Histrionic Personality Disorder (HPD) are skilful at getting attention; they will comprehend how to obtain it in every area of life.

That could be the way they look, dress or speak. They can be highly sexual or speak of sexuality and also flirty with everyone they come across. The individual with histrionic personality disorder can be sexually provocative and inappropriately seductive. They use their appearance to draw attention and seek out exciting new relationships. Psychoanalyst Wilhelm Reich introduced the concept of "character armour," which denotes defence mechanisms used to mitigate cognitive conflict stemming from internal impulses and interpersonal anxiety. For example, individuals with histrionic tendencies often tend to exhibit projection, splitting, displacement, and sexualisation as defence mechanisms. (Shapiro, D.,2002)(Lee, YJ, Keum, MS, Cheon, EJ, et al., 2020)

This disorder is very similar to borderline personality disorder, and a newcomer in the field of disorders could get mixed up between the two. Some elements of differentiation are comparable with borderline, but most are similar. The motivations behind the symptoms may differ. The mood swings or outbursts and impulsivity, for example, they share among others.

Histrionic personality disorder has been commonly linked with alcoholism; also, people with this disorder exhibit poor discernment. This disorder, similar to the rest of Cluster B, is considered ego-syntonic. Lacking the ability to see one's own actions or condition and its effects socially.

Histrionics have high rates of somatisation disorder, major depressive disorder, substance use disorder and conversion disorder. Personality disorders such as borderline, narcissistic, antisocial, and dependent can co-occur or be highly comorbid with HPD.

Histrionic personality disorder symptoms or character traits are as follows;

- The intense need for attention
- Dramatic & provocative behaviour
- Superficiality
- Speaking very vaguely
- Frequent mood swings
- Exaggerated emotional displays
- Emotions change rapidly
- Acute sensitivity to criticism
- Empty or shallow emotions
- Reassurance-seeking & gullible
- Impulsivity / self-dramatisation
- Bored or frustrated easily

Females are more likely to be diagnosed with HPD than their male counterparts. Most teachings refer solely to females when speaking of histrionic personality disorder. We will not be gender specific while discussing the topic here.

The histrionic resembles the narcissist. Both types seek attention compulsively and tend to be bothered when not everything revolves around them. Attention; Gaining and seeking attention, this aspect is key to understanding the histrionic; they will get it by any means necessary, even if that involves making up fictitious stories. This compulsion towards attention makes them professional victims, just like narcissists.

They want to be the life of the party, and if they are not getting enough attention, they may create a scene or make up a story. This individual is known for being easily suggestible and trying to fit in but ending up influenced by others. They are fully immersed in looks and will get any new treatment or plastic surgery that can add to their appearance. Histrionics strive to fit into social settings and misjudge events or interactions to the point of delusion. They sexualise almost everything, with actions possibly turning to the point of inappropriate behaviour.

The childlike behaviours, responses, or hysteria characterise the infantile histrionic personality disorder. The overlapping trait with this disorder is the shifting of emotions, which mirrors Borderline Personality Disorder.

These individuals can become highly uncomfortable if they are not the centre of attention. People with this disorder can be highly dramatic, excitable, animated and impulsive. It's all about status and what you can do for them; they are self-absorbed and can speak very vaguely, lacking in detail. They are not clear on their motives and lack insight.

These types of people would be inclined to speak about every detail of events without the ability to filter the information. Becoming the centre of attention is a key motivator, seduction or utilising sexuality as a tool for gain and attention. Individuals with HPD are known to shift emotions; at times, with obvious insincerity, they shift emotionally to counter their outside stimuli or circumstances.

"There is a marked overlap between the symptoms of HPD and BPD.

For example, both share the features of rapidly shifting and reactive emotions, impulsive behaviour, and strong expression of emotion." (Ekselius L. 2018)

They can be impressionable and easily led lacking critical thinking. The difficulty with this personality disorder is the overestimation of their relationships or friendships.

They could consider relationships to be more intimate than they actually are. There's an assumed intimacy that isn't there, which may lead to false allegations.

They are theatrical and have been known to bait a victim into a situation. Histrionics like compliments and tend to avoid negative feedback or attention.

One distinction between HPD and NPD is low empathy. Yes, Histrionics have low empathy, but they are so preoccupied with themselves or their needs that they overlook empathy, resulting in them showing low empathy. The personality disorders that lack empathy are Borderline, Narcissistic and Anti-Social, but it is not a part of the behaviour of the histrionic diagnostically.

Several factors may contribute to personality disorders, including HPD. There are genetic factors such as histrionic personality disorder that can run in families and be inherited.

Trauma from childhood could contribute perhaps to the loss of a family member passing away or abuse, either physical, sexual, emotional or all of the above—also the lack of boundaries or overindulgent, overly erratic or dramatic parenting styles.

The bar is set at five or more symptoms to be diagnosed with this disorder. They play the victim role and seek exciting new situations. Women tend to be diagnosed with this disorder more than men. If a clinician was trying to assess this disorder, it could get overlooked by other personality disorders and vice versa.

This personality disorder has a preoccupation with blaming others, making it a problem for others to recognise the truth in any given situation. This focus on targets of blame is a common thread within Cluster B.

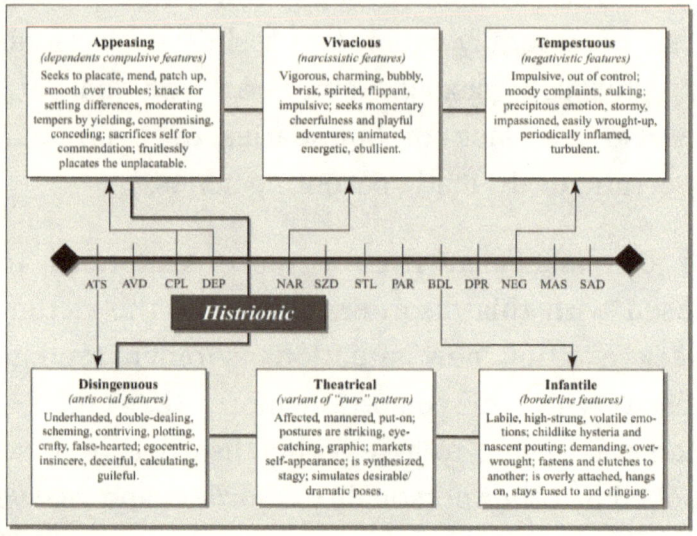

FIGURE 9.1 Variants of the Histrionic Personality.

(M, Theodore, S, Greossman, S, Meagher, Et, Al 2004)

Theodore Millen suggested that there are six types of histrionic personality. First, we have the theatrical histrionic variant, which is the pure histrionic. This is the most dramatic and notable histrionic. The theatrical histrionic is everything touched on about histrionics; thus far, it is the basic histrionic pattern. The chart shows the different palettes of histrionic, if you will, from the book Personality Disorders in Modern Life by Theodore Millon.

Theodore Millon went on to say that such individuals essentially live as commodities, marketing themselves as chameleons on social demand and changing the characteristics they display depending on audience and circumstance. (M, Theodore, S, Greossman, S, Meagher, Et, Al 2004)

These personality types posture up to be seen, bringing attention with fashion, sex appeal or self-appearance tactics. If they are not noticed, they will go back to the drawing board as they feel quite inadequate.

Then there is the infantile histrionic, which has the borderline features. Labile or easily susceptible, they can be edgy with highly volatile emotions.

This aspect of histrionic is marred with childlike hysteria and a nascent pouting and overwrought. Overly attached Hands-On and stays fused or bothered, clinging to a perceived or even a misperceived intimate partner.

Appeasing histrionics: the appeasing histrionic is dependent and compulsive. Seeks to placate, mend or patch up over issues that arise and would agree to appease even on things they don't agree with. These are the people pleasers, often putting others first in an attempt to gain approval. Settling differences to prevent further disagreement or conflict by allowing the other to get their way. A lot of codependent features with the compromising of oneself to avoid dispute.

The vivacious type of histrionic personality has narcissistic features. Vigorous and can be quite the charmer, outgoing and even socially popular. This type is also flippant and impulsive and seeks momentary cheerfulness. In social interactions, they can come across as playful, animated and energetic.

The tempestuous histrionic has negativistic features, meaning their attitude is sceptical and pessimistic. They tend to do the opposite of what is asked of others, highlighting an inability to get along. Also an impulsive individual with an out of control emotional reactive pattern, often complaining or sulking. This pattern of behaviour is periodically brought up, making others walk on eggshells in the process, as it can be quite turbulent.

Then, there is a disingenuous histrionic personality, which includes antisocial features. Two-faced, conniving, plotting against others. Very self-centred and egocentric with a personality littered with insincerity and deceitfulness.

> "The unprincipled narcissist preys on the weak and vulnerable, enjoying their dismay and anger. In contrast, the disingenuous histrionics seeks to hold the respect and affection of those they dismiss in their pursuit of love and admiration."
> (M, Theodore, S, Greossman, S, Meagher, Et, Al 2004)

Histrionics are often scattered in every facet of life. Relationships are that of chaos and disingenuous situations. Affairs and jealousy or behaviours that garner attention will be prevalent. This makes the histrionic feel safe and reduces their anxiety somewhat. They can be adrenaline junkies that choose illicit affairs or cheating, demonstrating deception and reckless behaviours.

Antisocial Personality Disorder, AKA Sociopath

Known frequently as the sociopath, Antisocial Personality Disorder (ASPD) is known for the lack of conscience. The ignorance of what is accepted, or what is right and what is wrong. With no regret or remorse, the antisocial would purposely make others feel sorrow or devastation. Like the rest of cluster B, the antisocial would specialise in manipulation and focus on hurting others in their lives.

They can be reckless in their behaviour and can be known for breaking the law. Even breaking the law repeatedly wouldn't be out of the question, with no concept of consequence or care for it.

There is immense difficulty in strategising or planning ahead, encompassing so many overlapping features of some of the other personality disorders.

Demonstrating aggressive actions against the people in their life, bullying, shouting, threatening or becoming physical. There is a certain harshness or cruelty to their actions that can lead loved ones to be bewildered. They use charm to manipulate others for their own personal gain and pleasure.

When they feel the time is right, they lash out and do whatever it takes to destroy that person. Antisocial personality disorder is known for inviting situations such as abuse, either spousal or child abuse or neglect, prison time, attempting suicide or trying to kill somebody. These extremes are dull in effect to the person with ASPD, with the limited ability to produce any empathy they feel nothing. They simply cannot understand how to care or be empathetic towards the feelings of others.

> "While people with Anti Social Personality Disorder often come into contact with the criminal justice system, research suggests that incarceration and other punitive measures are largely ineffective since people with the condition are usually unresponsive to punishment" (DeBrito.SA, Viding. E, Kumari., Et, Al,2013)

Antisocial personality disorder symptoms or character traits are as follows;

- Deceitful and untrustworthy
- Impulsive behaviours and irresponsible
- Lacking guilt or remorse when causing harm
- Aggressive, easily irritable or hostile
- Frequent mood swings
- Lacking empathy
- Reckless behaviour/disregard for others
- No conscience, opinionated and feeling superior

People with ASPD lack empathy, are arrogant and think down upon others. The relationships with others can be fundamentally centred around exploitation and coercive control.

They can commit harm to others with zero remorse for their actions. Individuals with Antisocial personality disorder have fluctuating emotions described as ambivalence. Ambivalence would be mixed feelings towards something or someone, conflicting reactions and beliefs. This could be an attitude towards a person that is simultaneously negative and positive.

Heightened states of emotional detachment or emotional coldness also displaying a callous attitude towards others. Like the rest of the Cluster B group, individuals with ASPD exploit others in harmful ways for their own pleasure or gain. Fine-tuned for the frequent manipulation of others, they deceive anybody they can.

Like in the name, they are comfortable around antisocial situations such as the destruction of other people's property, violence and starting random drama with people. Patterns of conduct issues stemming from their youth to beyond, often in trouble or had previous criminal behaviour. Antisocials utilise superficial charm, telling certain narratives or doing things for display purposes.

They have disdain for whatever they feel needs to be vocalised or a task to perform but will do it to try to establish an acceptable presentation. With limited guilt, they pursue the use of superficial charm to manipulate, adapting to the given situation.

The use of intimidation or violence is also a common means of exploitation for the ASPD. According to Bursten, "Most antisocials and psychopaths find the tender emotions incomprehensible; these individuals learn to adapt to a world in which emotional expression is the very currency of communication, developing a sensitive intellectual awareness of social conventions and an ability to size up interpersonal situations.

Their knowledge of human relations allows them to feign empathy when necessary, to deceive and manipulate". (Bursten, 1972) Use superficial charm to get their way and socially engineer their desired outcome.

Case Study

Anonymous

For anyone going through the struggles of being falsely accused, I really feel for you. Back in January, I was falsely accused of Rape, GBH, Possession of a Section 5 firearm, controlling and coercive behaviour and theft against my ex-partner. I was a serving police officer at the time in Lincolnshire and had been the victim of daily abuse for 7 months from her.

This includes daily punching, kicking, slapping, punching and eventually stabbing me twice with a kitchen knife. On January 14th 2024, I couldn't take it anymore as she put a knife to my throat and threatened to kill me.

This was captured on a voice recording, which I'll share. I called 101 and reported the abuse, of which the officer who was my tutor attended and stated that because I was trained in conflict management, male, and well-built, that she was not a risk to me and wasn't arrested on the night. I blocked all of her communications despite her ringing me on no-caller ID because she was infatuated with me.

January 17th rolled around, and I went to work, where I was arrested on suspicion of rape and possession of an S5 firearm (Pava Spray). I actually phoned my mum and told her that I was going to be arrested for rape as she had threatened to accuse me of rape if I ever left her. I spent 23 hours in the Grantham custody suite, of which I had intimate swabs taken and was eventually released on bail. My ex-partner, who I would like to name and shame but I'm unsure if I'm allowed to, was also arrested for making the threat to kill me.

She accused me of rape when she arrived at custody, of which she was bailed instantly and allowed to return home (get out of jail free card). After answering my bail, I was further arrested for GBH, theft and C + C of, which was false.

My ex-partner breached her bail conditions 6 times, of which I reported via 101 each time and didn't receive any visits from the police. She attempted to ram my car off the road, which was reported and again, I received nothing from the police. In March, I was told that both our cases were NFA (No Further Action). I was told the case of me as a suspect was known to be false immediately as they had checked CCTV, showing she was not in the area at the time of the alleged false rape. My case as a victim was NFA, as I was trained in conflict management and "should have resolved the incident better myself" after having a knife put to my throat.

I would like to add that I was told if I resigned from the police, the case with me as a suspect would be dropped, so essentially, it was blackmail when I was extremely vulnerable due to the mistreatment from the police despite working as an officer for 3 years. After the cases were concluded, my car was vandalised, my flat was broken into twice and various other threats were made. Surprise, surprise, the police did not attend to any of my reports. The system is utterly and completely broken, and I really would like to help others who are going through this, as it makes me furious that these accusers can say anything related to a sexual crime, and it is processed as such without any further investigation.

I have and keep for court cases Video 1 - In which she threatens to kill me as I asked her to leave my flat, of which she puts a knife to my throat. Also, photos of her with pill bottles and proof she downed all the pills inside. Almost to make me feel sorry if she ended her life then and there. These are photos she sent me in which she has a handful of pills from the bottle and proceeds to down them all in one go. She sent me these after I ended it with her. I also kept text conversations, such as I got off work early, of which she accused me of cheating. Videos of her calling with no caller ID; after I blocked her, she called my flatmate with her abusive, threatening behaviour. The final Video I have is when she had just stabbed me in my kidney, after which I turned around to face the wall and sleep.

Rula Odeh Alsawalqa from the Department of Sociology in Jordan mentions that they are living by the "principle of pleasure" and selfishness that makes them unable to sympathise, and they love power and control of what they have false beliefs about that fit their preferences. So, they tend to disregard the standards and social values, seeking to take advantage of the miseries of others by colouring and lying, leaving them unable to engage in social relationships and form a group of friends. (R, Alsawalqa, 2019)

World Health Organization 1992 ICD manual labeled AntiSocial Personality disorder as dissocial personality disorder. Symptoms of the disorder mirror those in DSM-IV see (Table;1-2).

Classification and Definition of Antisocial Personality Disorder

Table 1-2.	ICD-10 criteria for dissocial personality disorder
≥3 of the following required for the diagnosis
1. Callous unconcern for the feelings of others
2. Gross disparity between behavior and expected social norms, with irresponsibility and disregard for rules and obligations
3. Incapacity in maintaining enduring relationships, though having no difficulty in establishing them
4. Having a very low tolerance to frustration and a low threshold for aggressive behavior, including violence
5. Incapacity to experience guilt or to profit from experience, particularly punishment
6. Marked readiness to blame others or to offer plausible rationalizations for the behavior that has brought the person into conflict with society
Source. World Health Organization 1992.

(P, Tyrer, A, Farnam, A, Zahmatkesh, Et, Al, 2022)

Jeffrey Dahmer, Charles Manson, and Ted Bundy were all diagnosed with Antisocial personality disorder. Deceitfulness, compulsively lying, fraud or conning others, destroying property, etc. Any Anti-social activity that you can think of this disorder encapsulates. Impulsivity and failure to plan ahead, making rash decisions that can hurt others.

Disregard for others and even themselves in terms of safety or relating. Remorse will not be present if they choose to cause hurt.

They rationalise this as deserved or karma, displaying callous conduct in the process. Rebelling against social norms or how a person should act in a given situation, Antisocial personality disorder conflicts with every aspect of a person's life situation. Furthermore, there is no direct treatment or medication for this disorder.

Borderline & Narcissistic

PERSONALITY DISORDERS

Borderline and Narcissistic personality disorders are commonly attributed alongside each other. Both are two distinct but often overlapping mental health conditions that can present significant challenges. NPD is a personality disorder that creates a false sense of self within the psyche. Narcissistic injury is the source of a perceived threat to the self-esteem or character of the narcissist. This can occur with criticism or, a humiliating instance, or simply not getting the attention they need.

When the narcissist is challenged or invalidated, this could give birth to a narcissistic injury. This could potentially start a personal vendetta without resolution or mediation. Narcissists think they are superior, entitled and above everyone else in their lives.

They have no empathy and simply don't care if they hurt someone, as they have an inability to feel remorse or place themselves in someone else's shoes.

People with NPD exaggerate who they are and even believe their own hype, forgetting that they actually have deep-seated insecurities. This grandiose visual they have of themselves is likened to a character they portray.

If a loved one ceases to go along with this exaggeration, it could cause injury to the narcissist. There is a compulsion for them to use everyone in their lives as mere pawns or puppets, treating them like their peasants. The unfair treatment doesn't seem to register for the individuals with NPD (Narcissistic Personality Disorder) as they have a strong need to take everything they can in a relationship setting.

Whether that be the house, their partner's belongings or their children, this behaviour has no limit. NPD characteristics are highlighted in many of the case studies provided, and there is a common thread of similarities between them. Do not expect a narcissist to reason with you or show any consideration for your well-being. They share the qualities of the borderline, such as lambasting or attacking loved ones. Most people with NPD can hide their true selves while meeting people for the first time or perhaps even only seeing them at a minimum from time to time.

They are expert liars and have an inability to admit fault; this will all be used to take advantage of others without regard for consequences. Taking advantage of others is a speciality of theirs. The priority is always the same, which is inflating the superior sense of self of the narcissist. They hide so much behind the facade and can become highly triggered or injured if suspecting a person can unmask them. NPD individuals have an ineffable fear of exposure that is entirely repulsive to them: to look at themselves for once without envisioning their carefully constructed false selves. They have built up this grandiose aura and do whatever is necessary to keep this self intact.

Criticism or failure can depress the narcissist significantly. Just like BPD, validation is a crucial part of coping with life situations.

Public exposure or humiliation would be the type of validation the narcissist would try to avoid and fend off this injury in any way they can.

They are skilled; good at what they do, master manipulators with muscle memory or with ease with how they exploit the family courts.

Not only are there some similarities between the two, but many people with NPD also have BPD with some shared traits, such as;

Both live in alternative realities in which feelings create facts.

Both project their badness upon other people, who become their target of blame.

Both blame everyone but themselves; neither will admit they were wrong or made a mistake; neither will take responsibility for their words or actions.

Both are critical and judgmental, and both have to be right at all times.

Both may carry grudges, see themselves as victims, and expect loved ones to throw them a pity party.

Both are unwilling to listen to what they don't want to hear.

Both may become exceedingly jealous over little or nothing.

Both may feel intense shame, which they cover up with layers of self-deception.

Both often lie.

Both try to control other people and their environment.

Both are sensitive to stimuli that can trigger issues and lots of drama.

Both need plenty of attention.

Both have stunted emotional development.

Both are impervious to logic when they are triggered.

Both can be emotionally and verbally abusive.

Both have unstable or impaired relationships which involve criticism or blame and which often end with forcing the other person to leave.

Both may use manipulative or coercive techniques such as emotional blackmail, gaslighting, silent treatment, unreasonable expectations and magical thinking.

People with BPD are at about age two, and people with NPD are at about age 6

Both are still struggling with issues that most master in childhood.

(Mason, P, Kreger, R, 2020)

This past paragraph is from the classic Stop Walking on Eggshells (taking your life back when someone you care about has borderline personality disorder). It sums up the key differences between the two groups perfectly. The intersection between the two is summarised with a clear, understandable list of criteria, simplified and perfectly constructed.

Because BPD and NPD are so delicately intertwined, it can be challenging to separate them. They also both construct a pathological grandiose self and may overestimate their own abilities.

This is all a defensive mechanism to stay safe at all costs, even if the threat is only perceived.

The intersection of these two mental health disorders is destructive; sided with the fact that people can have both of these very challenging disorders. Devaluing and valuing a person or idealising and discarding are common traits within Cluster B.

These personality types do share similarities, and even a person who doesn't have a disorder on the surface can still demonstrate narcissistic traits—also littered with entitlement, forms of validation, and a distorted sense of self.

High-conflict personality types will use reactive abuse, creating uncertainty and struggle. Abuse patterns and manipulation will be discussed in the following chapter.

"Lots of all-or-nothing thinking Intense or unmanaged emotions

Extreme behaviour or threats A preoccupation with blaming others—their Targets of Blame."

(Bill Eddy, 2018)

Chapter 7
Hurt People, Hurt People

Do you push people away? Perhaps because of a fear of being hurt, abandoned or dumped. Maybe competition with others plagues you? Have you had early childhood issues that gripped your habitual moves even as a grown-up? Is there a repetitive pattern of self-sabotage that greets you at certain points in your life?

If so, it could be a trauma response, dictating your reactions to life situations. Unresolved trauma can surge through a person, with the outcomes resulting in anger outbursts or hateful actions. So many people have something unresolved that translates over to their present circumstances. Cluster B personalities have experienced an underlying trauma. Experiencing either neglect or abuse at a young age, physical, sexual, verbal or emotional. All of these experiences could ultimately develop into a personality disorder. There may have been childhood trauma, but not always.

There are environmental factors or a combination of biological and social factors. Severe childhood abuse or neglect can be damaging to a person's mental health regardless of whether a personality disorder is developed. The person would disassociate, and the personality disorder would become established throughout life. Or the neglected or abused child grows up and is resentful, thus abusing others.

Through life, they will be more dominant and avoid becoming the victim again at all costs. Defences are always up, and, at times, lashing out with abuse for others. This abuse could be aimed at a partner or even their own child, and on and on. People who have experienced harm or pain are more likely to demonstrate it to others. This is in no way a reason to stay in an abusive relationship or to tolerate outrageous behaviour. If you are experiencing coercion or abuse, love yourself enough to get out of the relationship.

Excusing behaviour is not the way forward; yes, we should be tolerant and love unconditionally. However, relationships need a level of safety and security. Only tolerate uncontrollable behaviour if there is something that is added to your life. If all that's added to your life by a supposed loving partner is areas like dangerous situations or court slander, who needs enemies?

Adversities happen to us all, and so does trauma! Unfortunately, it takes a highly emotionally developed person to surpass a dysfunctional past. These people can get on with whats done, living their best life, giving life a try once more. It takes years, and by no means is it a walk in the park. Let's try to be conscious of people's past issues and their mental health and sincerely wish them well.

That is an ideal outlook, and it is easier said than done, of course. Consideration and understanding fall by the wayside when you have been the target of blame, suffering from False allegations, Parental alienation, Constant abuse, Harassment, Manipulation, and Emotional Abuse.

This campaign of harassment should not be tolerated. How can you fix or justify past abuse by abusing the people in your life now? It makes no sense; it just perpetuates the abuse cycle.

These people go on to abuse everyone close to them who can be manipulated, including their children. Nothing can excuse such behaviours of abuse and grief.

Misery loves company. Never allow it to destroy others. Then you're just as bad as the neglector or abuser in your own early life.

These hateful people want nothing more than to take advantage of others. Gain leverage throughout life at the expense of their loved ones. There is no respect for the behaviour of these sorts, nor should there be, regardless of what happened as a life experience.

We all had, for the most part, challenging or unwanted situations that occurred. Trying to love, accept and be more patient doesn't work and can lead to years of coercive control and obnoxious, abusive behaviour.

This is codependency, which will be discussed further, followed by other unhealthy relationship dynamics. The following will be the main manipulation methods used by abusers of loving relationships, followed by an overview of coercive control, which these manipulation tactics perpetuate.

Codependency

Codependency is a dysfunctional attachment style regarding relationships. This involves an overreliance on another, perhaps for their sense of self-worth, esteem building, validation and identity. Seeking validation and approval from the other person is tied into codependency.

> **Codependency is when a person does everything for someone and doesn't take care of themselves;**
>
> **It weakens everybody involved, weakens them, and weakens the person doing it** (C, Doré)

This can be a constant approval needed as there is a leader and a follower in this dynamic. This would entail completely sacrificing one's own needs and wants. Some people rely on others to provide them with validation as they lack the ability to reinforce their feelings themselves. An unfulfilled, abandoned person has a resultant behaviour of attachment. This attachment is demonstrated through actions such as parental alienation and false allegations to keep the other partner around that bit longer in their life.

There is a leaching approach within this relationship. Taking everything from the other person and creating obstacles for them if this abandonment comes to fruition. They could use the likes of money or children as a manipulative tool.

These people are emotionally attached and bring this unhealthy attachment pattern into their relationships, which often ends pretty miserably. Attached love is manipulative and co-dependent; a codependent person tries to acquire love by coercing someone into loving them. By making this person dependent upon them by providing care and keeping that person in a subservient, weakened position where they cannot care for themselves. (Doré, C,2011)

There is an obligation concerning responsibility for someone else's emotions or well-being. Codependency brings an unbalanced reliance; do you pay for everything all the time? That is a co dependent relationship. It could be feeling sorry for someone and it results in doing everything for them while stuck in a one way output cycle. The relationship could be psychologically abusive with inadequacy and low self-esteem for the target. Unless you go out of your way to validate feelings or put up with abuse. This codependency looks like many different things but all-in-all it is an unhealthy attachment style. This type of relationship is parasitic in nature.

Relationships based on codependency are unhealthy and involve one person enabling the other's destructive behaviour or mental health instability. There may be unsurmountable lengths one has to go to please the other. In an effort to gain their approval, which is always only temporary. Tolerating an abusive relationship all the while sacrificing personal needs and happiness.

Relationships fall apart with this codependent behaviour, and it's pretty hard to articulate it when you are in it. Feelings of resentment and anger soon follow when it becomes quite obvious that you are taken advantage of and unappreciated. Additionally, there is a mismatch of boundaries in codependent relationships, leading to a cycle of chaos and arguments. This obligation to take care of and mend the problems of your partner at the expense of your mental health adds to the chaotic relationship style.

Any relationship can turn into a codependent one. One obvious relationship that ends up codependent would be the presence of a Cluster B personality disorder or high traits of narcissism.

The borderline character trait of smothering their partners would be another sign of a codependent relationship another couple of traits which may seem familiar by now are the lack of empathy, attitude of entitlement and a need for admiration. These traits create unhealthy dynamics, with the narcissistic partner exerting total control over the co-dependent partner.

Emotional regulation, which is prevalent within Cluster B, is another key aspect of codependency. If a person is in a relationship with a person who displays Cluster B traits they would likely be responsible for soothing the emotional outbursts.

This pattern develops unconsciously and continues throughout the relationship; in turn suppressing emotions, given in, taken abuse just to keep the peace. People with NPD seek to control and find out ways to manipulate others to meet their needs, leaving their partners feeling gaslighted, overwhelmed and drained. Some victims try to hide aspects of their relationship to others; to hide any abusive or codependent behavior.

If you find yourself constantly making excuses for your partner's behaviour, walking on eggshells to avoid conflict, or feeling guilty for asserting your own needs, you may be partaking in a codependent relationship.

Case Study

Aaron

My ex wanted to move on in the relationship, and I didn't stop her, although I tried to save our relationship. When it came to deciding on where to stay, my daughter wanted to live with me. My ex then tried slandering me by saying I controlled and manipulated her. That was found to be false in the family courts, so she then made out that I was sleeping with her while she was underage!

She confesses in court and in 3 statements that she wasn't in the area at the times I was alleged to have committed these offences. I was given an NFA (no further action outcome) by the police due to no evidence, which means they stopped taking the case forward.

The family court gave me 50/50 custody of my child. I drove a 600-mile round trip every other weekend to see her. Fifteen months later, I was charged with six counts of her BS. No second police interview! Social services and family court cut my contact off with my daughter, and my ex made disgusting allegations to family courts, who then, without any proof or evidence, cut my contact with my child. I have a top barrister working on my case and preparing seven witnesses and evidence of her manipulation of the courts to take to court.

Eleven days before court, the CPS (criminal prosecution service) went to court without informing my council of it and changed the date to a date the barrister couldn't make. I was given a new barrister who undid everything my first barrister had done and put together and doesn't call any witnesses. The jury found me guilty of 6 counts of sexual activity with a child! I had been with my partner for over 10 years.

The family court told me I could only contact my daughter once a month via letter. I haven't seen my daughter for 4 years now. I served 3 years in prison, and now I am on licence for 3 years. I am in the process of fighting our corrupt and broken system to prove my innocence as I have new evidence put together and seek justice for what has happened to me and make sure she and her lying friends face the full weight of the law, whatever it may be!

But more importantly, I want to be able to build memories with my daughter, who is now 12! Getting anyone in authority to listen and look at the evidence without it costing £90k is impossible. It's all hush-hush how men in this country are being sent to prison on nothing more than hearsay! These false accusers are walking away with £10k+ compensation each time, as well as revenge, that spiteful itch well and truly scratched.

NARCISSISTIC ABUSE

Individuals with Narcissistic traits display manipulative and controlling behaviours. Exploiting those around them to leverage their gain. Victims of narcissistic abuse find themselves introduced into toxic relationships. In denial at first, using tolerance until they become entirely burned out, confused and emotionally drained.

The aftermath of narcissistic abuse results in a severely compromised mental state—enduring symptoms such as anxiety, depression and complex post-traumatic stress disorder, among others. One area of research I wish were easier to explore is the connection between narcissism and sadism. If a person is sadistic, it means that he or she derives gratification from punishing, harming, or abusing others. My hope is that readers can avoid relationships with narcissists, especially those with a sadistic streak. (S. Meyers 2016)

Codependency breaks you down, and fending for yourself may become problematic after escaping the unhealthy pattern. These high-conflict personality types don't care how they do it; they aim for annihilation. There's no remorse here. Manipulation is what they excel at. If it's children, they'll use them; if it's stealing everything you own, they'll do it; if it's making up allegations to try to put you in prison, they'll pursue it. They will use the elements against you; if they can make you homeless, then homelessness will be the parting gift. They perceive then manufacture outcomes such as threatening or highly volatile situations; children, even weather or malnourishment, are weaponised.

If they felt abandoned or like the relationship was coming to an end, they would seek to end it first. They want to usher in painful scenarios for the other as a way of reflection if the scary situations you might encounter in prison cells or through the rough homeless life don't get you! The allegations, smear campaigns, or parental alienation will. This is to make the other look back and say that life was so better putting up with the narcissistic abuse; life is so hard now. This is when they possibly try to give you signs to make up, be their victim and hoover you back in. In fact, so many people do get back into these risky relationships.

The scary part is the impulsion that takes over the high-conflict personality type. It is a common saying about narcissistic personality disorder that no matter the bravado or the display of superiority, they feel empty and hollow inside beneath it all. The constant abusers must feel so low and dull within themselves that they have to resort to going out of their way with severe tactics to force a person to feel misery. For others, it can be easy to get along and negotiate throughout a relationship.

For the narcissist, on the other hand, the person suffering from the abuse needs to either accept the abuse as a regular occurrence or face the wrath of it anyway. The narcissistic abuse fulfils their needs; it reminds them that they are entitled and become validated through the pain of another. With no regard for children or family dynamics, caring solely for unrealistic constant validation; when it eventually does not come on schedule, however, punishment or revenge soon follows.

These are very dangerous character traits for anyone to have, the sadistic nature, for example, to seek out a life with a ferocious intention to ruin it. There are decent, innocent people who are in prison or suffering in some dreadful way, and the actual perpetrator feels nothing and has no conscience. Some people kill themselves and become trophies for these high-conflict people. At the very least, the cycle of emotional abuse leads to the loved one needing an immediate mental health evaluation.

They wholeheartedly believe that they are entitled to special treatment or privileges at the expense of others. They have a very fragile self-esteem and that is on display when in receipt of zero validation or admiration. No matter how unrealistic it is to demonstrate it to them, they will expect a constant need for attention and approval from others. This in and of itself can be almost impossible to keep up with.

Furthermore, buried deep under the surface is a fear of criticism or rejection. Victims of narcissistic abuse often feel pressured to keep up the praise and try to appease the narcissist in order to avoid conflict or emotional outbursts. They find themselves isolated from friends and family members, as the narcissist seeks to exert control over every aspect of the victim's life.

Triangulation
AKA Flying-Monkeys

The triangulation method combines the manipulative tactics of emotional blackmail, lying and moving the goalposts, gossip and outnumbering. Triangulation, or Flying Monkeys, is narrative changing; it is gossip and exclusion at the expense of the target. It is the use of talking behind someone's back to someone outside the relationship outnumbering them.

This then creates tension and drama, and the victory will surely be one-sided. Bringing in more parties into a relationship to purposely exacerbate the insecurity and problems. This could look like interest in other people as a tactic to get you to admire them more, as the evidence is there that there is competition now. Or triangulate to other people close by either one or several; that can help box you into a corner and become voiceless.

Relationships are a battleground for these disorders, so take nothing on a personal basis with regard to enduring these behaviours. This form of manipulation is the act of forcefully maintaining power and coercive control over others while playing the victim or darling role. Triangulation helps the narcissist control the other person and can strategise against them more efficiently.

Triangulation is the most common manipulative tactic, casting loneliness and isolation onto the target. This is a typical schoolyard tool bullies would use to single someone out in their school. The main goal here is exclusion.

This method outnumbers the victim in maintaining the narrative and control.

This outnumbering then selectively brings a third party or parties into a relationship in order to gossip, rumour, or introduce tension and jealousy.

It could come in the form of cutting ties or creating drama. This could be someone close to you. It could be someone manipulated into solidifying parental alienation by speaking on behalf of the narcissist in court.

Drama is the end result with a pile-on of gossip, rumour, and disdain. This creates an atmosphere which is highly toxic; the end goal is to control the dynamics of the relationship; building a team of sorts against the opposition.

Alienated children, too, will be triangulated from a very-early-age. Individuals with Cluster B often use triangulation as a way to assert their dominance. Seeking control over their partners, spouse, friends or family members. This allows them to create a diversion from the already deep-seated systematic abuse, all the while sustaining competition and insecurity. Triangulation helps them gain one over on the real victim. Most of the time, the flying monkeys think they are doing the righteous thing. They have been inundated with horror stories and believe in the lies. They are manipulated by this master manipulator. Weaving a web of all sorts of lies and slander.

Case study

Simon

My life is in the process of being destroyed by a gang of spiteful women in a tiny town. The smear campaigns have been horrendous, not only for me but also for my wife and children.

The constant false accusations and attacks from flying monkeys from the community have left me isolated and alone, unable to trust anyone. Before moving to a place I now refer to as the Salam Massachusetts of California with a combination of "hills have eyes" druggies.

I was a decorated Veteran and served my country with honour, only to come home and have my soul ripped out as you are dog piled for things I never said or did.

This group that all grew up together out here in this tiny town maintain control and drives out everyone they don't want out here. I think it's about the land and water here, very depressed and scared after knowing they were coming for everything I've worked my entire life for.

Flying Monkeys Continued

Flying monkeys side with the narcissist no matter the situation. Even if evidence is presented to them that is contrary, they are weak and easily led into becoming subservient to the narcissist. They spread gossip and rumours about you. They gaslight and manipulate you. They dismiss or trivialise your feelings over and over.

Flying monkeys can pass on information about you to help the narcissist harass you. Narcissists are experts in securing support and getting other people to believe that they are so nice. The outcome is the belief that their partner deserves to be treated the way that they are.

The best targets for flying monkey recruitment are vulnerable people who completely feed into these elaborate stories. This causes validation and a very strategic vantage point for the narcissist. With very limited or no contact between the people involved, the narcissist secures their dominance and control.

Keeping people at odds with each other, especially when both sides have different opinions and viewpoints installed by the narcissist, is not an easy feat. However, this manipulation method is very effective as the narcissist is altering people's perceptions. This is high-level manipulation.

The people involved have no idea what's really happening or don't want to believe an alternative viewpoint. The toxic nature of the narcissist is in plain sight, and nobody can spot it. It is also a form of proxy recruitment, which is a way of controlling or abusing the victim.

This would likely turn any real situation into a manipulation hotbed, having other people back them up. This situation of being outnumbered can feel overpowering, and nobody needs to hear the other side of the story. In fact, there is no place even to tell your side of the story as this process cuts people from your life. Triangulation can be quite tricky to spot and respond to. The narcissist enjoys creating drama and conflict between others, especially when they can gain from it.

People used and manipulated by the narcissist can be either family or friends from both sides or other people they could use as pawns to help create narratives, jealousy and or conflict. Children can also be used in this process, and it helps cement parental alienation as the result is always to turn people against the victim. It is all designed to diminish and control, creating further abuse. This manipulation tactic is used to perfection, and there are no bounds to how far this will go.

The goal here is to defeat the other not only at the present but also at a perceived future event perhaps through divorce court or a property dispute.

Triangulation helps sow the seeds of animosity bringing about a bullying atmosphere into the situation. Making the other person feel inadequate and unworthy with no way to speak up for themselves; helping reinforce the falling on deaf ears dynamic.

Fueling mistrust and resentment in an already damaged relationship might not seem like too much of an issue at first glance, and this behaviour could easily be dismissed. However this should not be overlooked as there are a number of false allegation stories that have a reinforced credibility with a flying monkey corroborating the erroneous story made by the accuser.

Triangulation brings about a rapport between the parties with a common objective over time to team up and be on the offensive.

Flying Monkeys is the title that encapsulates this behaviour. This is a term, especially for narcissists, which is derived from the behaviour of the Wicked Witch of the East from the famous 1939 film The Wizard of Oz. The term Flying-Monkeys is a fundamental description of the triangulation process and the narcissist's minions.

These flying monkeys are fed into the story, furthering the smear campaign narrative. They are enablers who fall for the manipulation and believe the falsehoods of the narcissist. Having misconstrued who the real victim is and who the real abuser is.

The narcissist knows how to tell an engrossing story and play people off against each other, creating division. Flying monkeys are ignorant of narcissistic habits or traits and become immobilised in this process of triangulation.

This can be likened to a double or parallel life. For example, in a break-up or make-up scenario, The Narcissist could beg their partner to come back and then apologise for the ill-treatment and controlling behaviour.

Then, the couple ultimately end up getting back together. Then, without even hiding it as blatant as can be in front of your very eyes. The narcissist calls up the flying monkeys connected to the drama. Making up stories such as they were begged back with promises of change, so much so that the narcissist had to take pity on them. Made up; dialogue that was never mentioned at all. After they hang up the phone, you go and confront the narcissist and tell them you never said that? You never begged or were pitied back? But even then, it goes in one ear and out the other ear. Their gaslighting just pushes the topic aside, or they won't respond to it at all.

The two parallel lives then being the partner who thinks they got back together but under false pretences. Also, the flying monkeys who believe a completely different scenario took place, and it's the pitiful or sweet-talking actions that mended the relationship, etc. This then keeps the triangulation process going, keeping apart any interactions between the target and the flying monkeys as a way to gossip and fuel discourse and hate. You will notice this style of relating to people when viewing the narcissist. They will constantly gossip about someone in their life while concurrently portraying themselves as somebody else entirely when interacting with that same person. They could pretend to be a chum, a friend, an associate and really secretly hate them. Or be a tyrant behind closed doors, giving their own family hell, meanwhile, going out the front door and being a darling neighbour or work colleague.

They like to control the narrative; they could be in a relationship with you all the while; be telling other people nasty, untrue things about you, and you would never know it. Not until you're served court papers and you start piecing things together. Their weird interactions, all start to make sense now; the things they said and the narratives they spewed to other people.

Don't be under the impression that this gossip is harmless; there is far-reaching potential for problems depending on the nature of the gossip. The Narcissist or cluster B individual can attack indirectly through other people just as they attack using courts. People can be perceived differently depending on the nature of the narrative convincingly spoon-fed over time. Remember, these people are master manipulators and hone in on this skill regularly, staying sharp in the process. Using a common boxing term as an analogy, too much time away from the boxing profession for long periods of time, they call it ring-rust.

Flying monkeys are people who are both vulnerable and recruitable and at ease falling into the manipulative tactics of the narcissist. They will side with the narcissist no matter what evidence is presented to them in an almost cult-like manner. Create firm boundaries if they re-enter your life, as you need protection and caution. You do not want to be feeding the narcissist information through the flying monkeys if there was no consideration for your livelihood or family dynamics before there will be little consideration going forward.

This process is also interwoven within the usage of parental alienation and is a very unsettling method, as its creativity can manifest in all sorts of damaging directions. The alienated children can get recruited into this triangulation process, hearing negative, damaging things about the other loving parent, which destroys the reputation of that parent.

The child would fear the narcissist and then be forced to pick a side and become emotionally damaged in the process. The flying monkeys are used as pawns, and that's their only use.

The narcissist is cunning and maintains one step ahead in a battle they create. There is power in numbers; triangulation is outnumbering the unwitting victim or future victim.

The Lure-Manipulation Hoovering & Love Bombing

Hoovering is a manipulative tactic used to bring a person back. This is common among cluster B, such as Borderline, Narcissistic and Histrionic personality disorders. It is primarily used to reel in the unwitting victim who has withdrawn from the relationship or situation. Coercive control reached its peak within the relationship. Enough is enough, and the lookout for an exit to this carnage became a probability. These victims have been tarnished, abused, screamed at and threatened. The flying monkeys and outnumbering left the victim with the option to either stay and remain subservient or to love themselves enough and leave.

This lure alternative would try to mask or turn a blind eye to the abusive nature happening throughout the relationship. If successful, it would create further control over the victim of a toxic relationship. This Lure typically occurs at a time when the person wants to remain separate after exiting the situation or contemplating it.

They repeatedly draw someone back into the relationship using this lure method once they have come to terms with the fact that their partner is trying to distance them. The term "hoovering" is derived from the Hoover or vacuum cleaner, which creates suction, forcing whatever debris to be sucked in. This method keeps the victim emotionally invested and dependent on the manipulator.

This may be the time false promises are made regarding behaviour but never kept. This lure method then is a mirroring of how the toxic person once was at the beginning of the relationship. They try to reenact the love bombing phase that was once present at the beginning of the relationship. This version of the love bomb fails in comparison and is indefinitely weak. This method is used by these personality disorders to further maintain dominance, asserting power and control over others. This is one of the last grasps of manipulation within the toxic relationship. Usage of what previously worked before, such as love bombing and making bold promises that their behaviour will change going forward.

Usage of guilt-tripping or reaching out under the guise of it being accidental or even playing the victim in order to draw the victim back in. The idea is to get back into the same pattern of codependency under the guise of a more secure, less hellish relationship. Children you have together could be used in this lure phase.

Love bombing is an attempt to influence another by showing excessive displays of attention and or affection. It's also a way to mask their true intentions and manipulate the person and those around them. It can be used at any point during the relationship, but it's typically more noticeable at the start of a relationship.

The overly pushed love bombing strategy is an intense indoctrination into a new narcissistic relationship. Categorically needing you with them at all times or sending texts seeking to hear from you. Leaving the person on the receiving end overwhelmed and very attentive but tricked in the process. This has the ability to make you open up about your insecurities, such as your past or your actions and secrets, stuff that they can use against you later. As it's a tactic exploiting gullibility, it's too good to be true, and it works. The first few months could be filled with admiration and over-the-top attention displaying love, but this is to hide the underlying personality disorder. It creates a starting point for dependency and emotional attachment in the relationship.

They may give exaggerated compliments or even give gifts. Displaying communication overload while saying they love you quite early on in the relationship. It may seem as if your new partner really likes you, but this is a warning sign that you're stepping into an unhealthy relationship pattern. They're hoping that you trust them without having to earn it. This comes from the premise that you trust the best characteristics within people. If you can distinguish between an act and sincerity, this luring technique will fail. Baby trapping is also tied into the love bomb; they will quickly initiate the lifelong decision of having a baby almost straight away. This major life event is then used as a mere trapping tool, an emotional trap. Now, there is no escape from the mental and emotional torture that will inevitably ensue. Going forward, how you react is your power. Harassment comes in many forms, and nothing is off-limits to the narcissist. Some people have a built-in response that they use to try to minimise the emotional supply the narcissist receives through any harassment, baiting or interactions that cause fiction. This method, some claim, works, but it differs depending on the narcissist. It may be a good reactive pattern in some situations but can be futile in others. It goes by the term "grey rock", which is a calculated response that removes the emotional connection from the interaction. Maintain a bland stance in any conversation that you respond to and simply observe.

When the narcissist tries to trigger you emotionally or make you engaged in a situation, the responses would be null and void. The response to toxic behaviour is unresponsive and boring, lessening the narcissistic supply. This may work in a relationship setting, but with a baby in the picture, the best approach would be the "yellow rock". This yellow rocking is the same method but with a friendlier approach, sort of like how you would treat a waitress or a public servant. These methods won't do much for custody issues as communication is warranted. However, this method may be useful if the narcissist is trying to make you breach an existing court order or baiting you into a situation. At first, the love bombing phase can be overlooked immensely as it does not display any signs of coercive control or attacks. It merely acts to hide manipulative or abusive behaviour. By hiding this behaviour, the victim will be blindsided.

Soon, they get introduced piece by piece to what a toxic relationship actually looks like. The narcissist will try to have a baby quickly; the child is used as a form of entrapment within this toxic relationship. This is a premeditated method of control in which the child will be turned against you in the future. Among the alienating experiences that are shared between you and the child, this child will also be abused just like you. For narcissists, everything is transactional; their own children are just a possession.

These manipulative actions and techniques are an approach that regular people just aren't ready for, and unbeknownst to the victim, they fall for it. Manipulating the victim's emotions and exploiting their vulnerabilities once they have become trapped in the intricate web. These subtle psychological methods of attack and control are quite similar to the intricacy of the web from a spider catching its prey. The manipulator is able to keep the victim under their influence and continue to exert coercive control throughout the relationship.

Hoovering, love bombing or any attempt to entrap and deceive a person's goodwill can have lasting effects on the victim's emotional well-being. The constant cycle of being pulled back into a toxic relationship is enough to let the trauma it incurred linger for longer than it should. This causes an influx of low self-esteem, confusion and insecurity.

Victims of this find it quite difficult to break free from the manipulator's grasp. Continuing to be subjected to emotional abuse and manipulation. In some cases, the behaviour turns criminal and can include but is not limited to stalking, harassment, or even physical violence.

Case Study Anonymous

My wife's sister passed away unexpectedly and suspiciously in May of 2020 in Monroe County, TN; she left behind an 11-month-old and an almost 18-year-old son and a recent ex-husband, along with two sisters and both parents. Also in this aftermath was her unemployed drug-dealing car part-stealing boyfriend, who was the father of the 11-month-old. Knowing this man was in no way fit to raise a child, we consulted with attorneys about our options and did not have much to go on to launch a case to remove the child until 1/21, when dad attempted to take his and the child's life.

We quickly went in for emergency custody, being that we lived out of state I flew to TN and retrieved the child and brought him to our home out west, during this time we paid out of pocket for medical evaluations for the child who was so malnourished and below every benchmark that the attending nurse-who was reduced to tears at the site and situation of the child had no other choice but to refer us to our states CPS for a home visit.

When the CPS caseworker visited our house, she had the same reactions, we were ordered to take the child for a hair follicle test, those results showed exposure and/or ingestion to several prescription drugs, the same ones that the father was prescribed.

Unfortunately, we would be ordered to return the child to his father by Monroe Co, child/family court before we had the drug results; when these results were provided to the father's attorney and my attorney, they were never presented to the court as they were waiting for a hearing date to present them.

Then again suddenly and quite unexpectedly in 11/21 the father passes away somewhat mysteriously and that was when a former stepdaughter of the father stepped in and took (kidnapped) the child she was only supposed to have the child for the weekend as the father died on a Friday night, and was supposed to help DCS identify family to place the child with.

We had been interacting with this person ever since the childs mother died and she knew we had a case open for custody but never called DCS back to tell them, then the responding case worker said a paperwork "mistake" resulted in them never following up on the childs whereabouts or well being, so the "stepsister" without any legal standing went and filed for custody and competed with our filing, and did everything in her power to keep the case from going to court for as long as possible; when we finally got our day in court (April 2022).

They allowed her to file for adoption and froze the custody case, since the judge was too lazy he just allowed this to happen and said he didnt want to decide on anything cause either side would appeal and it would be a waste of court resources and we could just fight for adoption, how is that applying case history and legal proceedings for family members?

We were allowed to take the child for 7-12 days visits in our home and told we should be lucky that was allowed; even though we are the only biological family members seeking custody of the child, we were treated like criminals by this court with not ever committing any crimes in our entire life. Sadly, after this much time and money, we have had to give in and allow for the adoption of our nephew by non-family members; and now will have very limited contact with him for the rest of his life. It is a shame how the system has treated us including collusion by the court-appointed guardians, attorneys, judges and DCS. We don't even know where to go to voice this or take other legal action. Thank you for taking the time to allow us to speak about this. I am sure I have left out many other details, but it is difficult to recall this story in its entirety. We believe there is some level of profiting and child trafficking taking place in Monroe County, TN, these non-relatives have done nothing; but live off the system and profit through the child's dead mother, who, at a point before her downward spiral, had a somewhat productive/successful life.

GASLIGHTING

The term gaslighting originated from a play in 1938 called Gaslight. This play depicted a marriage that was based on deceit and abuse. The character of the husband tricks the wife, convincing her that she is utterly insane and drives her to a mental institution. In this play, he alters some aspects of their environment, and when she brings up the fact that there was a change to the environment, he makes her believe she isn't remembering things or losing her mind with delusion.

One of the things he did was take an old-fashioned gaslight that operated with propane, and he would dim these lights. When she would bring up the fact that the lights were dimmer and different, he would respond with I don't know what to do with you; there is nothing wrong with the lighting. This play-turned-film formed the term as we know it today: gaslighting.

Gaslighting is a subtle, psychological, manipulative tactic; It seems harmless at first or even just odd and eccentric displays of behavior, but this is a manipulation feeling out process. A probing of responses and boundaries, this tactic is used to control and confuse a person. This directs the person into states of doubt; they will second guess their own perceptions, feelings, memory and even their own sanity.

Gaslighting has dramatic effects on the victim, cementing uncertainty and self-doubt. If you're in an abusive relationship, you might not ever get to take a minute, sit down and consider these facts. It's actually abusive, especially if you're constantly on your toes dealing with comments and nonsensical narratives with the intent to gaslight.

This method is subtle but very effective. It can make you question yourself and teach you to take less notice of your perception. It is a boundary detector; it is used primarily to test limits and reactions. To Gas-light is to sow seeds of doubt in a person and try to convince them that what they see, they do not see; what they hear, they do not hear. This is a projection or deflecting method and convinces the other that there is something wrong with them.

It's a way to exert power and control over others; manipulating the victim can make them more dependent on the gaslighter for validation and approval. When a person is gaslit, it establishes disorientation, so much so; that they do not realise they are being manipulated. Gaslighting undermines confidence and causes doubt so precisely; so obvious, we see it yet, we dont realise it.

Gaslighting is one of the first psychological attacks used if it is not the first. It is one big game, soon the manipulation tactics will evolve; the gaslighting being the groundwork of observation; of reactions, decisions and sort of a character reading. This is a prodding, and the victim is left isolated, perplexed and vulnerable to further manipulation. Gaslighters may flat-out deny that something happened, even when there is clear evidence on the contrary.

If this continues at a high rate, the victim may overlook instances where there are clear mental health symptoms on display. This then will also minimise the victim's feelings and experiences. As if their concerns are invalid or unworthy of attention. By undermining the victim's sense of reality, gaslighters can maintain control over the relationship and continue to manipulate and harm the victim.

This manipulation tactic implements the use of confusion and misdirection. For example, after an event of inappropriate behaviour, this behaviour could be the target is on the receiving end of abuse verbal or other, so much abuse that a reaction has to happen to answer this abuse.

The gaslighter will follow up by changing the subject, deflecting blame or shifting the focus of the conversation to confuse and disorient the victim. This subtle display of manipulation will keep the victim off balance, questioning themselves and tolerating more. This then allows the gaslighter to maintain their power and dominance over the relationship.

Gaslighting is a sneaky tactic used to exert control, deceive and size up the opponent. This method subtly exploits the vulnerability of the victim and also serves as a measure of how much the person will tolerate and accept.

This gaslighting can also distract from other manipulative tactics that are used against you or even what is to come. It's done to nullify and to get rid of the person's perspective in favour of the manipulators. It's a validation technique to its core and is quite familiar with Cluster B.

GET OUT!

How do you feel when this person is around you? Do you like spending time with this person? Does it feel like their maturity is lacking? Do they deplete you? People don't want to have to end a relationship, even a terrible one. More often than not, they want to stick with a facade or try to repair it. Admitting that you're in a toxic relationship will be the first step forward. If the relationship is always going one way, well, then it's unhealthy. The my-way or the highway attitude, this style is deemed one-sided.

A relationship is a relation between two people. This is communication, agreement, and a vote of such actions to take in unison. Being constantly put down or exhibiting codependency equals an unhealthy relationship. If you're in a relationship that is making you insecure or it's incredibly abusive, get out.

Coercion is the use of making someone do certain things by threats or even force. This could come in the form of isolating you from others and auditing everything you do, monitoring you or depriving you of new ventures such as new life commitments like work. This behaviour views the victim as mere property; your money, your time, and everything else are theirs. They can humiliate you or make you feel miserable and still expect you to tolerate them.

The control dynamic concerning relationships shows their inability or lack of confidence in being loved or liked for who they are. Regardless of the reason, don't pity them and stay with them. Realistically, they need to be single as all they know is dehumanisation. This coercion control method is used systematically within the abusive relationship. If this rings true to you, get out of the situation or the "relationship", if that's what the abuser calls it. Coercive control can get physical, and any real domestic abuse victim has faced it.

Threatening consequences if you don't meet their demands. This could be leeching you for your money so that, inevitably, it is no longer your own. Threatening future behaviour or telling stories riddled with inconsistencies to strike fear and panic. Even threatening you to engage in sex, these demands are all simply control. There will be no balance or control over your life anymore if you are in a coercive relationship. Any move you make, they will sabotage. Any instance that they can manipulate and sabotage on your behalf, they will, as the mere idea of you leaving and being happy will irritate this controller.

These people are cunning, and they know that their behaviour is wrong. Relationship dynamics have evolved, and so has coercion.

They know full well that courts and police are against this behaviour. However, they also know that their policies towards it are outdated. They want to continue this coercive control should this abusive relationship come to pass.

This is the planning stage for false allegations or the gathering of evidence from any reactive abuse, etc. This coercion will continue, and it will be fully legal. The police and courts will enforce this coercion for the abuser. This is the last laugh, and any repercussions from here onward will be unjust, like the rest of the relationship.

They methodically plan future events and what-ifs. Speculating on how they will get back at you should you get sick of the coercive control. They will graduate the abuse into the courtroom and enforce parental alienation if they can. They will foresee all of this before it occurs. A person who lives a life of purposeful abuse and coercive control has tested every limit and boundary possible. They know methods of control more than regular people. They weaponise every detail against their victims. It is plausible then to assume that they know how to utilise the court system against another.

They are skilled at turning events and situations into weapons. They know that if they go to court and mention that they are the ones being abused, when the alternative viewpoint comes in, it's just word against word.

No regard for children or the well-being of anybody else. They want to cause suffering, as that's all they know. Whatever brought them to that dark place in life is irrelevant; these are the most dangerous people you can associate with. This controlling behaviour is then prevalent when manipulation is lacking. They play mind games and manipulate with ease to get what they want at that specific time. They will manipulate you, the courts or others.

Watch out for signs of triangulation or living parallel lives at your expense. Talking bad about you puts you on the defensive. Making you inferior and outnumbered. Tricks like gaslighting might seem harmless at first, but pay close attention. This technique is used to test your will and your boundaries.

How much will you tolerate? Do you bring mistreatment up, or are you going to let it slide? Do you remember this or that? It is done to break your mental state down so you live more like a puppet than a free-thinking individual.

Hoovering will be used when there is an instance of distancing. Perhaps the behaviour is becoming intolerable. This luring method will be used to catfish you into more drama. Furthermore, Love bombing is underestimated, as this is the strategy to reel a victim in. This phase is fleeting and demonstrates their knack for acting. They must find real love intolerable or are unable to show it. They merely act it out for a couple of months, even just to cement the relationship. They will use this to trap you so you can never leave. This is when they rush to get pregnant before you get a glimpse of who they really are.

This warning is not only for innocent people trying to meet a new spark or love interest. It is for every person who has been through an abusive relationship pattern. For example, even if you are borderline and your abusive partner is narcissistic, get out of the relationship. If you are a self-aware individual able to admit you have a personality disorder, thank you. There are plenty of content creators these days, either self-aware narcissists or borderline, etc. We need more as it's not to single out the entire spectrum of Cluster B. Rather, the high conflicting-attacking abusive behaviours from these disorders.

No person should tolerate a vicious attack or an array of attacks. This is simply principle and morals. Watch who you allow into your circles. Try to interpret their behaviour and their state of mind. Abusive relationships don't start as abusive; they start filled with intensity. This intensity turns into smothering. Isolation, jealousy and volatility soon follow. Frequent breakups and makeups, the relationship having ultimatums. If the relationship strips away empowerment, it is abusive.

If you are in an abusive, coercive-controlling relationship dilemma, Get Out!

Chapter 8
Inside the Psyche of the Parental Alienator

This topic is a delicate one. In fact, if you do not have children of your own, you will not completely understand the magnitude of parental alienation. Parental alienation seems to be sweeping courtrooms at a rapid pace, with the cases continuing to increase. More and more people are speaking up about it, but change has yet to come.

The energetic bond between parent and child is ineffable, and nothing can describe it. Making it a prime target for would-be abusers controlling relationships. The joy of parenting and nurturing your child brings about purpose in your life like nothing can. People can't seem to co-parent effectively.

They remain in dispute, but at least one parent is unable to act amicably. More often than not, the unwilling child is ushered centre stage and ripped apart by two parents who the child loves equally.

This child will be brainwashed early on in this manipulative mind game process. The child is no match for the psychological attacks of the alienator. This child will face grief and pain. This child will also face the coercive control that the alienated parent once felt. Parental alienation is a form of severe psychological abuse.

The child will be inundated with hearsay to dehumanise the alienated parent. The alienated child will be triangulated against the other parent. This repetition of systematic manipulation over time will eventually lead to the child thinking that it's their own feelings and thoughts about the parent. They are accompanied by peer pressure and the influence of the alienator. The children are trained early on with hate and to repel the opposing parent. Unfortunately, even if the kid figures this out and resents the years of alienation, the damage is still done, and time is still lost.

This encapsulates the petty, childish behaviour of getting the last laugh and trying to torment the other parent. This parental alienation, then, is simply a strategy and an abusive family dynamic. This child will become a mere puppet from the mental and emotional abuse alienation causes. Followed by attachment issues and or emotional instability going forward. This child is emotionally beat-down, suppressing love for their parents since they can remember. This suppression of emotion will affect them dramatically and cause ongoing problems later on in their lives.

This alienation, then, is a hostage dynamic of sorts. The child's authentic self is buried and held captive by this control. The child does not have the mental capacity to process or handle this orchestrated manipulation. They will be forced to go along with this facade, and long-term life choices will be made on their behalf.

A healthy upbringing for children promotes a good visual and influence of both parents in the child's life. The mother and the father influence development and act as role models for children as they mature. This unhealthy dynamic ruins any normality regarding the child's development.

The alienating parent will do everything in their power to reframe any kind gesture or nice thing the other parent does or says. This experience will mentally and emotionally damage the child. Altering the functionality of their relationships for the rest of their lives. This learned inauthenticity will dominate their reactions and behaviour from here on out. This child suffers from being nothing more than a mere pawn. Alienating parents let a conflict get in the way of the child's upbringing. These conflicts are usually as simple as jealousy or just as a means of punishment.

This behaviour is unnecessary just to hurt the other parent's feelings. These abuse dynamics show the immaturity of the alienator.

Painting the other parent as all bad while they want to be viewed as all good. Alienation also happens because of their ridiculous idea of being the number 2# parent. What if the child likes that parent more? The opposing parent can be viewed as competition. Again, this is how ridiculous it gets and how mindless alienators are.

Then comes the explanation of the alienation process; that might seem like a relief to tell that child someday. Once you mention your reason for not being around in the past or speak of the other parent in a negative light, then you are now on the alienator level. These children are ignorantly caught in the middle of a tug-of-war between parents, either way, demonstrating nothing but dysfunction.

There is no justification for purposely ruining a child's development by excluding a loving parental figure, which ultimately results in damaging the child's emotional well-being; this happens all too often. The act of alienation rips the heart out of a loving person and destroys any normality in their existence. That's why it's the perfect course of action to take, to be weaponised, with lasting effects on the victim.

Out of all the attacks or manipulation methods that can be used against a person, Parental Alienation has the worst impact and manipulative effects because it involves using an innocent child. This is a well-known deceitful practice but is not well-known enough to warrant any legal change or ramifications. Parental alienation is the term used to describe a situation in which one parent manipulates instances where a child would be banished from the other loving parent without valid justification.

Parental alienation is a sophisticated abuse process; the intent is to forcibly choose the child or children's side amongst either parent without consent. Either by manipulation or by avoiding child access from the targeted parent. Make no mistake about it: parental alienation is a form of abuse, and parents who engage in this tactic are abusers. It's like a form of Stockholm syndrome for the child. As they mature and grow up, they feel threatened to ask questions or pick any side other than the alienating parents. Children can be coerced or coached into saying disparaging things about the other parent for leverage in court.

These alienators seek to hurt the feelings of the other parent and lack empathy even regarding their own children. In order to be involved in this form of abuse, one has to have narcissistic tendencies.

The child becomes an emotional and mental hostage to the alienator. Some reasoning behind their actions would be the fact that they are triggered or feel a slight form of possible rejection.

As an ultimatum maker and a revenge ploy, they use the baby hostage method. They view the idea of having a baby with someone merely as an investment into a future relationship due to their insecurities.

The feelings of inadequacy force their hand to use parental alienation to serve as a harsh punishment and a source of emotional negotiation to accept them and their abuse going forward.

No relationship? Well, then, no child or children in your life.

Court orders, such as restraining or protection orders, are used as a smokescreen to the outside world.

They make it appear that the person put up with abuse and needed a court order to create the space when, in fact, the person on the receiving end of the court order wants nothing to do with them.

Here are seven common alienating beliefs that occur in false allegations:

Some of the criteria involved regarding this fallacy of thinking is that the alienator would be coming from the premise of;

1. "I am afraid our child will love you more than me and will want to live with you."

2. "I want my child all to myself."

3. "If you don't want me, you don't get our child, either."

4. "I want to exact revenge on you, and what better way than to deprive you of your child."

5. "I don't want my child to be anything like you."

6. "I've been the real parent in this family, not you."

7 "I don't want my child to love their new stepparent because I might be pushed out."(Parlato, F et al.,2023)

Another would be "If you don't put up with me or my behaviour, you won't have your child either". This hostage-style takeover of a child often occurs during high-conflict divorce cases and breakups.

Where emotions run high, and parents seek to use their children as weapons or pawns.

Fathers are usually the victims of parental alienation as women are granted guardianship at birth, but alienation also frequently happens to women. The victims are left overwhelmed and emotionally distraught and unfairly portrayed as the scapegoat.

The results of alienation on a child have devastating effects and can lead to long-lasting emotional and psychological damage. Some damage would take the form of attachment functionality and trust issues. If we look at the statistics, between 70-94 per cent of incarceration, violent crime rates, behavioural problems, substance abuse, and high school drop-outs can all be traced to growing up without a father. Parental alienation isn't just a swing at the targeted parent; it's a massive blow to the child or children. It's purposely done to break the hearts of the significant other or break the bonds between parent and child.

Parental alienation can also be used as a way to gain an advantage and control in custody battles. It starts with limiting visitation or access to the child. As the child grows up, their fate is to be pitted against the other parent.

The alienating parent may be able to secure sole custody or, better yet, convince the child that the other parent is no good and doesn't love them anyway. In court proceedings, it's quite common that the child is coached to say things such as "they would rather not see you anyways", regurgitating what was fed to them.

Alienation is a complete and utter purpose-driven breakdown of communication and cooperation between the parents, with no intention to resolve conflicts and reach agreements on co-parenting issues. Courts that are exposed to this callous behaviour should consider changing custody arrangements to protect the child from further emotional harm. However, the incompetence of the family courts and child services is on full display. They haven't caught up yet and are recycling the old methods of dealing with child safety.

Case study

Anonymous

The father who made this submission wanted to remain anonymous. He mentioned that he had fought day in / day out for 14 years to be in his kids' lives. They live very close, but he remains alienated, unable to have any type of bond or relationship with them. His ex-wife has used manipulative tactics such as parental alienation and has distanced them from him since 2011. His eldest will be 18 years old in January 2025, and he hasn't seen her since she was 4. The effect of this emotionally breaks him, and he would not even recognise her in the street if they passed by one another.

He went on to stress that, he has spent nearly 100k fighting to see them since this all began. He tries everything and always seems to get nowhere, ending up with the same result. He and his ex-wife have to go to court again in September.

He emphasised that he has done anything and everything in his power to see them. His ex-wife tells them that she has always allowed him and his family to be around them, but they chose not to be around, which couldn't be further from the truth.

They saw a reunification counsellor for 6 years (after multiple botched prior attempts when she would pull more stunts to keep it from happening). A reunification counsellor would typically work with parents and children to improve communication using interventions and a range of modalities.

His ex-wife has lied about him in court in her affidavits; they haven't made it to court since she submitted the affidavit.

He has written communication that proves she is indeed lying about him.

He is a deaf man, so everything is communicated via text or email. He just paid 5k for another psychiatrist to do a custodial evaluation and alienation assessment on the case; now, he has to come up with another $3500 more to pay for this to proceed further.

In which he feels is more like a donation because the psychiatrist will be the one giving the court recommendations on how to move forward. He initially reached out to tell what he could of his story and sought advice, further resources, reassurance, and help.

Parental alienation is widespread within relation fallouts, such as grandparent alienation, but it is mainly a cornerstone of co-parenting relationships. When one parent actively works to decimate and undermine the relationship between the child and the other parent. This is the aim and could stem from pretty trivial matters; such as attention. This targeting will ultimately create a toxic and hostile environment for co-parenting. Decision-making for the child's well-being is now non-existent, with ongoing conflict and tension arising between both parents.

Parental alienation is a heartbreaking phenomenon which is grown exponentially in recent years. So common are the stories of that one parent who manipulates their child to reject the other parent or tries to stop access to see the child altogether. There is no valid reason other than a petty conflict or resentment. There is no attempt to solve or work towards resolving this conflict. These alienators seem conflict-driven, focusing on disrupting the child's well-being. Loving parents need to be aware of the early signs of the alienation process. Unfortunately, it is usually too late by the time it is fully realised. We must recognise when it is happening and take cautious steps to address it.

Parental alienation becomes evident when the child suddenly and inexplicably begins to reject the parent for no valid reason. The relationship before this sudden change was previously close and loving. Triangulation will have the child parrot negative comments or criticisms about the target parent. Phrases or comments that they have heard from the alienating parent, as well as the usage of triangulation manipulation, influence the child's behaviour and actions.

In cases of Parental alienation the alienated parent may notice that their child is being coached, coerced or manipulated into saying damaging things. There are stories of persuading the children; for example, to make false accusations of abuse or neglect. These accusations are often used to alienate the child from the targeted parent further. Victims of this should be on the lookout for any signs that their child is being coerced. The worst case scenarios are the constant court battles excluding the parent from the child's life.

If law-fare is the case, the parent needs to be aware of any further slanderous or damaging accusations. Parental alienation is the known term, but in most of these cases, it is not alienation of the children at all; it is stealing the children. The children are mere possessions; alienation is a side effect of the steal.

Parental alienation impacts relations profoundly and in the most negative way imaginable. The exclusion makes it difficult to communicate and co-parent with the alienating parent. Exclusion will break the bond of the child and parent at a pivotal time in the child's life, missing key milestones and watching the child grow up.

As the alienating parent continues to poison the child's mind against the other parent, the targeted parent will succumb to isolation and depression. This vicious tactic has no bounds, and once it is in motion, there is no alternative route or way to navigate it; the great loss is experienced by the targeted parent. This chaos further fuels the conflict, creating more animosity and distrust.

Parental alienation is psychological abuse that reinforces torture and suffering. There is no mental gymnastics that can be performed to escape the devastation. The effects on the alienated children will be lifelong, facing restriction from a loving parent and now in the grasp of a control freak. These effects are what the alienator simply does not care about; in fact, they enjoy passing the torch of misery.

When a parent engages in petty alienating behaviours, either triangulation, bad mouthing the other parent and restricting access to see the child; the innocent child is put right in the middle of a high-conflict situation. This brings about shock as this person is willing to use a child as a baton; and nothing else constructive crosses their minds. This conflict profoundly impacts the child's mental and emotional well-being causing issues that the alienator uses as a way of getting back at the parent who cares, passing on heartbreak anyway they can. It also ruins any relationship or even friendship with both parents in the long term. This can impede future relationships for the child when they grow up, or even lead to the development of mental disorders or gender identity issues.

Children who are subjected to parental alienation go on to feel states of confusion, guilt, and loyalty conflicts, not to mention depression, even very young children. The insurmountable pressure to choose sides between both parents leads to a breakdown in their relationship with one or both of the parents.

This can have a detrimental effect on the child's self-esteem and sense of identity, as they may struggle to reconcile their feelings towards each parent. Children look up to both parents their entire lives before their first recollected memories. Even in the womb, a baby's brain development is affected by arguing or fighting. This affects their ability to feel safe and create strong bonds. During the time the child looks up to their biological parents; they mirror them connecting spiritually and emotionally to them. There is already an established energetic guardian bond that parents have with their babies that is fulfilling and purpose-driven for each parent. This is why a Cluster B-type personality would use parental alienation as an attack stratagem.

Children are led by their parents, and they look up to and admire each parent equally, with no judgements or biases. They inherit qualities from each parent and are easily influenced by the parents, for better or worse.

So many grown adults have issues in life, be that depression related or perhaps they require a psychiatric appointment. The psychiatrist will always pose the question and bring up the relationship with parents or what it was like growing up relating to both parents. This subtle aspect is the most common theme that affects people's current life issues. Moreover, these life issues are centred around and connected with one or both parents.

Unfortunately, people today seem to lack a moral compass or dignity, among other things, and care little about the effects on a child. They constantly compete against the other parent, perpetuating toxicity within the family. Living in chaotic environments, children suffer as they need approval and never quite feel fully validated by their parents.

Furthermore, this would leave the child not feeling wanted or loved at all; they'd feel rejected as they were only used and accepted by the alienator if they behaved unfavourably to the other parent.

The alienating parent may use the child as a pawn in their efforts to hurt the other parent, which works wonders for the alienator, but it also demonstrates the lack of love towards the child by that parent. This can create a toxic environment for the child, as they are caught in the middle of an ongoing conflict and subjected to manipulation. It can't be emphasised enough that parental alienation is one of the worst forms of emotional and psychological abuse. This abuse has lifelong effects on both the child or children and the targeted parent.

All of this bad parenting has significant implications for custody and visitation arrangements. This area of the court is used as a way to further control, using the child to make a point or make the other parent miserable.

The family court system lacks the ability to punish or even acknowledge this common form of emotional abuse. They remain ignorant of the parental alienation abuse tactic. Parental alienation is complicated with an unlimited amount of hearsay, text messages or scheduling issues to sift through; full of conflicting narratives from both parents.

For the victim of parental alienation, protecting their relationships with their children can be next to impossible. In an ideal world, adults should be mature and level headed enough to negotiate and maintain a civil co-parenting relationship. The only issue here is that these personality types don't do well at negotiating; they don't accept responsibility, and they stop at nothing to fill the opposing parent with as much misery as they can manufacture.

In cases of parental alienation, it's a life sentence; and for others it is a death sentence. This tactic enforced with help from the family court has such an impact, that there are countless people who give up and commit suicide because of it. Despite evidence of manipulation and emotional abuse, the legal system look beyond it. Leading to frustration and helplessness as time is ticking by; and loving parents relationships with their children are on the line.

This law-fare tactic is used to wear down the other parent emotionally, causing strain and defeat. The sorrow caused by missing the most important moments of your child's life is immeasurable. Family courts don't consider children being purposely alienated for no good reason. Parents can be fueled by animosity from this heart breaking control method that they overlook how to effectively advocate for themselves in court.

It's pretty difficult for most people even to try to comprehend using a child as a weapon. Begin to get into the psyche of the alienator and start to see the child as a tool or object to utilise for your own personal gain or hurt; it is nearly impossible, and that's because you have empathy!

Even the term parental alienation isn't recognised by most people; it is a relatively new phrase. It's until it happens to you! That's when you take a step back in awe, confronted with all the unnecessary obstacles you must overcome.

That's when you notice the situation you're in is based primarily on coercive control and manipulation, and guess what? It works, leading to irreparable damage. It is a combination of quickly getting with the wrong person, often with some underlying mental health conditions, and also the outdated, easily manipulated court systems. They systematically allow issues like these to occur without any inquiry or investigation of such practices as safety or protection orders. Justice doesn't exist if it can be manipulated quite easily by slander and spite. The family courts should not be able to be used as a mind game; children need better, evenly distributed parental rights and justice.

DEDUCTION

The sickening display of intent regarding parental alienation as a tactic has ruined many parents' lives across the world. These cases highlight the need for more education, care and better handling of these sensitive matters by the courts and the third party child agencies involved. The family court in inundated with inaccurate proceedings and incompetence. We need to be learning from these erroneous court proceedings and most importantly the victims who experienced parental alienation.Personality disorders; specifically Cluster B (borderline, narcissistic, antisocial and histrionic), these are the personality types most likely to become parental alienators. The alienator will demonstrate extreme narcissism, salivating at the conflict driven, emotional turmoil.

Cluster B is the calling card, if we want to delve into the psyche of the parental alienator we must look at this cluster. This cluster, is so argumentative and drama latent, that the recorded numbers of people who have a personality disorder within it, are all wrong.

These people avoid diagnosis, they will not self reflect or consider a second thought regarding their actions. If a person is not diagnosed with cluster b, and they alienate children; this message still rings true. This cluster is known for falsely accusing and sooner or later it will be known for parental alienation. It is impossible to make the life choice of deducting from your own childs life unless you have narcissistic traits of some kind or another.

Diagnosed or not people under the umbrella of Cluster B are the usual suspects for this parental-alienation Phenomenon. People with one of these personality types are set in their ways. Diagnosis means a loss of thier identity; very few are self-aware. The numbers are much higher regarding the diagnosis of such disorders. Not everyone who has disorders like these even know they have it or ever get diagnosed. The person who knows that they have a disorder from this cluster, and remain undiagnosed; this type is the most dangerous kind. It demonstrates the tenacity to rummage through life, not bothered by hurting themselves or others. In fact it is their super power; they play god serving others; ex partners or their children with harsh life events that will break hearts, unable to mend.

They have children to use as pawns to emotionally and psychologically break the other parent; most people can't take the torment and leave altogether. Cluster B individuals would likely use lawfare to intimidate, such as fake protective orders. They would continually insist to the police that their partner has breached the order when they haven't. Moreover, they would make up stories in the hopes that police and courts would believe them, with the sole purpose of getting their ex-partner in trouble. Usage of situational attacks, leaving torment in their wake; Now their essence is fully felt, now they are validated.

They will be intolerable, making every aspect of co-parenting difficult. They will enforce preventive measures to the parent-child relationship while publicly telling others that the parent just doesn't want to see their child.

The (abuser) which is what they are, as they are cutting off a healthy influence and loving bond on behalf of their child or children. Remember, we are not talking about a protective parent here, trying to keep a child from harm as if the other parent has a record or represents a valid danger, which is wholly justified with an apparent safety concern.

That is the structure of law that's being manipulated here! That same law is used by abusers and perfected to the point that it wouldn't be shocking to postulate that these personality types think this course of action through well in advance of getting into a relationship to have children.

These personality types don't look upon people or relationships as others do; they don't appreciate them, and they couldn't, not if they remain scattered with these types of symptoms. Narcissistic traits, for example, would only demonstrate thinking about what they can gain from this relationship, what money, possessions or status this relationship gives them. Then it's an abrupt discard and onto the next, but if a child or children are involved, it's the same modus operandi. Take, Take, Take, I, I, I. There's no room for error. This is their only function. Also, Narcissists can't self-reflect; they cannot learn from past mistakes that occurred in previous relationships and adapt to a change going forward. They are armed with an array of callous manipulative behaviours that they function with throughout their life.

They are cunning and overly proud of their strategies to outwit others, wreaking havoc and taking the credit.

They are manipulative and think so far ahead, studying their entitlements or best approaches towards a soon-to-be court case, divorce case or custody case, examining their best chances to win, collecting evidence months, if not longer, in advance before their unwitting partner knows what hit them.

This would act as an ultimatum; if my partner doesn't do such and such, doesn't stay or put up with this coercive control, then the element of surprise will be fierce. That surprise will startle and stun for months, leading to an unprepared and highly reactive person.

That surprise is a court order of some kind, law-fare, police harassment and yes, you guessed it, parental alienation. If it's a protective order, they would bait you in and steal all of your possessions, money and children in the hopes that you breach your order, and with the built-up stress, some people probably do.

But beware, this is not only what they want; it legitimises their false court order. Being a loving parent towards their children is the last thing on their minds.

Case study

Denise

I want to tell you what I observed in a Loudon County, Tennessee case. It wasn't my case, but it is one example of how well the children are considered. My mother was diagnosed with cancer in 2005. Within days of her announcing it to our family, my daughter announced she was marrying the man she was living with. During my mother's illness, my daughter's behaviour became increasingly bizarre. As my mother lay breathing her last, my daughter demanded to carry through with her wedding, which was planned to take place at my home. I had no choice but to arrange food, drinks and guests, but when the time for the ceremony came, my daughter told me they did not have time to get the licence and tried to coerce my neighbour, who is a minister, to perform the ceremony illegally. The couple exchanged vows before the guests without a licence. (They never legalised the union.) My mother passed away a few short hours afterwards. After my mother's funeral, the couple went on their "honeymoon" in Gatlinburg, Tennessee. My daughter had scammed money from her biological father to pay for the trip. I received a call from my daughter informing me she needed cash to pay for damages to the hotel room! I don't recall what her story was.

Just because they were threatening to call the police unless she paid hundreds of dollars for damages incurred during their stay, I explained there was no way I could help her. Financially, I was struggling to survive and feed the two children at home. I'm not sure how they were able to get out of the trouble, but she evaded arrest—a trick she has done many times.

A week or so later, I answered my phone to hear him screaming. I could hear her yelling in the background. He told me that she was chasing him around their home with a huge kitchen knife. I told him to call the police. When the police arrived, I asked repeatedly to speak with them but was ignored.

My daughter had locked herself in the bedroom and told them it was HIM chasing her. The poor young man was arrested and charged. My daughter dropped the charges later, but they will be on his record forever. While living with HIM, my daughter called, begging for help after being arrested for shoplifting at Target.

My other daughter was working for a local Sonic restaurant. I asked if she could help her sister. (I was still under the delusion I could help my oldest daughter.) Once she had the money in hand and knew there was money in a savings account, she proceeded to steal every dime she could from her sister's bank account. Had I known, I would have had her arrested. My daughter was seventeen, and I was listed on the account. I was not informed until years later by another family member whom was confided in. Working for a rental car company in a strip mall, my oldest daughter called me in tears.

Her boss came into the office and discovered three vehicles were missing. My middle daughter had accepted a position at the company as well, and my first thought was of her. I was quickly assured that she was not involved nor suspected of wrongdoing. My oldest was their main suspect. After hearing various conflicting stories, I told her that her best course was to cooperate and be honest.

By this point, I was well aware of her mental problems but felt helpless as I was limited by what I could do. She was over eighteen. She refuses to admit a problem with drugs or mental issues. I would like to point out that drugs were only a crutch. One of her many excuses for her horrible deeds. (I think my favourite excuse is, "I learned everything from my mother." And "My mother gave me opioids to do the dishes." Excuse me, little girl, but can anyone who knows me believe that dribble?) An incredible actress, she has always been able to manipulate others and bend them to her will. If that failed, she would use blackmail or bribery. People will readily admit they are terrified of her finding out they said anything. Not wanting to turn her attention toward them like she did me.

My daughter left the young man and moved in with his friend. Eight months later, she had her first child. My oldest grandson was born with opioids in his system. My daughter talked her way out as she did after the second one tested positive. My son-in-law owned a very nice two-story home when we met. He drove a newer truck. He enjoyed the job he held and was happy. My daughter lost everything he owned in the first two years of their marriage, including getting him fired from three different jobs.

One of her favourite tricks is to find a place to live, paying whatever it takes to move in and wait for the eviction notice. While she lives there, neighbours will begin to complain about her actions. Police are called, and reports are made. Family and friends who saw the truth about my daughter started calling me and reporting what they saw and knew, including concerns for my grandsons. I heard a rumour that she had waited until her mother-in-law went to work one morning and sold the woman's patio furniture collection before her return.

When I happened to sit in the pew before my son-in-law's family on a court date, his mother confirmed the rumour was true. We were in court for their divorce hearing. She had left him after he refused to take out another payday loan for her. She packed up the two small children they had at that time and went to a battered women's shelter, claiming that my son-in-law beat her. The battered women's shelter took her and the children in and retained an attorney for her. Which partially explains why I didn't want to turn to them myself. I felt that others would need the services more than me. By that point, I knew my daughter was mentally unstable and worried for my grandsons.

I told my son-in-law I would testify at the divorce hearing on behalf of the boys. My daughter found out I had offered to testify, so she took out a restraining order against me to try and stop me.

But the officers didn't find me in time to serve the papers. I showed up in time to hear Judge Rex Dale ask the bailiff about the documents. "Have these papers been served on Malissa Evans?" The bailiff shook his head, "No, your honour, the address is Anderson County." Hearing my maiden name, I stood up. "I'm here, your honour, but that is my maiden name. My daughter knows I married her father but refuses to acknowledge it." "Did you know about these papers?" I was honestly dumbfounded. "No, Your Honour." "If you weren't served, why are you here?" "I am not here to testify on her behalf. I'm not here to testify on his behalf. I'm here to testify on behalf of the children." I stated in a calm, clear voice. He had the bailiff hand me the papers to look over as he started the case. (See the documents provided.)

The disgusting lies and insinuations infuriated me for a long time. 1. I have never owned property in Georgia, as she claimed. 2. I was not even in the state of Tennessee during the dates listed. I allegedly tried to break down her door and kidnap my grandsons on her statement. 3. I have NEVER drugged my son. And that's just the top three. Thanks to her continual false allegations and the investigations I have endured, I have lab reports I carry in my purse to refute the lies of drug abuse of my son and myself.

Unfortunately, I was never able to prove my innocence nor discuss anything with the judge. My daughter quickly dropped all charges and did her song and dance. When it was revealed that she was, in fact, staying with the first young man she accused of abuse, the judge was going to award custody to my son-in-law. When the very person who told me I "needed to put him (meaning my son!) somewhere." stepped up and offered to allow her to stay in his home. My father has separate issues with me to be revealed at a later time. I TRIED with every ounce of my heart to speak with the judge.

My daughter's attorney came rushing up to where my husband and I stubbornly sat, refusing to leave until we spoke with the judge. "It's okay; you can go," she simpered. "All the charges have been dropped." CHARGES! I was NOT concerned about charges! How dare she? "We want to speak to the judge," I said as calmly as I could as my husband sat nodding his agreement. We were never given the opportunity to be heard. Our testimony was crucial evidence to be considered. Yet we were blocked by every angle. She was allowed to walk out with two innocent children to abuse. That's when the calls, harassment, and investigations increased. We have been under investigation by multiple agencies since the date of the charges she tried to file.

Since that day in court, my daughter has reconciled with her husband. They went on to have two more children. I have discovered that my son-in-law passed away recently due to cancer. My heart goes out to his family. He was a good man. I will always believe he reconciled on behalf of the children he so loved. To offer what little buffer he could. My heart, kisses and hugs beg for my grandbaby's forgiveness. Yet, my only excuse is that my son should not be punished for someone else's crimes or insanity. He is no angel, either. (And please don't think I would ever choose one child over another.) However, allowing her further access to her brother would be a tragedy. The only threat used against me to be found effective was adequate indeed. To know my greatest strength and weakness all rolled into one—my innocent son.

To continually have to be on guard for his safety is my top priority. Her constant remarks to others have not fallen on deaf ears. "If something happens to her (meaning me), I'm going to take everything he's got and put him in the cheapest place I can find." I still remember his cry of pain when I caught her with him, face down on his bed. Her knee was in his back as she wrenched his arms up. This occurred right before his abuse by the school in 2007. "She's given my inheritance to my brother," she gripped when the trust fund was established specifically for him. She has stolen medications from my home. My medications and my children were taken when I was at the grocery store. I had been giving her money at first when I could "to help pay bills". Then I stopped that and paid the bills at the office.

Finally, I had to realise that I was contributing to the madness. I have stated more than once: "I would love to be a part of her life, but I WILL NOT be a part of her death." Since refusing to support her habits, my daughter began her campaign to hurt my son and me whenever she can. Why am I explaining all this? Am I just wanting revenge or retaliation? Hell, NO! I'm ashamed of myself for not fighting harder! I have always thought of the innocent ones first. Do I have anger or hatred for my daughter? She is mentally ill. It's taken me a long time to deal with that. Accept it. I'm sure she doesn't care about my posts, pain or the trouble she's caused. Her only concern is for herself. Yet I will no longer bear my shame in silence. Silence suffered in fear.

Not fear for myself, fear for the most innocent of all, my son and children like him. For the innocent grandchildren who will never know how much I love them. For all the other children to come seeking safety and justice. I will be silent no more! This is just one example I have experienced in a Loudon County courtroom.

My daughter is a sociopath. She has never accepted responsibility for any crime she has done. People who come across her or are in her life are terrified of her. I really don't care what she has done and is doing to me. I only pointed out a few things that she has done to others. My point is that the JUDGE refused to listen to testimony critical to the children's custody. The case was finalised, and they were sent home with her to be abused!

The person who sets out to become an imposter, filling the courtroom with lies and false allegations, is an abuser. The person who designs the blueprint to eliminate a child or children from the life of a loving partner is an abuser.

The abuser cannot maintain composure and has an innate function of behaviour almost built into their DNA, such as cluster B personality types. Furthermore, they are hardwired to initiate this abusive nature to other people, including children or animals. These people will create ultimatums and give their partners physical and verbal abuse or keep them ingrained within their manipulative games. Should the victim of this break from this manipulative cycle or is suspected of possibly doing so, the abuser will bring charges, build a case to the courts and exclude that safe parent from the equation, either as a way of eliminating a possible future threat opposing the abuse the child will face going forward or to merely hurt the other parent as a form of punishment or both.

We are talking about revenge from different angles, such as law and the breaking of a loving bond without consent. Once it gets to the parental alienation stage of the fallout, your mind can wander about how dirty the allegations can get to justify the alienation. When a child is born, both the child and each parent share a deep biological bond that they navigate throughout life. To remove this positive bond or biologically wired connection is devastating and indeed leads to sombre depression. This is what the aim of parental alienation is: the ability to emotionally affect the other parent long after they're gone, contributing to their torment.

There is no trying to co-parent, there is no turning the other cheek, but rather, how can I cause as much grief as humanly possible?

> "There is some evidence that loss of contact with one's children is a contributor to parental suicide" (Shiner et al., 2009)

OTHER POSSIBLE REASONS OR OUTCOMES THAT CONTRIBUTE TO PARENTAL ALIENATION;

When considering the parental alienator, their unique attributes and behavioural aspects, should we thoroughly examine the building blocks of what makes up a parental alienator? They mirror all the symptoms from the Cluster B category. These symptoms highlighted in earlier chapters such as abandonment issues, paranoia and delusional thinking. Hypothetically, the alienator would suspect; think ahead through rumination, the possible outcomes relating to their outrageous behaviours. The what-if scenarios with their partner or children. Possibly, this conclusion will be based on past relationships, friendships, jobs, family, and so on, and it will be a summary of all the social rejection stemming from behaviours they exhibit that they cannot manage.

This would give them the idea or feeling that perhaps soon, their own child will end up picking sides just like so many people have done in the past; that choice would be a unanimous decision of the other, more stable parent.

This would be the last straw. Put yourself in their shoes, think like they do for just a moment. To lose your child due to the behaviour that you deemed acceptable to lash out to you're loved ones, this wouldnt be a loss of just a son or a daughter; it would be a loss of validation.

This would encourage any form of parental alienation, going as far as damaging the other parent's credibility and eradicating them from the picture by any means necessary. They would want the other parent to feel in danger of even wanting to spend time with their child or children. This fear would stem from the possibility of what the alienated parent could do next, bringing a shock value of dirty tactics to the mix and demonstrating a complete lack of empathy along the way. They would invoke possible unforeseen outcomes, creating distress. They would invoke the fabrication of stories to establish safety or protective orders, including false allegations and allegations that meet the criteria in a court system to abolish the other parent from visitation or access.

The superior feeling of victory against an opponent with the ability to manipulate a judge and attorneys for example, putting their opposition on the back foot. That's what the other parent is to them, the opposition, and the best interests of the child aren't at play here due to the lack of empathy. A Cluster B type personality will look upon their partner as their opposition even when they are trying to love and support them.

The inability to realise that things can improve between them, even if they have arguments or fights, for example, there is always room for growth and improvement. But cluster b is incapable of this transformation; the impulsive nature of these personality types brings about these combative outcomes. Also, the narcissistic personality type would want to be the first to strike due to possible narcissistic injury and the probability of the other parent whistle-blowing the first narrative of what is actually going on; which, is repulsive to the Narcissist.

> "The potential risks to children raised in fragmented families that have been identified in the literature include poverty, mental illness, physical illness, infant mortality, lower educational attainment (including greater risk of dropping out of high school), juvenile delinquency, conduct disorders, adult criminality, and early unwed parenthood" (Scafidi, B.2008)

Coercive control throughout abusive relationships will continue through the parental alienation process. If the relationship ends, so does the high the abuser gets from initiating abuse; therefore, the abuser would seek a path to continue the assault. They would seek to take everything from you: self-esteem, your mental health, funds, possessions or house, and automobiles if they can-and this trend will not stop there; It'll continue with your child or children.

Jealousy is another significant aspect to consider; Regarding Cluster B personality types, jealousy is a potent motivator. This could be jealousy of the other partner or wanting someone else with the sole intention of making, their partner jealous. This jealousy could be built up due to suspicion or even just the prospect of a break up. It could be fiction. For example, if the relationship is falling apart, sadness over it would lead to delusional thinking of unwanted events, which could be real or perceived. For instance, the borderline would be a typical example of unhealthy attachment styles towards their partner. They could become increasingly jealous of situations involving others over innocent interactions like post deliveries, shopping exchanges of money at a till, or anything social that involves their partner engaging with another. They can misconstrue any social interaction as a hint of future abandonment, displaying seemingly absurd reactions to regular interactions on the offset. They compile a view of suspicion and ruminate on possibilities, typically worst-case scenarios. This occurs and fosters jealousy regardless of whether the borderline is in a state of idealisation or devaluation. Children, too, can be a cause of jealousy between father and mother: who is the favourite? This goes through the minds of these personality types. The possibility of the child favouring the other is a crushing blow to an individual who feels emotion that intently.

Even if it's co-parenting and the child spends equal time with each parent, the parent with BPD' for example, well, their thoughts would linger about the child favouring the other parent with a mindset of pure delusion. Devaluation is another significant aspect; if the borderline is going through this phase, they will want to impulsively cut off, severing any ties with their partner. The only problem here is the child is hit by the crossfire, as this means steps are taken to pursue parental alienation. Devaluation is a decisive motivating factor for BPD and can be intense and disproportionate to the situation. It is mixed with the impulsive nature of the borderline; some absurdities can come out in courtrooms with the attempt to keep you from your children. These compulsive personality types cannot adapt and reason for the greater good or for what's best for the child or children. That's why mediation will be ignored and shut down immediately, even if the relationship didn't end in a nasty manner. The ability to negotiate is lacking within cluster B. Family court proceedings and child guardianship, for example, are negotiable processes. The Borderline, Narcissistic, Histrionic and Antisocial personality disorders reject any negotiation and ensure a toxic outcome. Fueled by toxicity, they will not tolerate any form of agreeable stances or positive relations. Their motivation is centred around gain; any perceived loss is detrimental to who they are. They will be unpredictable and vile and demonstrate that throughout court and life.

Parental alienation or the exclusion of a safe, loving, and fit parent is misunderstood and unheard of, in today's society. Most people don't consider the possibility of it ever happening, and awareness of the topic is quite scarce. The courts don't legally recognise it, but they are aware of the abusive tactic. There are no repercussions or penalties-exercised for lying under oath or creating these narrative-driven, false allegations. There are no systems or laws put into place that seek to eradicate parental alienation as an outcome for co-parenting families. The family court is a business that thrives on cases centred around broken families. Furthermore, the family court does not know what coercive control looks like. How could they if they fail to recognise parental alienation patterns in these court cases that span years? Coercive control and domestic abuse are what these court orders claim they are tackling. Yet it is clear that they are ignorant of what coercive control or domestic abuse, looks like. People lie, children are mere puppets to abusers, and courtrooms are a battleground. This alienation then, furthers coercive control within the abusive and domestic relationship. The court system as of writing is still ignorant of how these relationship dynamics work.

Chapter 9
Defamation

Demonization II

It is important to remember the women of Domestic Abuse. These women were abused, used and in domestic violence-relationships. Manipulated and aggressively pressured within this relationship dynamic with coercion used against them; maintaining control. These life experiences involved getting beat up routinely, abused, or screamed at. Threatened and harassed or even stalked. In clear danger of a lunatic boyfriend who would stop at nothing and destroy the family home while leaving the woman helpless, in fear and sorrow.

Objective number 1# is the safety of our women, mothers, daughters and wives. We need laws to protect our women, which is why we have implemented such laws to protect and keep them protected specifically.

The women living in fear of events of a domestic dispute need all of the support granted to them. This is a harrowing life journey, faced with fear, torment and erratic behaviour in the place you call home. These women have stories of incidents laced with aggressive partners in which they are always physically at a disadvantage to their male counterparts.

"People who have a higher tendency for interpersonal victimhood feel victimised more often, more intensely, and for longer duration in interpersonal relations than do those who have a lower such tendency" (Gabay, Lifschitz, Hameiri & Nadler, 2020)

This would be the one group of women who would respect and endorse this writing. That's solely because these women en masse are being; impersonated. Their life stories are becoming (just-stories) that can be mimicked for manipulation purposes. Most of these real cases are not heard because of the saturation regarding phoney stories of domestic abuse. These aren't just stories; they are real conflict situations and genuine fear. These women didn't need to make-a bruise with makeup.

Imposters

Court orders meant for safety and protection are now often used to harass and alienate parents. The scorned and spiteful imposter knows precisely the amount of harassment they are inflicting. The type of harassment where they can take a back seat and let the police harass you for them. Getting phoney court orders gives them the power to do or say anything, followed by a barrage of police situations. This could be a text message to see your child or a fake story they make up to make it look like you breached the false order. This breach could also be a simple look, possibly if you look at them with disdain.

Then there are the supervised alienation visits that usually take place in a supermarket for two hours now and then, and it's all over a false report. Alienated from your children, in yet another control pattern from the abuser. Naturally, you are not going to have a sparkle of love gleaming from your eyes towards the false accuser. These orders were created for the real victims; they were intended to keep the victims safe.

These victims did not seek to punish or get creative with how to enforce the orders; they just wanted protection. They didn't try to make it look breached or have ridiculous fears such as from a text, a few words said or a look.

Mental health screenings aren't conducted for these court orders, regardless of how absurd the behaviour is, in front of police or judges. There is a lot of legal jargon and misunderstandings about the orders. It feels like the rules are made up on the spot; they lack practicality. If the court order says you can see the child and text to arrange to do so, the person with the mental health disorder can call the police. They can complain about your text and have the police come to get you. A text message stating a date and time more than seven days in advance and nothing else. These irrational behaviours go unchecked. They are put into practice by an incompetent police force. The police don't bother to help advise or even make sense of such orders, they treat you like a career criminal. They prefer to harass a caring parent who's worried about their child instead of doing real police work.

Some of these court orders need mental health screenings to hear claims, allegations and stories that lack any real timeline or evidence. If there are no threats, physical danger or previous assaults, then it's not a real case. If it's just an opinion-based court order, it should be screened, mediated or even evaluated for mental health before becoming a court order. Parental alienation is a childish game that these people play, and court orders are initiating this activity.

It's the courts that are so full of cases that they aren't even bothered to audit these claims and weed out the highly suspicious cases. How are we going to lessen the cases if we allow these judges to merely glance at the paperwork and enforce the full effects of the law on innocent people? Go visit your local family courthouse; pick a day and a time. It's full to the brim of ongoing cases or people lined up making new cases. There is an infinite number of cases, and our courts can't think of a better system to process these claims. One really important act we should teach court administration is to read the claims made. They don't even read them. The claim turned case goes straight to the judge; they add it to the system and clean their hands of it.

The majority of the cases are children bitterly taken from loving parents to annihilate the parent-child bond.

Some of these so-called protection order cases are made over a bad feeling, a disappointment, or a delusion. A good majority of these cases are people with mental health issues and or domestic abuse imposters. These court orders were made for the safety and security of victims of abuse; the outcome would surely favour the victim, and the prioritised safety would ensue. Therefore, it puts a win-win in the minds of any would-be imposters.

These personality disorders are in their element, acting like somebody is infatuated with them. When in all actuality, the person is trying to escape. These court orders are a place of refuge for these PDs; as now the story for them continues and they can act out their fantasies of being wanted, desired or honoured. Retaliation for supposedly being wronged in some way. These people are after your items and possessions, and that includes your children. This order immediately results in parental alienation and a continuation of a control dynamic using the children to do so.

Once the court order comes into effect, there is nothing in the order that states fairness among possessions owned and returned. They don't want to listen or seek proof of ownership as the orders were not made to apply fairness in a relationship.

The court order was put into place to punish the other party for wrongdoing. There is an instant unspoken guilty verdict, regardless of the evidence or lack thereof. If the order instantly punishes once it comes into effect, then, of course, people will try to take advantage of it. People will always seek leverage or personal gain.

The real-life situations and real abused women need support and clear guidance with quicker response times. They say imitation is a form of flattery, but concerning real victims of domestic abuse, it is not. Impersonations of these victims are an insult to everything that they've been through. These types of impersonators can introduce an innocent victim to the criminal courts and be left with the probability of a stint behind bars. We need our courts to recognise abuse comes in more than one form. They operate on the premise that abuse is always physical, with a clear bias towards men. Men can be in abusive relationships, too. It's the behaviour of abuse we need to focus on, not the gender.

Every single employee of family law, courts or mediation needs further training on the actual term of 'Abuse. What is Abuse? What is considered an abuse of power or control? When does it go too far and turn into abuse? What actually is abuse, and what does it mean? The courts don't know. They haven't even given it much thought. The truth is abuse is used to propagate coercive control. This is why the term walking on eggshells means something to everybody.

Either you recognise the phrase or remember it from the title of a classic book. This phrase encapsulates that control. Suppose a person steps away from the abusive relationship for whatever reason. Friction boils over, and at the next minute, we have a restraining order, protection order, or safety order. What is the outcome of this order or any breaches of such order? How will the person on the receiving end of any one of these court orders feel? They will feel like they are walking on eggshells!

Remember, we are discussing the abusers who lie here. I think we can all agree that people lie. Not the courts; apparently, an abuser wouldn't dare make their way into a courthouse and get a court order summoned. Ideally, courts need to identify abusive patterns within these relationships.

Abuse comes in multiple forms; playing the victim or impersonating an actual victim is one of them. There is a particular thrill to it, and any gender can do it. It is turning into a first come, first serve with these court orders. This act of falsification of such court orders is a disgrace and a disrespect to real abuse survivors.

A toxic relationship turns abusive at a rapid speed. How far this abuse goes varies case by case. If we recognise and admit that we are in a controlling relationship, we can try to prevent future allegations and forebodings. Purchase a body-cam or record any instances of these impersonators in action, and watch out for traps that could be set, such as baiting you into something incriminating.

When your court case comes, emotions can run high; try not to overreact and focus on your evidence to refute the allegations. This may include collecting emails or screenshots of text messages. This digital evidence needs to be backed up onto a cloud with any other evidence gathered.

This is necessary just in case anything is purposely erased. If someone is going to go as far as to manufacture phoney evidence and pretend that they're being abused, they would likely destroy any abuse or coercion they've displayed that may be recorded.

Abusers take many forms, such as the role of playing the victim. Any child service callouts or other unfit parenting records displayed by the abuser will be valuable. Playing victim can cement the toxic behaviour needed to further the coercive control. Playing victim helps open the door to getting away with this abusive behaviour, and accusations can fly at ease as a result.

ULTIMATUMS

Remember that you can be with someone who is actively building a case against you, all the while staying in a relationship with you. It's unfathomable to think, but let it sink in. Your spouse or partner can be in the process of building a case against you while carrying on with this so-called abusive relationship for however long they want, and whichever way they will ultimately spin it.

This all boils down to ultimatums: if you don't stay with me, I can make your life a living hell. If you don't accept this coercion and ill-treatment, you will be years without seeing your child or children. All while waiting for a fake court case concocted as punishment for your decisions or failure to validate emotions. Borderlines, for example, perceive the end of a relationship as inevitable, especially when you're in the devalued stage. They would purposely ruin the relationship or quickly end it to eradicate their perceived vision of being on the receiving end of the relationship-dumping. These matters seem trivial, but make no mistake about it: these cases flood our court systems.

Ultimatums can be absurd; they don't have to be logical. These can be expectations that are impossible to live up to, even if you want to stay with the abuser and avoid future ramifications or legalities. Quite common, the ultimatum of parental alienation is your fate unless you acquiesce to the coercive abuse. It all doesn't make sense and doesn't have to, not in the eyes of the courts; the repercussions will still come to fruition, whether it's a conviction or even time spent alienated.

When amid a case, cooperate thoroughly and try to build your case. Get all the help you can to navigate through the emotional rollercoaster of false accusations, court pressure, police harassment and or parental alienation.

According to Wakefield and Underwager, False accusers are likely to misperceive the behaviour of others and to react to stressful situations in maladaptive ways. Depending upon the specific personality disorder, they are characterised by instability of mood, impulsivity, inappropriate emotional overreactions, a need for approval and attention, and difficulties handling anger and conflict. (H Wakefield R Underwager 1990)

Any one of these symptoms is the sweet spot for a severe punishment. This punishment would be justified by their idea of approval within the relationship. It will probably shake things up and get you to fall in line.

There is no concern about how their target will be perceived following accusations or having issues with the law. On the contrary, this is the disturbance that they believe will help with regard to controlling their target.

This road is an uphill battle; it doesn't get any easier. Get back to living life and focus on yourself. Communicate this injustice, and be open and transparent if you have trustworthy companions around you. Be cautious and remain guarded to avoid leaking any information to flying monkeys. Feeding information to mutual friends or family could be just feeding info to the abuser. Try to make a routine or activities in your day-to-day actions, such as exercise, meditation, walking or whatever it is that gets you through the tsunami of negative emotion.

A list of false accusations or a barrage of police harassment brings forth a lack of belief within the system. Read books on various mental health conditions; familiarise yourself with symptoms and become aware of these facts. Some people don't have apparent mental health conditions at face value, but that doesn't mean they haven't adopted the dangerous traits of these conditions. It is essential to be aware of what these destructive disorders are capable of.

They can play a part in some serious legal ramifications. Weaponizing the legal system against their victim with the falsification of allegations. The use of intimidation against the victim by means of, possible prison time, depending on the accusations. The stripping away of your home, possessions and funds is standard. The detaching of the family dynamics, removing your children, and no longer being a parent. The slow burn of the court case with nobody caring to listen to an alternative viewpoint can all be demoralising.

There are plenty of court cases that are legitimate and need to be heard. There is a fundamental need for court, law, and order. Although this will not be the topic of debate here, we will discuss a loophole that continues to take place. There are very dishonest people in this world who commit crimes, lie under oath, or commit libel and slander. These liars need to be held accountable. They are not all cluster B-type personalities, but a vast portion of them are. All cluster B personality type behaviours should be known and recognised within courtrooms.

Even if a person does not have a disorder, the high conflict nature or behaviour they portray should be evident. Some good people have disorders that can integrate within society and give all power to them. Even people with Cluster B have issues with other people or their partners who also have Cluster B.

Why should we pretend that the cluster is not conflict-driven? Credit is given to every person who sought out treatment under the umbrella of Cluster B. For example, there are a few insightful, self-aware borderline or narcissistic people out there, and let's hope that number rises.

However, ignoring the statistics, facts, and overwhelming similarities between Cluster B Personality Disorders and criminal activity would be naive. Jordan Et Al. Found comparable patterns among female felons entering the prison system with higher rates of mood disorders, alcohol and drug dependence and borderline and antisocial personality disorders than among the community sample.(Robins, LN, Regier, DA, 1991)

Yes, we need to care for and support people with cluster B. Alternatively, we know that people would be at a disadvantage in court if they admitted they were even thinking of getting a diagnosis or shared the qualities of a disorder. But we also need a healthy awareness for the innocent, good people out there—an understanding of the likelihood of false allegations, abuse or coercive control and parental alienation.

The courts are easily manipulated and will remain so, with zero vetting for allegations against a person. This cluster takes chances, seeks power and control and can use these halls of justice as viable alternatives to continue their abuse.

The prevalence of severe personality disorders (PDs) among prison inmates in general has been assumed and measured to some extent in male prisons and forensic samples. (Blackburn, R.,1998) A longitudinal study of 717 youths found that adolescents with symptoms of DSM-IV Cluster A and Cluster B personality disorders were far more likely than any other adolescents in the community to commit violent acts during adolescence. Criminal behaviour such as arson, assault, breaking and entering, initiating physical fights, robbery and threatening to injure other people (Johnson, JG, Cohen, P, Smailes, E, et al.,2000)

"A weakness in the control of anger and impulse can lead to stiffness, rape, or physical attack, which is seen in Cluster B of personality disorders, leading to severe social and interpersonal problems" (Esbec, E, Echeburúa, E, 2010)

The person with a personality disorder struggles when confronted with obstacles in life, perceived or actual. For the borderline, it's the intense emotions, unstable relationships and impulsive behaviours. Suspicion, mood shifts and manipulation are Cluster B attributes. When there is an inability to regulate emotions, self-destructive behaviour follows. Self-sabotage is an unfortunate action/re-action dynamic in anyone's life.

You don't need a personality disorder to experience this downfall. With personality disorders like Borderline, it's not only self-sabotage that is concerning but also the acting out in regards to sabotaging their significant other. This is where the legal battles, usually one-sided, commence.

The seeking of deliberate destruction for a partner to teach them a lesson. How dare they think, do or say such and such. Revenge is served cold within a blind courtroom, unable to see the real victims. The risks of violent behaviours seem to be identifiable via the significant role of a personality profile, including PDs and clinically significant traits of personality. (Esbec, E, Echeburúa, E, 2010) (Candini, V, Ghisi, M, Bottesi, G, et al.,2018)

The symptoms involved within the Cluster B umbrella make it challenging to maintain healthy relationships or make sound long-term decisions.

Impulsive decision-making can ruin a life; the desire for a borderline individual's ex-partner to die, for example, could be a justifying fantasy. If that person has not validated enough or there is a suspicion the relationship could come to a screeching halt, then the delusion goes to the extremes within the borderline.

If an upset or jealous personality type starts to conjure up ideas of revenge, ways to ruin their ex's life or social standing, they do not hesitate. False allegations have serious consequences for the victim, legally and personally, and the perpetrator could care less.

As we know, false accusations can significantly damage reputations and lead to lengthy legal battles. People need to become aware of the potential of people with these personality disorders. Again, not all people are equal, and this is not to focus solely on the inadequacies of Cluster B while ignoring the treatment options. This highlights their potential nature regarding high-conflict breakups or sour relationship situations.

Any disorder with a track record of making false allegations is highly dangerous.

These allegations commonly occur when a divorce or a breakup is inevitable. If perceived rejection continually occurs, they could give you hints of the allegations, "What if I say this?" "What if everybody believes that?" and so on. They get ego inflation as they sense fear from others as to what might come of their actions. It only seems right to gloat about the steps they're willing to take and watch people crumble as they're told their careers, livelihoods or even children are compromised. Advertising the possible repercussions if you don't do things their way.

Unfortunately, this taunting style happens out of the blue and surprises the unwitting victim. Now would be the perfect time to press record and catch some type of recording of what is being threatened.

As this cluster B personality type is close to the edge and ready to play damsel, they are very cunning; if they have threatened the use of making faking allegations, more than likely, they will not verbalise the threat again, too many times. They cover tracks and delete any abuse or wrongdoing on their part. They would likely show up to court with one mis-spoken, angry text message from their ex-partner. Deleting the hundreds of abusive texts before it from themselves., People have to be replying to something, How this is not seen as suspicious is baffling. They can fabricate evidence, splice audio, or get creative. Triangulation will aid in helping them bring their opposition down. They possibly already gathered evidence months or years in advance.

These people plan court cases. They lie under oath and try to manipulate the system just to justify a mere feeling that wasn't validated some time ago. This is not what real victims do; they don't plan cases, try to trick the legal system, or threaten hearsay. They require safety guidance and support; the Cluster B personalities just require attention.

Picture the real cases of domestic abuse involving safety or protection orders. These life situations are intimidating for the victim who has to implement these orders. The victims are in a state of panic and fear; they need the law to back them up. They are the real victims of physical abuse, coercion or more. They are usually the woman who has an over-aggressive boyfriend who demonstrates chaotic behaviour. They have horrible, unpredictable partners who present a clear danger. These real cases have been exploited and impersonated. Impersonation is an insult to everything these women have been put through. This book will tackle these impersonators; we are going to speak about the unspoken.

In the court of public opinion, there is an abundance of issues that are debated regularly. We already know and frown upon a plethora of topics; wife beating, stalking, child abuse or taking advantage of a woman are all frowned upon, for example.

The people who make false allegations or protection orders are Not in fear; the victims receiving the phoney orders are the ones put in fear.

These false accusers are grinning and snarling without a care in the world. They know the odds of destroying through deceit and lies is a winning gamble. These people should be frowned upon, mental disorder or not; what's right is right, and what's wrong is wrong.

They put themselves out there and play a part, a role, deliberately delegitimising the real cases. These people are impersonators, professional victims and outstanding actors. There is dignity and depravity, and we will single out the latter to be discussed here.

No Comment!

17-year-old Jay was hoping to study history at University; outgoing and friendly. Everybody likes him and has good things to say about him. He loved selfies and would take random selfies with friends, cheering them up if they felt down in the dumps.

Everyone has good relations with Jay. They usually like watching films or playing PlayStation together. Jay is a popular kid with no care in the world until the spring evening in 2015 when Jay arrived home distraught after an incident with a girl he'd been seeing. He said to his family that they were involved in foreplay; he was lying next to her, and he'd got on top of her, and she just froze. He sat back, assuming something was wrong, and he kept asking her what the matter was. She said that she wanted him to go home. So he did, but he knew something was wrong and left spooked. He was visibly shaken.

Texting and phone calls between parents ensued, and one phone call was made using a loudspeaker. The girl's mother then, out of nowhere, grabbed the phone off of her and said they'd put in a rape allegation to the police.

I'm going to effing get him done, speaking about Jay. Following this, Jay called the police to figure out what was happening, yielding to the law. He was told to come by the station and that a complaint had already been made against him.

The questioning was about to begin; Jay and his older sister met with his solicitor before it did. The solicitor emphasised that there are so many inconsistencies with the story! He simply advised Jay to just say No-Comment.

There wasn't much of a story to begin with, so the police doing the questioning needed evidence or a confession. No comment was the wise action to take, but it can be difficult when confronted with false allegations or situational-attacks. They went into the interview room. Jay's sister recalls, "When the police officer came in, she was all guns blazing. She didn't hold back. Did you rape her? Did you force her? Did you penetrate her?" The way she worded these matters was an awful tactic to use against a teenager.

It was used to break him, make him feel something emotionally, or get a reaction out of him that was detrimental to his case. Jay's sister went on, "It made Jay want to answer, and the more times he said no comment when he wanted to answer these questions, the more the tears were streaming; I could feel him shaking under my hand. It was probably one of the worst experiences I've ever been through in my life. He was treated like a criminal. I thought, look at him. He's a boy" Following his interview, Jay was released under investigation; those close to him could tell he was going through it.

Jay's sister mentions that he was just a shell of a person from that moment. I've never really seen a boy Bellow cry and just be as distraught as he was; it was like he'd had his soul ripped away," Weeks followed with no update from the police. They eventually had to call the police to see if any of these inquiries had an update. The police then told them that the girl had dropped the allegation and that there would be no further action. Regardless of the result of the investigation, Jay wasn't the same. The despair remained, although the charges went away.

To be branded with something like that changes a person. Jay's sister appears in the documentary and news reports on this case; I Am Not A Rapist Devastating consequences of False Allegations-true crime central.

She mentions what was done to her brother and, regarding false allegations, "If you haven't done it, it's a big thing, so we were all very, very distraught."

After two weeks, the girl dropped the charges, but Jay, described as a 'gentleman' and 'intelligent', had already 'spiralled completely'. The police said Jay had gone to the store and bought his favourite energy drink, his favourite bag of crisps, and a rope. Later found by a dog walker.

Jay was found hanging from the tree they played at as children. He took his own life near the family home in 2015, a few weeks after the false allegation, even with the allegation being dropped by the accuser.

He wrote a suicide letter to all the people he left behind in life who loved him dearly. Part of the letter reads: 'Mum, you have been the greatest Mum'. Five days later, Jay's mother had a mental breakdown. One year later, at the time of the anniversary of Jay's death, Jay's mother hanged herself. (S Linning, Dailymail 2020) (True Crime Central, 2024)

True Crime Centrals; I am not a rapist also features the story of Liam Allen. He received false allegations of rape, tieing up the victim, holden down the victim, taking the alleged victim to a tree and raping her. This case lasted 2 years until the defence team got hold of the phone to get a log of all the messages, including those she had erased. This batch contained 40,000 texts and WhatsApp messages. These messages revealed that the alleged victim pestered him for casual sex. She said she liked sex with him, and she was painting herself out to be an innocent victim of rape by this horrible man.

However, the text messages revealed she had sex with him numerous times, and she mentioned that she had rape fantasies; she likes sex in the open air. She pestered this guy for sex, the jury heard after months and months of looking at him like he was a monster. This was a 12-count indictment; this man could have been convicted and got 12 years, had his life trashed, and on a sexual offence register forever.

In the majority of cases, false allegations are only officially recorded if the complainant admits their allegation was untrue. The cases in the documentary, like many others, such as the last two cases, aren't recorded as false allegations. (True Crime Central, 2024)

"To a large degree, a particular collision of genes and temperament with a suboptimal or hostile environment may explain the development of borderline personality disorder" (Mosquera, D, Steele, K,2017) If you research Borderline personality disorder's symptoms for a diagnosis and your partner exhibits five or more of the signs, they more than likely have the disorder. But you should never speak this directly to them or point it out, as this can offend the person greatly.

The same goes for narcissistic personality disorder or a person displaying narcissistic traits. It would just chink the armour of their delusions of grandeur. Self-diagnosis is imperative despite what anybody says. It is helpful if you can interpret the signs of BPD or even other disorders like it. Expect serious issues like allegations, and at least you will be better prepared for chaos when it comes. One way which shapes a borderline, for example, to make false allegations is through the individual's unstable sense of self and intense fear of abandonment—struggling with feelings of emptiness and inadequacy, which can lead them to seek validation and attention through making these false accusations.

The attention is almost high, and it's exhilarating. There is an inhumane factor that can arise within this disorder and many others like it. This cluster has some of the variables, for example, histrionic personality disorder or narcissistic personality disorder, that share similar qualities. Or the infantile histrionic is considered the borderline histrionic.

A loving relationship can abruptly get out of hand; what if the end is near? Who cheated on who? Or who flirted with who? Feelings of emptiness arise, and then they stop at nothing to get their partner locked up in prison for no valid reason. This transition from love to hate in an instant is commonly termed as splitting, the all-good or all-bad distorted perception. It is like a scale of perception but in terms of extremes.

The stalking and harassment caused by behavioural disorders need to be addressed and looked at not only by everyday citizens but also by law officials or police. Regardless of the disorder, there should be a certain stigma or shame if a person tends to use unjustified tactics to punish or cause harm to their ex.

There is no knowledge about abusers using such tactics. At least, it's not in the minds of everyday people. The victims of these abusive relationships stay quiet and just accept it.

Narcissistic abuse is a theme lately and is gaining traction. Still, in most cases, with personality disorders, people take the abuse and never speak of it as if it never happened, trying desperately not to relive it. High-conflict personality disorders need discussion as they cover a large percentage of these false allegation and parental alienation cases.

Additionally, the inability to regulate emotions, their impulsive nature, and a whole host of manipulative attributes motivate them to act out on intense feelings of anger and betrayal. This connection is prevalent between needy personality disorders and the likelihood of making false allegations.

We must navigate these toxic dilemmas better if we are currently embroiled in this situation. The next chapter will move on to the legal system concerning the family courts and their knack for parental alienation. To discuss the inaccuracies of how they operate, we will need to look at a few relatively straightforward red flags that they deal with and can implement some assistance to.

The following case study is quite controversial and heartbreaking at the same time.

The person who submitted it seems articulate and is trying as best they can. A woman sent in this case study, and some of the names were changed to protect her identity, as these case studies are a lesson or a learnable window into the lives of others.

They are also highly upsetting and can remind us of when things went wrong in our own lives. These case studies become a way to gain insight into how courts and child services operate and how they lack ability and merit. In the following case study, there are quite a few instances where they did have to intervene as drugs unfortunately ruined the family.

There is no issue with social services in this case study. They did what they could with the situation at hand. The problem this book is conveying is the easily exploitable family courts and or child services—the unjust act of punishing another with the usage of manipulation and abuse.

Parental alienation, narcissistic abuse, and methods of how they manipulate and operate in relationships are trending lately. The next chapter highlights the family court's inadequacies and the areas overdue for improvement.

To look at what cases they overlook and the incompetence they display, we will look at a highly volatile case in which they did have grounds to execute methods of child protection. This case study is added to highlight some of the hard evidence that would help build their case and confirm how they operated.

This is learnable from the standpoint that not every case is this bad, and we still have parental alienation booming. We have cases in court, that are unsettled and going on for years without resolution.

The following case study highlights some of the things the caseworkers and the child services or courts have to become accustomed to. But what about the cases that aren't remotely this bad?

What about the cases that lack any evidence? Or the cases with no realistic outcome? The cases that just remain cases for years and years; It is as if the court itself is the punishment, and that's precisely what it is.

Case study Anonymous

On March 29, 2022, around 11 am, my water broke, and I called Wayne back from work so we could go to the hospital. Jayden wasn't supposed to be here until April 26 as a scheduled c-section. So, Wayne called his parents to meet us at the hospital so they could take Liam. We all met up, and Wayne and I went into the ER, where I was promptly admitted and rushed off to the operating room as Jayden was in the breech position or upside down, which is typical for the early stages of pregnancy.

This resulted in the doctors bringing me in for a C-section immediately. They put me under as he was coming out too fast, and they had to cut me open. So, at 1:01 pm, Jayden joined the world. He was whisked off and put with his dad while I was stitched up and sent to a recovery room. I was really out of it for the next 2 days. I was in and out of sleep, and a lot was going on. The Office of Children, Youth, and Families (OCYF) was already involved as I am on methadone, and so they were already there. They tested my urine and found opiates, fentanyl, methadone, and THC in my system. I had a lapse 2 days before Jayden was born, using dope.

I do have my medical marijuana card, and it has helped with all three pregnancies. They also tested Jayden for drugs, and there was none found in his system.

He was taken to the NICU (neonatal intensive care unit). Later on that day, I had him as they were treating him for being early- Not for withdrawals, and there was no (Neonatal Abstinence Syndrome) NAS scoring on a regular basis as, again, he was not showing signs of withdrawal.

So, on the 2nd night in the hospital, a few of the nurses finally realised that I was more out of it than I should have been. I was unable to wake up and stay awake for any amount of time. So around 11 pm (I believe), they took me for a few tests and whatnot. It was then found that I needed a blood transfusion. I think I got two bags of blood...

Once I had that done the following day, I felt so much better. I was discharged later on the 3rd day. In the 3 days after Jayden was born, all kinds of people came to my room, attempting to talk to me and having me sign stuff, even though I was clearly out of it and unable to totally understand what was going on. What I do know is that after Jayden was in the NICU for 6 days, they allowed us to bring him home. He had been treated for being premature and jaundiced.

They (OCY) say they allowed us to take him home only because Wayne was with me; I was not the only caretaker. I guess they thought that I was getting high around my kids and whatnot.

The thing is, I had only gotten high that one time in the 8 months I was pregnant- and even before that. Jayden came home on April 4th or 5th, and we started settling into our life as parents to a special needs child and now a newborn. I couldn't wait for those moments. Jayden did have what was called a 'sacral dimple' right above his butt crack, so we had to see a specialist just a few days after he got home.

We had in-home nurses coming in twice a week, and Wayne's mother, Tammy, came and stayed a few days with us. Everything was so lovely and perfect.

In the early morning of April 22, I was awakened by Jayden for a diaper change and bottle. So, I did just that; taking him back into my room, I sat down on my bed with my feet on the ground. I proceeded to feed him while I listened to The Simpsons on my TV. Once the episode was over, I removed his bottle from his mouth and stood up to place him in his bassinet... and that's when I noticed how cold and limp he was...

I turned on my light and saw how grey he was... I sat him on the bed, waking up Wayne, and I called 911. On the phone, they told me to make sure his airways were clear and start tiny, delicate compressions. Paramedics came and took him right out, Wayne following behind them into the ambulance.

I had to call my friend Elisha to sit at the house with Liam so I could be with Jayden. It took about 30 minutes or so while I was waiting, worrying and scared, I smoked a joint. It Is my medication that I do have my card for. So, once she got here, I took off as fast as I could to Hamot ER. I got in there and found where he was. Wayne was waiting outside the door, watching a team of nurses and doctors work on my tiny baby.

I was then approached by a detective and an Erie police officer. Wayne REFUSED to talk to him, but I was scared that if I didn't talk that, I would get into trouble. I told the detective that I was uncomfortable speaking with him without a lawyer present, to which he claimed that he did not know of any lawyers that would want to get up and come down to the hospital at 2:30 am in the morning.., so I reluctantly went with him.

I told him everything at the end; I felt like he intimidated me into talking with him and that I was not at all comfortable speaking with him. With that, the interview ended. I went back to the room where Jayden was still being worked on and was again approached by a woman who said she was the on-call OCY Caseworker and wanted to know what had happened. This time, I told her that I was not going anywhere and that if she wanted to talk, it would have to be right there. So, I repeated the story to this caseworker.

Once Jayden was stable, and we were able to go in and speak with the doctors, we were informed that he was being kept alive by machines; although his heart was beating on its own, everything else was being run by machines. We were told that a team was on their way up from Children's Hospital in Pittsburgh to get him down there attached to everything keeping him alive. And so, Liam was again taken to his grandparents while we tended to what we needed to down in Pittsburg. For the next 11 days, we talked to doctors, nurses, bereavement support, caseworkers, a priest, and more doctors and nurses... we had been waiting for the phenobarbital to clear his system, and it took the full 11 days to get down to levels where he should be having reflexes and signs of life, and there just wasn't.

We had gotten him Baptised. Liam came down with his grandparents so they could all say goodbye. On the afternoon of May 3, we were informed that there was nothing left to do and that he was a vegetable with no value of life. So, we had to make the very difficult decision to take him off of life support and hold him close while he passed on- his little body was finally able to stop... Once he was gone, we hurried over to the Ronald McDonald house that is attached to the hospital for families to stay while their sick children fight for their lives.

We went and packed up everything we had in the little apartment space we were given and left Pittsburgh behind us, leaving Jayden behind us. That night, I went and got high as soon as I got home. I knew Liam still needed me, but I just did not care that night, and I tried to do enough dope to make sure I wouldn't wake back up... but I did. And so, on May 4, 2022, we were attempting to settle back into the life of a family of 3. But there was so much pain in those first 2 days. Liam came home and ran right into the nursery, looking for Jayden... That about killed me.

The caseworker then was Ms Keller, and she was not licensed or fully trained as she was demoted, taken from working "in the field," and made to go back to training. (That is what a different case worker told me and Wayne the first time she had come to our home after taking my case.) * On May 5, 2022, OCY caseworker Ms Keller and another case worker knocked on my door. I allowed them to come into my home, and they then asked to make sure we had everything Liam needed.

I checked for food and got it. I checked for safety and got it. I checked. He had his own room and was age-appropriate; I got it. So once they were done with that, we were then told that we had to submit to a drug test and go to a urine screen the next day. Wayne, knowing his rights, refused to submit to the testing, stating they had no reason to be asking for any of this.

Then they told me that I would also have to submit to a urine drug screen, and when I asked her if I asserted my rights and said no, what would happen? That is when she told me that if I did not do what they wanted me to do, Liam would be removed right then and there that night. I was so scared of having my child removed from his home that I told her that I would go and submit urine at Esper Treatment Center the next day when I went to dose, even though I knew it was going to be dirty since I had used, just 2 days earlier when Jayden passed.

I dropped a UA on May 6, 2022, and it was indeed dirty for fentanyl, opiates, methadone, and THC. On May 16, Ms Keller and 2 Erie police officers showed up at my door with a court order to remove Liam from his home. I was NOT ready for that to happen. They had done NOTHING to try and keep him here with his family. They just TOOK HIM. She did allow me to walk him down to her FILTHY car to buckle him into her backseat... where there was NO car seat or even a booster seat. Liam was four and a half years old at the time; he has special needs and HAD to be in a car seat... I offered her mine, which she declined. Liam was stuck with this woman from that early afternoon until he showed up to his grandparents around 7:30 that night, having had NOTHING to eat and was in a VERY soiled diaper.

May 16, 2022- The morning of this day was when the court ordered emergency protective custody. They have two things in common: one is that 'removal of the child is necessary for the welfare and best interest of the child,' and the other one states that 'reasonable efforts to prevent removal or provide reunification were made.' (Which they never did) On May 21, Liam was moved from his grandparents' house and placed in a foster home with a woman named Sandra.

He was there for 2 days before he was moved once again, this time to Edmond L. Thomas Residential Shelter. It's a place meant for kids 10+, NOT a 4.5-year-old. We were able to visit Liam every night for 1 hour. And we were there EVERY SINGLE NIGHT. We did eventually find out how he was being made to go to his room, where they would lock him inside; he was forced into a place that isn't meant for kids his age.

At ELT, we visited every night. Once a week, my Project First Step Caseworker would come to our visits to observe, and Sandra would visit almost every day as well. Then, he was able to go to Sandras on weekends so he could get used to her. She also allowed us to meet up with her and Liam on Sundays before she took him back to ELT. We met, and after about 5 weeks or so (?), Liam went with her full-time.

After that, she would no longer do our Sunday outings because she did not want to have to report back to OCY about how the visits went. She stated that she was there to keep Liam safe and healthy, not babysit our visits and do reports. So, he's been with her since, I believe, the beginning of August 2022. We were able to visit him weekly with supervision. The stipulation with that was if I looked like I was high or smelled like Pot (I do have my MMJ card), then the visit would be terminated.

That never happened. So the first hearing we had was shortly after OCY picked him up, and that is when I found out about the whole "lack of care and control" and that I had a lapse – but I never mentioned WHEN that happened. Since the first hearing, I was never able to get my public defender to actually talk to me for any length of time. We would have just a few minutes before we walked into court. May 20, 2022, is when I got the dependency petition saying that Liam 'is without proper care or control.' With this, I allowed the man named Mr Ryan to come to my home to make this family plan. While he was here, he began to get almost verbally abusive towards me, and I told him to get out of my house.

The argument was over me telling him that he could sit there and tell me that what we were doing was mandatory. That ANYTHING OCY tells you that you must do something, you HAVE to do it. He was trying to tell me that it was NOT mandatory- and that's when he began to argue with me; I asked him to leave, and now, all over my paperwork, they are claiming that I REFUSED to do the Family Plan. They decided that if I didn't want to work with that man, I would have to refuse, even though they were more than able to send someone else in his place. June 2, 2022, is when I received the Order of Adjudication and Disposition, which started off with all the misinformation amended. However, NONE of these amended 'facts' were never changed in any other paperwork.

I have been on methadone since Jan 2016. I found out I was pregnant in December 2016 and had Liam in August 2017. I was clean from the hard stuff. I did smoke pot, and I now have my card to be able to do so legally. I was clean and on methadone, doing great. I do have a prior history with the agency due to mostly false reports. 09/01/2017- GPS- The Agency received a referral that I delivered an infant to term gestation and was transitioned to the NICU secondary to hypoglycemia. It mentions both mother and child were positive for marijuana and methadone.

In April 2022, The Agency received a referral in regard to the victim child arriving at the hospital critically ill in cardiac arrest and was transferred straight to Pittsburgh Children's Hospital. The victim child was removed from life support and passed away on May 3, 2022. This incident is still under investigation while The Agency awaits the coroner's report.

In that report was the FINAL PATHOLOGICAL DIAGNOSIS I. Sudden unexplained infant death of a one-month-old male infant II. Reported history of co-sleeping with parent III. History of premature birth by caesarean section at 35 weeks gestation (medical record) IV. History of neonatal abstinence syndrome (medical record) V. Reported history of household smoking (tobacco and marijuana) and opioid use

VI. Consultant neuropathological examination shows global hypoxic/ischemic injury to the brain. VII. No evidence of skeletal fracture at the time of autopsy. VIII. Negative viral cultures, non-contributory bacterial cultures, and negative metabolic screening. IX. Non-contributory electrolytes X. Postmortem toxicology is positive for phenobarbital in blood and urine (consistent with hospital-administered medication).

OPINION: Jayden, a 1-month-old white male, died as a result of Sudden Unexplained Infant Death. MANNER OF DEATH: Undetermined. Deputy Medical Examiner Pathologists FINAL DIAGNOSIS: Subacute Global Hypoxic/Ischemic Injury, Severe.

As of September 2022, the Agency recommended refraining from the use of illegal/illicit drugs and alcohol and participating in random colour code urinalysis screenings through the Esper Treatment Center. Which was occurring, but I just missed some due to unforeseen circumstances.

Despite doing my best to get and stay clean, I have been unable to at this point in time (October 2022). Liam is currently seeing a doctor for medication pertaining to his Autism and ADHD. He has regular medication management appointments. In addition to medication management, Liam has a support coordinator, a behavioural health technician, and a blended case manager.

At some point, the foster mom, Sandra, stated to the caseworker that Liam had had an increase in sexualised behaviours recently. He will climb on top of women and try to push them down and will move his hips in a thrusting motion. He has also been reported to grab women's breasts and ask them to take their shirts off. This is something that was never an issue when he was home. This has only been reported one time in the Jan 18th court summary.

However, this was not brought up in the court hearing. Liam is supposed to have a behavioural health technician, but due to severe understaffing, this has not happened for very long. He did have one who lasted less than 2 months. Liam is STILL on a waiting list for a BHT. I have refrained from illicit drugs as of January 2023. They asked me to participate in and follow through with all recommendations made in drug and alcohol treatment until successful completion and demonstrate the ability to obtain and remain in recovery. (As of November 2022, this has occurred; OCY is lying about me not completing this) Also, I want to continue participating in and completing Project 1st Step, Family Engagement through Erie Homes for Children and Adults and Family Behavioral Therapy through Family Services.

I have completed a psychological assessment and attended all medical appointments and provider meetings for the child. OCY reported to the Judge that there has been NO progress with me, and that is just not the truth. I have been busting my ass to do everything they wanted me to do while trying to deal with the loss of Jayden and the taking of Liam. It has not been easy. On May 9, they are going to try and terminate my rights involuntarily. This is NOT right. They also changed the goal from reunification concurrent with adoption to just adoption. It's not right. OCY keeps a case open for 22 months, and they don't usually change the goal at the 8-month mark, which is what they did to me.

They also used the removal of my child as a first choice instead of working with us and keeping him in the home. Then came the hearing to Involuntarily Terminate my Parental Rights.

I started that hearing on May 9, 2023, with the Senior Judge; she is the one who went through with the CPS goal change to adoption, stating in court that my addiction would be the thing that takes me out. On January 18, 2023, before the hearing, the Judge requested that I have a drug screen done.

Knowing it was still going to be dirty, I submitted it, and EVERYTHING on this test popped up: drugs I have never even touched before. I admitted to the THC, Fentanyl, Opiates, and Methadone, but I would not admit to the use of cocaine, PCP, amphetamines, benzodiazepines, or barbiturates, as I have NEVER done those before.

The Judge was having a hard time understanding how I was standing there that day, convinced that I had done all of those drugs before coming into court. She really doesn't seem to understand how drugs actually work, and neither do any of the lawyers who were involved in my case. The case worker referred to my son as "feral" and "spastic" during 2 of our hearings. She met him TWICE in the 14 months she "represented his best interests" – once while he was forced to stay at Edmund L. Thomas, and then the second time was literally just 3 days before the second part of the IVT hearing. She has no idea who my son is, and she has never seen how our family was together. My son was NEVER neglected or abused, and OCY did NOT prove anything in court.

I am not sure why a Senior Judge is allowing a state agency that is supposed to keep families together; how he is okay with them ripping my family apart, causing my son to be traumatised, as well as the rest of his family, they broke laws and violated rights. As of January 27, I have been given clean urines.

I have also continued with Family Based Therapy, Drug and Alcohol, Mental health therapy, and medication compliance; I am also completing IOP and Back to Basics. Since the goal change, OCY has refused to communicate with me. They pulled me out of Project First Step, even though I was doing great in that program. OCY had zero intentions of helping my family from the moment my son Jayden was born.

They have lied several times, violated my sons' rights as well as my own, and they have broken laws. No one will help me, and so I am attempting to be as transparent as possible because I know that my son was wrongfully removed, and my rights should NOT have been terminated. My appeal will be going in as soon as my public defender gets it in, right around the 30-day mark, as she likes to wait till the last minute to get anything in that should be put in quickly. I am at a loss. I have given my son everything, and when Jayden was born, we could not have been happier. They ripped my family apart; they took Liam from his home just 13 days after his brother passed.

"We're talking about something that could affect half of America!

Hundreds of thousands of children are winding up in the hands of abusers,

and family courts are missing this"

(Phillip C McGraw, 2024, AKA Dr Phil)

Chapter 10
The Easily-Exploitable, Family Court!

We need to audit and change the structure of court procedures. One day in our lifetime, it could happen. If pushed to a degree, we could see reform within the legal system. Bringing not only the standards of the family courts up to par but also the criminal courts. Ideally, we should move into an effective, knowledgeable, and more compassionate family court system that prioritises the best interests of the children involved in custody disputes.

According to Judge Judy Sheindlin, when speaking of this family court debacle. Society must demand that people grow up and accept responsibility.

The folks who insist that we continue to tolerate abuse by self-described victims should get the message- not anymore. (J,Sheindlin,J,Getlin,1997)

She went on to say that "so many people are refusing to take charge of their lives, the social service programs designed to be a safety net can no longer handle the load. They are overwhelmed by numbers. These days, everybody is a victim."(J,Sheindlin,J,Getlin,1997)

This means putting aside personal biases or grudges and creating a safe and nurturing environment in which children can thrive. Forced mediation in cases that aren't adding up to avoid the parental alienation strategy. Also, the focus should be shifting to the needs of the children, ensuring that their well-being is the number one priority within a messy breakup.

"We acknowledge that domestic violence is real, and something needs to exist for it. But putting in place laws that can be applied without evidence destroys families and children. That is not how to do it."(Parlato,F et.al,2023)

Another critical aspect of improving the family court system is to provide more resources and support regarding custody disputes. A court date should not be set up immediately; there should be more of a process or vetting of each case or claim.

Jumping into a court case straight away without any assessment of the case incites an abuser to get the first word in. They know the wait times and the adjournments help nourish parental alienation. They know a false protection order is basically bulletproof. They have free rein to alienate a child and to keep their opposition guessing.

Case study

Anonymous

The court system is really messed up, and attorneys who don't care about your life are only interested in enriching their pockets. Around July last year, I was in a child custody battle with my ex-wife. I hired an attorney, but for six months, I wasn't getting anywhere, so I hired another attorney in April. Unfortunately, the odds were still not in my favour. These attorneys were just out to extort and get rich from heartbroken parents. Considering how much I had spent, and with my kids obviously being neglected by their mother, I had to think outside the box.

I got in touch with a digital forensics company named Neechi. At that point, I had spent close to $9000 on attorney fees and had become disillusioned with everything going on around me. Amidst the hesitation, I gave them a try, and in a couple of days, they got me evidence of child neglect and more. I found out she was using drugs and leaving the kids anywhere she wanted, even with people she hardly knew, including questionable characters, just so she could go get high. One of the people she left my kids with any time she needed to get high was a convicted sex offender.

My daughter had a broken hand one time, and my ex claimed it was an accident. I found out my daughter was actually beaten by my ex's boyfriend at the time. With the evidence I had gathered, I got a lawyer and just pointed him in the right direction. I got full custody of my daughter and the rest of my kids. The system is broken and rigged to favour women. You have to think outside the box to stand a chance. My mental state is still recovering, but I know I'll pull through.

THE RED FLAG SYSTEM

In Ireland, the current process for making a protection, safety or restraining order is as follows: the person waits in queue, fills out a form, sees a judge, then briefly nods and claims it's true. The judge doesn't even bother reading it; he or she skims through it, and then voila! The court order is officially granted and would immediately come into effect. This order is exercised by the police, and they would be responsible for following the court order without question, regardless of the content of the court order. The police don't read it either and couldn't care less about false reporting. Talking to police about court issues can only be done hypothetically, as they are not even informed on cases or particulars.

An ideal alternative route to this pretty serious process would be as follows: The person waits in the queue, he or she proceeds to fill out the form, sees an appointed highly trained mediator or overseer, reads the court order and goes through it thoroughly. An assessment between parties would take place before any court proceeding.

There would be two pathways here. The first would be the scenario of circumstantial, petty, revenge-style court orders with no evidence of abuse. The accused does not have a criminal background, which is not currently taken into account or even searched during the inception of all of these orders.

The story as a whole seems either implausible or unreasonable. Well, then this case would be sent for further investigation before any court order or court date is issued between the parties involved. This can either be a direct result, or there could be an interim style order listed for a few months to observe the behaviour between when the claim is made and a month or so later, let's say.

The second scenario would consist of evident panic and an incoherent, fearful story. This person either has some visible markings or perhaps evidence or details of a previous domestic assault. The background of both parties is taken into account, but to a lesser degree, as there is already evidence to support the claims. The background of the accused, such as anti-social behaviour or past aggressive convictions, is checked. This type of situation would go straight to the judge, who would complete the protection/safety or restraining order and then delegate police to act on the court order immediately.

In the initial meeting with the appointed gatekeeper before the judge, some things would be taken into account. The accuser's background is considered; if this is an individual who has falsely accused before, then it's taken with a grain of salt. If this person is constantly using the police to harass the accused without merit, it does not go to the next stage, which would be the fulfilment of the court order from the judge.

If it's some single older woman who constantly rings the police, fire department or ambulance for call-outs for no reason, for example, that'd be classed as a red flag. Both criminal backgrounds are quickly checked, highlighting anything beneficial to the claims or false claims.

If it's a person with no real story or timeline, and the entire document is hearsay or slander, that's a red flag. If it's a woman claiming she has been beaten black and blue from pillar to post but hasn't got one photograph to support the claim or one police report or medical report on the system from the past that corroborates her story, then that's a red flag.

If the person making allegations wouldn't be in favour of a potential polygraph test in the future, that is also considered a red flag. Furthermore, Red flags should not be ignored; the whole process is overlooked these days. We can discuss what could be potential red flags, but what is the one thing that is needed the most? It is the lack-of-ease, to make the court order to begin with. This process, or any process, would be beneficial and bring justice much faster to the real victims.

Using these domestic abuse stories as an identity, transmuting them into a form of punishment, lessens the seriousness of these situations and takes away from the real victims. Courts should be looked upon as a serious matter, yet they are being used as playthings. Unfortunately, the family court system that we have today is easily exploitable and has become a literal joke.

There needs to be a deterrent from misusing our court systems, and there is none. There need to be repercussions from making false allegations, and there are none.

People's actions should be documented from when they came into the courthouse to make the court order to their demeanour. The severity of their claims and an analysis of how they behave following the claims. Mental health assessments should be considered if a person is making ridiculous false allegations that don't make sense. All orders against another person should be categorised under a class of mild to severe.

This would minimise so much of the backlog of court cases that are currently pending. Without exaggeration, every claim that turns into a court case is a top priority. The problem with this is you can freely go into your local family court and claim the most ridiculous talking points about your partner, and it gets put into action. There is no rational concept of people lying; there are no repercussions.

Think about that: no penalty whatsoever if it is found out to be mere harassment of a targeted ex-partner, for example. That's why these courts are being exploited in such a way that they are leaving a backlog of cases that the court officials can't keep up with.

If the claims for a court order are ridiculous, for example, A court should not be executing safety, protection or restraining orders. They could pivot the situation they have in front of them to include counselling services, mediation programs and even couples counselling. There should be a red flag if a parent is not accepting to attend the mediation service, rejecting any form of contact or deliberately trying to cause distress using a child.

If red flags keep appearing, mandatory support groups with educational resources should be available to help parents navigate the complexities of the legal system. We need to be able to come to more amicable solutions and reduce the trauma often accompanying custody battles. The minor cases of delivering heartbreak to another need to be identified and eradicated.

In most cases, the qualifications and training of family court judges and mediators need to be reevaluated. A new way of handling these sensitive custody disputes needs to be implemented. We must listen to the voices of those who have been affected by these outdated practices.

The outdated family court favours in terms of sexual bias, choosing mothers over fathers. This bias can result in extreme neglect for the child or worse, all because of a stereotype of who the better caregiver is. We must challenge these dated stereotypes, parents need to be looked upon as equals, displaying parental integrity and morals. No bias should come into play within these courtrooms.

These are family courts? Creating a family should be the top priority, as well as being balanced and impartial. Anti-family is these courts, Trying everything to help ensure the child's separation from one parent. One parent should not be excluded from a child's life without good reason or because a breakup brings about resentment. These family court cases are really just cases where parents are unable to co-parent. We need to support and teach or even implement how co-parenting will be established going forward from case to case.

QUESTIONING

When a person takes a trip down to their local court to file an accusation, one key feature is exempt from the current worldview. This one aspect would deter many of these cases from ever being formed. The entire process, including reports, observing red flags or categorising case by case, would be entirely avoided by one simple act? It's called questioning.

A person does not have to be bright to make a court order; conversely, they can get the courts to do their bidding with zero IQ. There are vast amounts of people who would claim falsehoods, but if given the hassle of questioning regarding these falsehoods, they would automatically decline any questioning, showing they have something to hide.

Not similar to cross-examination or an investigation style of questioning? Just a conversation, the recorded dialogue of questioning.

Instead of telling an outright lie (that is, one in which all details are falsehoods), they change only specific details in a truthful account or simply conceal vital details in the account.

Differences between embedded or concealed lies and truths are small, and thus, it is difficult to detect these kinds of lies. (B.M,DePaulo, et al.,1996) (A,Vrij, P.A, Granhag, S.B, Porter, 2010)

Let us see what these people have to say; listen, ask and converse. Believe it or not, this is not performed; most deceitful people might second-think abusing these court orders if the courts were not as gullible. Additionally, any real abuse survivor facing threats or intimidation would have no problem answering questions because they are coming from a place of truth. Once the person completes the form, they should be brought into a room with questions posed.

This is not only ethical but could be implemented with ease. Why should we ignore the court cases that are backlogged to infinity? There is a massive problem here: court cases are constantly adjourned, prolonging the alienation of the children and creating further conflict between couples.

Case study

Richard

Ex-wife Monica (Native Spanish), Daughter Sandra March 2020 I was away working, my daughter is 2 months old, and I have slight COVID symptoms; my wife did not let me home for 2 weeks even though it was the advice and the hostel I was staying in illegally let me stay. I have the name of the hostel; I also have the news reports stating that hotels and hostels were closing in Spain. I have messages to my younger brother stating what was happening.

April 2020 Monica finally lets me stay, tells me to quarantine for two more weeks in the attic and secure the door with rope so they know if I leave the room. I have a character reference who knows that I was locked in a room and can vouch that this happened.

July 2020: My mother-in-law tells me to leave the family home as she doesn't want me to stay any longer. I have no job and no home during covid.

I eventually sought out a solicitor in Spain due to the alienation that occurred indefinitely and the exclusion of any fatherly role. He wanted to obtain and assess the complete court file before recommending action. In the end, he said my options may be restricted.

Where a child has hardly seen her father (and no matter that's not his fault or that the mother has deliberately made things difficult for him), the court will first want to see that there has been a regular visit regime through a meeting point and receive a report from the meeting point's supervisors which recommends that visits should be moved outside the confines of the meeting centre.

At the outset, his firm requested €4,500 as a funds provision/retainer. "If we end up in court for you", he said – "which looks likely from what you write – fees, expenses, and VAT will be more than the amount of such retainer". So he said, "I am concerned that you will not be able to afford us".

I got in touch with another lawyer on 6th April, outlining my case. He advised that it was better to go through the Spanish courts, which I will do one more time. I just want to know if the UK/Ireland (I am both nationalities) could do anything, as I feel the Spanish system is biased against me.

I was also abused and mistreated by my ex-wife and family from 31 August 2016 to July 2020. I did not go into detail with the lawyers, and the court is unaware of this, but I have evidence of this, too.

It was recommended that my best option be to seek legal advice in Santander or Torrelavega, as it is my child's jurisdiction. Apparently, this will be easier for me and will make it easier for my lawyer to deal with the case.

I was having difficulties with the Punto de Encuentro and the courts there, which dealt with divorce and modifying the measures. I was advised to find a lawyer in that jurisdiction.

I have both British and Irish nationality and sought to know my daughter's rights as she has been denied the chance to have a relationship with her father. At the end of July 2020, I went back to the UK temporarily, as agreed with Monica, as my mother is also ill.

August 2020: My older brother exploited my mother out of money and forced her to keep his girlfriend as a lodger even though he was not living there. (I have emails and letters proving that this was the case.)

August 2020 quarantine in the UK is in place for 14 days, so you cannot go back and forth to Spain freely. It is not stated how long this quarantine will be in place. In September 2020, I ended up in the hospital with a stress-related illness. Monica did not send me photos of my daughter and ignored my calls until she verified with my mother that I was indeed in the hospital. (messages, photo of me in hospital)

In September 2020, I found a job in the UK. I agree with Monica that I can stay and ask her to send me the certificates. (Proof in email and on messenger that she did this)

In December 2020, I went to Spain and took two PCR tests, at over 300 pounds for both, to be sure I could travel. As I have a three-week holiday, then a variant of the virus comes out, so there are so many countries stopping people from coming from the UK. I had to leave quickly and saw my daughter and Monica for two days, but I had to go in a rush as I thought travel may have been stopped. (In the media, there are photos) of Monica and Sandra. The quarantine is now 10 days, so I will do this once I return to the UK.

In February 2021, my passport and paperwork went missing from home (I suspected my brother's ex-girlfriend, but there was no proof). (pictures of new passport)

March 2021, I am concerned that I will not be able to go back to Spain as I now have no green residency card. I spoke to Balcells, and they told me to have my ex-wife send the family book and meet me at the airport when I finally return to Spain. April 2021: I was offered employment in Spain to start in August. (email)

In June 2021, I asked Monica to send me the family book so I could return to Spain; she stalled, saying she was sick for a few days. I asked her again, and she refused. My friend Jackie asked her, but she declined again. It is not the procedure at the time for entering Spain, but to be sure. (WhatsApp messages both from Monica and Jackie) June 2021 Hand in notice quickly; work happens to be very understanding (email) My mum is in hospital. She sends a voice note to Monica, pleading with her to send the family book. (I have the voice note on my phone.) (Have messages from social services proving that mum was in hospital during this time.)

In June 2021, I returned to Spain and saw my daughter on the first day with no issues. The next day Monica was causing conflict, and I called her a bitch. The Next day, I asked to see my daughter; Monica said she was unwell. I called again in the evening, and Monica said she was at the civil guard. I asked Monica why she had done this, and she said that she was alienating our daughter. (have WhatsApp messages)June 2021: A Civil guard came to my hostel, took me to the court and provided me with a lawyer. I go to court (local civil court) and am given an interpreter. I was there for 6 hours, not told when the case would start or given time to eat, etc. No proof was found, but Monica wants to escalate it to penal court, and that is set for July. (report by civil court)

I went to penal court, and the lawyer told me to accept a deal to pay 720€ and a restraining order for 4 months. I then refused. The lawyer comes back to me and tells me I need to accept 360€ as it could be worse if I don't. He assures me that I will not have a criminal record. I get a new paid lawyer. I am told that Monica has already put in a demand for a divorce, and she wants 400€ a month and for me to see my daughter supervised for one weekend a month. My new lawyer told me that I do have a criminal record and that my last lawyer deceived me as he would have been paid whether we won or lost.

September 2021, I have not seen my daughter in 3 months; I ask my sister-in-law if my daughter is okay, and she says she is. The date set for the divorce hearing is the 1st of December 2021. In October 2021, Mum got really sick, and I returned to the UK for two weeks. I ask my sister-in-law for photos to show my mum (she ignores the messages) (I have the messages on my phone)

November 2021: Time for restraining order finishes. I messaged Monica to ask to see Sandra, but there was no response. My brother messages Monica with no response (messages on the phone).

December 2021: I go to court. Monica has claimed that I abandoned my daughter, but there are photos of us screenshotted on WhatsApp calls and call records on my phone. Monica's lawyer said I had not contributed anything financially. I said that I had a receipt where I withdrew money for Monica at Christmas and copies of things I had bought her, totalling hundreds of euros on Amazon. He was not interested and didn't want to see them. The court ordered me to pay 200€ a month plus expenses, and I could see Sandra twice a week (unsupervised) as long as I found a flat and had a car to collect Sandra. (have the report)

In January 2022, I asked to see Sandra for her 2nd birthday and offered her money by email to Monica, and Monica replied that I shouldn't message her and that I should go through lawyers. (I have the email.) There was a report asking that I see social services in Spain to see if I am fit to see Sandra unsupervised (I have the email)

In February 2022, all the flats I looked at were out of my price range, and I tried to get a mortgage, but they kept stalling me. (have WhatsApp messages)

In March 2022, I became very mentally unwell and quit my job to work online teaching. I have not even seen a photo of my daughter in over nine months. I messaged Monica at Christmas asking to see Sandra, but I only received a message saying that I needed to go through lawyers and not talk to her. Social Services saw Monica the day before me. I sat down with social services, and within 5 minutes of talking to me, she (social services) said that they would be recommending that I have supervised visits. I asked how she could make that decision based on a few minutes of talking. She did not give me an answer. She told me I should work in a supermarket or do whatever it takes to stay in Spain, as I told her that I feel unfairly treated in Spain and think that returning to the UK is the best option; she promised to speak to Monica and try to get visitation sorted. I emailed social services and asked what Monica said about visitation; she goes off-topic and is not helpful, and she never fulfilled her promise of calling Monica and arranging visitation (have emails). I returned to the UK, and my job in the UK happily took me back, but I was in a lower-paying job than I had previously.

April 2022: The report from social services to the court is negative. It has statements from my ex-wife that I was not made aware of and is baseless. Recommended that I have supervised visitation. (have the report)

June 2022: Go back to court for the final divorce hearing. I am called a foreigner by my ex-wife's lawyer. The judge lets Monica speak, and she says that I have done nothing for my daughter. I try to speak, but I am castigated, and we are all told to leave the court while the lawyers talk with the judge. My lawyer told me I would need to pay 250€ a month as I had not paid the extras. I said that I had offered money and been ignored, but my lawyer did not listen. Video calls and supervised visits were agreed upon. (Have the report)

In July 2022, I got a report that stated that I needed to visit every weekend for one hour a day. The court was made aware that I am in the UK. My lawyer asked me to go to the Punto de Encuentro Santander for urgent visitation. I was told that I needed an appointment when I got there. I returned the next day and said that I had no Spanish phone number. They finally agreed to interview me. I was told that I should get visitation rights soon. The Punto de Encuentro told me that I could not use them and that I should contact Punto de Encuentro Torrelavega and said that I didn't have to be interviewed again. I noted that Santander is more manageable for everyone as it is closer to my ex-wife and more accessible for me. They said that my daughter's jurisdiction is Torrelavega, and it is not a matter of distance. (have email)

The August 2022 Date is set for me to see my daughter supervised (through a two-way mirror) in September. They told me that as it was a court order, I would need to go every week. I said that I lived in London, that it was impossible. They said that they would call me back, and they agreed with my ex-wife and me that I could visit once a month. (I have the agreement.)

In September 2022, I saw my daughter for the first time in 434 days of fighting to see her. We got on very well, and everything was good. Patricia (an employee at PDE) told me that it went better than she thought it would have gone. Ask a few people about visitation video calls, as the court report mentions the first day of the holidays. I asked Monica, and she did not respond (I have emails)

October 2022 Sandra cries for her mum, and Patricia has to console her. The next day, everything was fine.

November 2022 I get a letter from the police in Spain saying to call them. I called them and they said that my car (it had been with my ex-wife for 2 years) was in the town and had been there for ages and I needed to move it straight away. I said that I couldn't as I was in the UK, and my ex-wife must have dumped it there. I said I was going to Spain that weekend to see my daughter, and he agreed to see me.

I went to the police station and asked if I could sue my ex-wife for leaving my car in the middle of town with no warning, as I did not know of this. He said there was no need to sue as he could get the car towed. All of my belongings were in the car and he would keep it until I came back in December. I agreed not to sue.

In December 2022, I collected my things by taxi, had to throw a lot of things away against my will and put some things in a warehouse. (The police sent an email of my belongings and messages to the warehouse.) The car had apparently been there for 6 months, and I had bad asthma due to all the dust for a week after.

January 2023 I visited every month without fail; I have to pay for up to 4 flights at a time as no direct flights on Friday evening or Sunday from London to Santander. Costs me up to 200 pounds a flight. Sandra cries for her mum. Patricia stays the whole time and says to me not to worry as she has been on xmas holidays and it is normal as her routine has been disrupted.

Patricia tells me that she is leaving and wishes me good luck. I spoke to the new lawyer, and he said that the video calls mentioned are ambiguous and the order by the court is not good at all, and said that I should go back to court.

In February 2023, I sent an email to the punto de encuentro, stating that I was concerned about my daughter's welfare as I was treated horribly in my ex-wife's house, and I am concerned for my daughter; I got no response. (have email) A New woman (Maria) in the punto de encuentro told me that she was not interested in the email I had sent. Told me that I needed to come every week, as stated in the report by the court initially, and said if my daughter cried, it was my daughter, and she would take her straight to her mother. She said that I am not a good father and that she is not interested in how difficult it is for me to come every month. She said that my mother's illness is irrelevant and that I should prioritise my daughter over my ill mother. She said that I needed to go back to court to modify the document. I then went to see my daughter.

I was, of course, nervous after this. My daughter picked up on it and cried a lot. Maria took my daughter out as she promised, and I heard my ex-wife laughing to the security guards, "She doesn't want to see her father today". The next day, I pleaded with Maria not to do that again and that I was sure I could calm her down, which I did successfully. (I have emails of all flights booked and hotels paid for and costs, and I have proof of every child Maintenance payment.)

March 2023 I saw my daughter Saturday and Sunday with no issue. Maria was not there but two other workers were and everything was fine. I looked through my emails and saw a report sent from the court by Punto de Encuentro, which was very negative, saying that I only speak in English with my daughter. This is untrue and xenophobic. Nothing positive about me. Mentions that Monica is very close with the punto workers and that she is very enthusiastic for Sandra to see her dad. I sent it to my new lawyer. (I have the report.)

April 2023 I spoke to the new lawyer again, and he told me how much I should pay him and that I should come to Spain next Thursday to set my demand through a notary. I want video calls three times a week and to see my daughter unsupervised during holidays. I have emailed him my set holidays (email) I emailed the Punto De Encuentro Torrelavega and asked why there was no follow-up about my concerns for my daughter. I have not received a reply. (Have email) I emailed the punto de encuentro stating that I wanted to make a complaint about one of their workers in Torrelavega, Maria and how I could do this; I did not mention her by name. Not received a response. (Have email)

These court orders are being misused en masse, beyond the intended purpose for which they were created to combat. A protection order is now a method of control or dominance in a toxic relationship. These orders will likely be implemented when the recipient has loosened the shackles, if you will, and have become difficult to control. There is a premeditated forced-humbling element to this toxicity also. In the false accuser's mind, they think the recipient of the circumstances may feel like their life is over now, with the alienation from their loving children or due to depression from the court orders.

Sick and tired of the police harassment and false allegations, maybe it's a better alternative to just put up with the coercive controlling relationship, turn a blind eye to the abuse and tolerate it again. In doing so, this would severely compromise safety and even freedom if the false accuser would go on to make another claim. A lot of these cases are still pending while the accuser is back in a relationship with the real victim, which makes the court order a form of fear and blackmail. Either that or after months or years of the fear, grief and torment hit enough, they just drop the charges.

The person is weakened, and the court orders help destroy them in every way. The whole point for the majority of these fake orders is to break an individual, and it works to perfection. This also helps with the hijacking of homes, property, possessions and life savings. The constant loss is completely depleting, which is why they use these orders targeting the most vulnerable target of all: the children. This tugs at a person's emotions and excludes them from seeing their child growing up, missing key milestones over the case being adjourned over and over again.

A control freak would want to control every aspect of a victim's life, and by manipulating the court services, they can choose to do so when the time is right. These people are controlling from the get-go. They are the type to search your internet history or phone constantly; it's that level of control.

What can we expect from the loophole of these easily exploitable court orders? Incompetent police will be at the forefront, and they will treat you like a gangland criminal with not a shred of evidence to support a bogus claim. They will be used as a form of harassment either when you are still in a toxic relationship or after the order is implemented.

If a person is still with an abusive partner and notices the police calling over practically nothing, it will be a sign that the partner is planning a legal battle. This cements validity, and should the background of the couple need to be checked, instead of an empty screen on the system, it will show up as a police domestic call-out.

This constant threat of prison will be enough to worry and dismantle any clear thoughts on how to assess the volatility of the situation. If the court order is set in place, then the real abuser, at any feasible time, can ring the police and make it look as if the real victim has breached the order. This adds to the penalty, and prison time can occur. Even a look or eye contact can be enough for this domestic abuse imposter to call the police and say they feel threatened. Avoiding eye contact at all costs would be beneficial in this situation, as the look of disdain would be a reasonable default look. After all, this person has only walked the path to steal children and anything else they can, with the callous motivation to keep pretending the order is breached. Keep the fear perpetuating in the mind of the real victim, that constant pressure of prison and the problem it brings.

Furthermore, judges don't take parental alienation or false allegations into account. They merely execute every allegation without question and collect a handsome paycheck for doing so. These cases lead to delay after delay, never reaching a final hearing, leading to annoyance and exacerbating parental alienation. This real victim just wants to see their children and put the abuser in the past. Even when the judge happens to notice questionable behaviour during the case the trial keeps going ahead or will be adjourned. Such as extortionate alimony requests or unfounded claims, even caught lying, will mean nothing to the outcome of the case. The courts are easily exploitable; they are not concerned with who the victim is or about the welfare of the children. The incompetent family courts' only concern is the lucrative money racket these recurring relationship feud cases are.

> "In the United States today, more than 23 million children live in a single-parent family. This total has risen over the last half century and currently covers about one in every three kids across America." (The Annie E. Casey Foundation 2022)

The inadequacies of court procedures and policing need to be examined. Along with the third parties that coincide with the family courts, such as child services or groups that work on mediation matters. There is a pattern of inefficiency or lack of competency with the stated protocols for such systems.

These key areas need to be examined to gain an understanding of what is going on in the legal system.

The legal system across the board, regardless of which nation, all seems to be tallied the same backward way. These family courts are indubitably business models, endorsing the use of bullying with law-fare and or the punishment of child alienation. There is quite a money racket within the divorce courts; which can be lucrative for those involved like attorneys and judges, etc. In the United States alone there are so many reports of divorces costing well over the $100,000 range.

These figures, in hindsight, show we are generating a fortune but for all the wrong reasons. It's a common fact that divorce court is a staggering $28 billion a year national industry, with an average cost per couple of about $20,000.

Family fragmentation costs U.S. taxpayers at least $112 billion each year or more than one trillion dollars each decade. This $112 billion annual estimate includes the costs of federal, state, and local government programs and foregone tax revenues at all levels of government.
(Scafidi, B. 2008)

The average person who suffers from abuse at this level is shell-shocked, and rightfully so. They would keep the trauma buried deep inside, and that's how they control it; they suppress the trauma.

The issue with this is that this degree of punishment is not spoken of nearly enough. False allegations go hand in hand with parental alienation, and if you've faced them, then you are a victim. That's why there is difficulty reliving these life events. Unless we can speak about this law-fare abuse and make it common knowledge in society, it will never change.

To use law-fair tactics as a way to intimidate and further coercive control is entirely wrong and demonstrates severe ongoing abusive patterns. Not to mention the purposeful waste of court time and disrespect to the people who have real issues such as domestic abuse or rape; for example, faking allegations about someone is undermining any of these real cases!

To take away from all the real victims out there and steal their stories and likenesses just for revenge purposes should be frowned upon. This pretending, acting and creative form of attacks is quite peculiar indeed. It takes a special type of individual to perform or even construct these matters accordingly. They utilise normal aspects of society, such as the court system and police force, and use them as weaponry.

Chapter 11
Being Innocent Is Not Enough; Don't Be Complacent

As aforementioned, made-up accusations are immediately believed with a presumption of guilt for the accused. This allegation alone serves as a form of punishment. Real people who do suffer and have real cases are not the topic here; remember this discussion is strictly on false allegations. Of course, should an allegation be raised, it should be investigated properly and should sufficient evidence be present, the law should require punishment. The problem with real cases is that they drop out of charging a person usually because it never gets investigated; part of the reasoning for this is the lack of policing. There are too many cases, and the phoney cases aren't getting addressed or realised, and this stifles the real cases. This discussion is about the false cases; who causes them? And theories on how to prevent this stagnation in our courts and policing.

Phoney court Orders & The Culprits

A high number of these false cases are by people who have made multiple accusations over long periods; this never gets addressed. Some people are repeat culprits of false allegations and it is never highlighted. There are good people out there getting in trouble with the law over a lie. These cases need to be eradicated if we want some justice for the real cases; the 1# priority should be eradicating the phoney cases that plague our justice system. A large number of these culprits are people with narcissistic traits and people with interior motives of gain.

People with personality disorders either Paranoid Personality Disorder (PPD) from Cluster A or Borderline, Narcissistic, Histrionic or Anti-social-Personality disorders are the likely accusatory type. The ultimate goal here is to disorientate the victim, playing off the emotions causing great distress and worry, and now your mood will equate to that of the borderline. Legal orders such as protection, safety orders and restraining orders are misused en masse by people who need a mental health evaluation.

The gullibility of the family court system is second to none, without question. Without review or conversation about the allegation, it simply becomes implemented by the courts. A simple cross-examination, either when the allegation is made or during the process of waiting for the court dates to align, could simply rectify this matter, preventing most cases. Each court order between a couple or a breach of that order should warrant questioning over the subject matter.

Purpose-driven parental alienation needs to become a circumstance that the courts actively try to prevent from occurring. In cases where allegations are made between a couple with no children, they can easily rule out the alienation strategy.

There needs to be a separation of these orders in terms of priority. Severe, mild, minor and questionable, AKA nothing/falsehoods. Some orders should be prioritised and put into action, but they still require some cross-examination to figure out the gains or punishment modus operandi.

The majority of the cases that line up with falsehoods, when observed, become quite clear that there are specific gains to be had through the system. Even with no children, there can be gains such as property, money, or possessions; also, compensation is worth nothing depending on the jurisdiction and country.

The common association in each case where the courts are being manipulated and used for gain involves children. Children are a key motivator. If the family courts were structured fairly, they would tackle parental alienation at its core first. There are improper practices in how these family cases are handled, and the courts don't seem to be progressing any time soon.

There must be justification for the immediate outcome of a protection or restraining order against another parent. When these claims are made, most of these orders should be temporary. The minor ones last a mere month or two, discernment based on the severity case by case. If it's a mere argument or a petty breakup, the cooldown period between a couple is usually a few weeks. Anger, resentment and jealousy cool down in time and naturally revert to everything becoming normal again.

It is the court orders themselves that exacerbate hatred between most of these couples. There is so much wait time for each court case; preventive measures should be taken to tackle this. An out-of-court examination of the substantial proof and statements regarding the issues should be executed.

We can find common ground or perhaps identify real severe cases we need to keep an eye on before any date is even set by the courts. If aggression is involved and the witness statements or evidence points to violence, then this should be prioritised and given a court date.

In 2019, the National Registry of Exonerations had 143 exonerations. 101 of those exonerated were from perjury or false allegations. Figures are taken from the National Registry of Exonerations, which was founded in 2012 in conjunction with the Center on Wrongful Convictions at Northwestern University School of Law. For more information about wrongful convictions or more figures and info about such convictions, look up the National Registry of Exonerations. (The National Registry of Exonerations 2019)

The Silver-Bullet technique is used to gain leverage and control of the court narrative. This is an abhorrent allegation of abuse in a multitude of facets. There is no chance to duck and take cover, as it only takes getting hit by one stray bullet to lose the case and custody.

Emphasis on truth and lies may not be shown in court to weed out any phoney cases utilising this silver bullet approach. The court system at present considers every single case and treats them all equally when, of course, they are not. With no screening or vetting of people and their claims, how do we know the validity of these cases? We don't. The cases drag on, lasting months or years for court dates to proceed and reach a verdict.

This time-lapse the courts allow to occur is spent honouring abuse. Children are left with abusers; all the while, real victims are vilified and left to suffer. Who said it first? Or who alleged this or that first? It is a childish approach, but it seems to run its course throughout the incompetent family court.

There is no consideration of what is said, why it was said or if there is a motive behind what is alleged. It is approved by the court system automatically, resulting in a mountain of cases that lead to court stagnation. This area has not been tackled and needs to be addressed first, starting with vetting case by case.

Judy Sheindlin, better known as Judge Judy, mentions a story in her book Don't pee on my leg and tell me it's raining. This was from a father who was in an overnight access agreement with his daughter. Judge Judy looked disapprovingly at the father, who insisted that he had tried to coax the girl to sleep in her own room.

That night, however, she stayed with him. The mother's attorney believed the case was won as it seemed suspicious and highly inappropriate behaviour. Judge Judy asked the mother where the child slept when she was with her. "Why, with me," she answered. "She's always slept with us". "When the couple separated, the daughter continued to sleep with her mother.

But Mom set new rules for Dad. When at his house, the daughter had to sleep alone. It was a cunning way of manipulating the child and her father. Over the last decade, I have had perhaps thirty or more such allegations come before me. But less than 10 per cent have had any validity because, more often than not, mothers are simply trying to punish men. And they are supported in this by a dubious industry comprised of thinly credentialed, so-called "experts". (J.Sheindlin,J,Getlin,1997)

Case study

Chris

Triangulation was an option for this woman, which helped reinforce parental alienation; she had her sister involved in the lies. Chris is a loving father and husband, an author, supervisor, and security guard working alongside the police. He is well respected and has known his abuser since his early teenage years. They settled down and had a family together. As soon as things were not working out anymore, the marriage was ending, and Chris found someone else. Right away, he was confronted with a situation that was out of his worst nightmare.

Almost instantaneously, he was accused of rape and abuse. Once she found out, he moved on and found someone else. The timing of the false accusation didn't matter much to her as his mom was terminally ill from cancer at the same time.

She got the court-injunction order, A protection order without him knowing about it while she and he were sharing the same bed. With that type of court order, he is not supposed to be in the same house, but again, he had no idea of the court order until six weeks later.

To his surprise, she got him arrested for rape and domestic abuse following an investigation for 10 months, all the while social services backed her up. She had an accomplice in bad-mouthing her husband in her sister, who could corroborate her phoney stories.

She claimed rape more than once and said he threw hot coffee on her. Painting Chris out to be a domestic abuser and perpetrator of rape, delegating him to a class he does not belong, trying as hard as humanly possible to get him locked up.

Evidence-wise, she had a text from 2016 from him calling her a name, which raised eyebrows as that's almost a decade ago. She claimed her current phone was broken and that she could not retrieve up-to-date messages. Keep in mind they have been together twenty years; this was all there was; why did she keep messages that long, almost planning this case as an alternative route? She got called a name in the message!

What she did to Chris was on a different level: branding him forever, having him worried about impending jail time and ostracising him from his daughter/kids, family and friends. The older kids that they have together are now brainwashed against him, known their dad; Chris as a domestic abuser and rapist like everyone else who is in earshot of these allegations.

This woman did the very same thing to her ex-partner before Chris; she has accused her ex of similar false allegations and is creating quite a decent-sized trophy list of men's lives she has destroyed. Upon questioning both parties, police found Chris's story to be more credible, mentioning, "You're not the man she says you are" after being questioned.

This woman isn't clinically diagnosed with anything, showing all the hallmarks of a disorder or a comorbidity. She got all the made-up dates wrong, and she later admitted to the police that it was all a bunch of false allegations. This isn't a happy ending. There is more; this highlights exactly how the system will work if you are confronted with a similar situation.

She claimed he raped her on a date on which the same date he had a video of her being extremely aggressive to him, but the police didn't buy it. She claimed that it was a different date and proceeded to simply change the date. But they weren't even around each other on that specific day; he was in public and seen on camera in McDonald's and also at the daycare centre with his daughter, an easily provable fabrication that's when she kept changing the timeline to make it fit, but ultimately gave up and shrugged it off as just a fake story in which she'd hoped worked.

But it did work; Chris was petrified of getting locked up in prison and wanted nothing more than to spend time with his daughter; now it's impossible for him to explain to her over a phone call; why they can't see each other?

Ultimately Chris was labelled a domestic abuser and rapist. Suffered parental alienation from his child for an entire year and more, merely seeing her in a contact centre in which he pays £300 a month to do so. Chris has taken a loss of £40,000 so far from solicitor fees, child support, contact centres and divorce.

The upcoming course he has to part-take in costs £2000, which is a (DAPP) domestic abuse and perpetrators course. If he does not go on the course, he faces the fate of seeing his daughter in a contact centre until she's sixteen; she's currently nine years old.

So, taking the course is worthwhile as an alternative to that fate. There is an ultimatum to this; in order to take the course to begin with, the prerequisite is that he will have to admit a guilty plea to all the false allegations made against him.

In the meantime, he will have no choice but to accept the unacceptable and bow down to these false allegations just to see who he wanted to see all along: his daughter. This tactic is a presumption of guilt or branding oneself of guilt without being guilty.

There is no consideration or notion that a person can lie, and even with the admission of faking the stories, he will still have to be coerced to take the guilty plea just to merely part take. Noting that you have to recognise your behaviours as a domestic abuser and rapist for any chance of reform.

Cafcass is a UK organisation that gets involved when parents split up; they interview the mom, dad and child. The reviews for this organisation are appalling, and this organisation and others around the world need re-education and further training. I encourage any reader to check these reviews; there are so many complaints about being biased and also breaking up families. They split families up and create further animosity, showing displays of gender bias and unprofessionalism.

At one point, a third-party group was in charge of checking the homes of Chris and his ex. His home appeared clean and well-organised, while hers was chaotic and filthy. They mentioned this as a safety concern in the report, but Cafcass pushed it aside, focusing on mere sexism and bias discernment. Chris brought up the fact that this woman was publicly releasing all his medical records as she works in a medical profession in which he was looked upon as a bully trying to damage her work reputation.

In conclusion, this case is current, and the contact centre said he's a brilliant dad and put in reports on his behalf. He has lost family, friends, and the only person he really wanted to spend time with, his kids, a victim of parental alienation. He suffered a full year in which he did not see his daughter and then a further year and a half in visiting through a contact centre.

They allowed this man to get slandered, a rapist, an abuser etc and called him a bully among other things. When the child was 6, this woman left her child alone and went on holiday for two weeks, leaving the child behind. Chris had to be plan B and take care of the child, and he didn't mind. Chris's ex didn't care about safeguarding the child or even bringing it up in the case; it must have been a good holiday.

There was no consideration for the child, and if Chris is as bad as she made him out to be, why care for a holiday and not blow the whistle? This woman had a high sex drive, threesomes and lesbian sex, for example, and when he mentioned that, it's called slander, but what about the rape and domestic abuse being said about him; that's not considered slander or even questioned.

Chris brought up the point of the holiday to child services, but they weren't interested and didn't care for an alternative viewpoint. She has done this to the older kids also and now brainwashed the kids against him. They see him as a domestic abuser and rapist. He lost his family, his friends, and reputation and was frightened time and time again of the threat of arrest and imprisonment. Her family had known him since he was 14; he was her childhood sweetheart.

The bottom line is that the family courts have found him guilty; he's not allowed to deny any allegation made. When his little girl says, "Daddy, when can I come to stay?" it breaks his heart as he can't tell her why.

Ultimately, after police quizzed her, she was caught out in her lies. Chris currently attends group meetings and is ostracised from his children, but he will continue to be, regardless of how things play out.

These courses typically last from 6-9 months; Chris's course will last 6 months, and then a report is put through with Cafcass, who usually extend it or prolong it, so it's undetermined when there will be some normality in this man's life. According to DAPP (Domestic Abuse Perpetrators Programme), 9 out of 10 mothers refuse contact after the course.

Succeeding in eluding any mediation or access to the children reinforces the parental alienation that companies like Cafcass promote. The new Cafcass policy from late 2024 is as follows: "FCAs and Children's Guardians will no longer use language such as 'claims' or 'alleges' in reports to the court, using instead the words of children and adults who are victims of domestic abuse. It is for the court to determine the facts." (Cafcass New Domestic Abuse Practice Policy; Published: 9 October 2024) The implication arising from this report is that the unofficial principle of 'contact at all costs' is not as all-powerful as it once was. Another alternative is forcing out-of-court settlements or mediation. In this forced manner it helps avoid the parental alienation technique. Keep in mind that there are no preventive measures by the court system to prevent parental alienation.

Furthermore, possible mental health screenings should a person raise the red flags of a given criteria. The parents' mental health is an important aspect that is shockingly not taken into account. Rewarding mentally ill parents for concocting a fake allegation can lead to child neglect and abuse. This outdated court structure at present is complicit in turning children over to their abusers. That's not to discredit real abuse cases; on the contrary, we still need to act upon real cases.

Abusers come in many forms and seek leverage to win by any means necessary. There is abuse that needs to be dealt with, and court orders should be exercised proficiently to support the victim. However, to garner this protection and support of the victim, we need to figure out who the victim is. More often than not, the victim is on the receiving end of an allegation. This then uses the current structured court procedures as an advantage against the real victim. Cases that demonstrate severe grudges or animosity are never evaluated, examined, or even taken into consideration.

According to Gabay et al., professional victims (TIV) Tendency for Interpersonal Victimhood, these people exhibit the following victim mindset traits: Routinely seek recognition of their victim status. Positions their alleged victim status as elite moral superiority. Has a lack of empathy and interest in other people's pain and suffering, especially people the professional victim has harmed. Obsesses about past alleged victimisation. Furthermore, "No actual victimisation need occur for the victim mindset to develop".(Gabay et al., 2020)

The Exit -

More on coercive control

At this point, enough people have fallen victim to the gullible family courts, and something needs to change. The family-court displays incompetence with an inability to restructure how it operates. They are not serving justice and are okay with serving out misfortune and unfair rulings instead. Some too many people haven't seen their children in decades, all because they are name-called and made to look bad at a hearing.

The real cases of abuse shouldn't be too hard to distinguish from the false cases. The problem we have is that it's as if these cases don't exist; or, to put it another way, it's as if people don't-lie. They are not considering the false cases whatsoever. This is because we have been running on the same laws since the family court's inception. This has worked then and up until a point, but these days and for the last few decades, we have new elements of abuse.

Why do we have a court system if it can be manipulated at ease, with no repercussions? Why do we give immunity to these untrained judges and expect them to reach verdicts at a high standard? This broken and corrupt system was more than likely purposely built in such regards as extorting money and causing friction among families. The money racket of these courts is so high that the chances of it changing for the better are slim to none. The children and conflicting couples are not taken into consideration; the money acquired is, however, along with decisions on a whim.

> "Nearly every six days in the U.S., a child is killed amid a custody dispute, family court lapse, or other mishaps. Each death is a tragedy. Collectively, these cases reveal a national crisis in the family court system that regularly misses warning signs and exposes too many kids to abuse and death, advocates say."(Alltucker, K, USA TODAY, 2023)

An individual with a Cluster B or Paranoid personality disorder will become zealous, seeking out a court case, creating allegations and using the court or police as a means to further coercive control over a relationship. Either make up stories trying to make it look like there is a breach of an order when there is not.

No repercussions for harassment or bullying through the police service. Even in times when it's evident that they are false allegations. If you don't acquiesce to their coercive control or intolerable behaviour, they will more than likely go this route.

If a person is diagnosed or not, has a disorder or not, the behaviour is apparent and should be noted. Harassment using methods that are out of the scope of everyday thinking happens every day. Careless lies are told with no remorse for how they may affect a person. Gleefully excited at the thought of the hurt caused by incarceration, parental alienation and so on. Another possible outcome would be to bait their victim into something.

There are many ways this can play out, such as reactive abuse. If they abuse, scream and shout at you for long periods, eventually, you may shout something back. Whatever the bait may be, this damages your credibility months before any court case.

Another way to do this is that the Cluster B type personality would get the court orders against you and try to cause anger in you to react emotionally. A person naturally gets angry with the fate of not seeing their children again and gaining a possible criminal record. Defeat in the courtroom in the upcoming case would be guaranteed as this could be real evidence, such as an angry call or text. Our children bring out intense emotions within us by becoming forcibly detached through phoney slander; this becomes an irritant. The systemic usage of irritation after getting hit with a fake court order will increase the shock and panic, and they know it.

They will steal your home funds and your possessions if they can. They will refuse mediation services; it's completely nonnegotiable. Stealing your children in the process will emotionally light you up; this will be a bad look for you. One moment, you're in a chaotic relationship. The next, you're still in it but not with them physically. They won't even bother negotiating for you to obtain your belongings back, as a real domestic victim would do. A real victim would want nothing more than to get rid of the abuser; here's your stuff, here's your money, taking the leave me alone stance. This use of Law-fare is purposely used to tug at heartstrings and create stress. This person doesn't want you to stay away from them or to leave them alone; this person wants to punish you for not staying in line with their demands.

This could either be a full-on attack by law-fare or a beta test of what's to come, depending on your reactions if you acquiesce, for example. The individual who is making these fake court orders wants you to focus on them and seek out a reaction. The traumatised Law-fare victim will know first-hand terms such as parental alienation, which was unknown to them before. The weaponising of children and false allegations start to become fixated in thought, fearful of what else this mentally unstable person could do next. These victims of False reporting are psychologically attacked; the mental warfare they face is ineffable. Not only of what has just taken place but what is going to happen in the future regarding their children or future allegations or punishments. The destruction of a devalued or discarded source of supply will commence. This punishment not only goes too far, it goes till there is nowhere for it to go. People crack under pressure, but this punishment cycle is like no pressure that came before it in any given person's life. The end goal could be the aforementioned treatment until the choice is made to seek an exit route. Suicide is an option that comes to mind for the person who faces ongoing harassment of this degree. Knowing this then makes it murder by proxy; it's a suicide with intent for that outcome. It is intended for jail time and despair, and the icing on the cake could be the exit.

Case study Mother of Sianna

This journey has been stressful for me. The process has been painful. The past has haunted me. I needed to take a step back, regroup and pray about this, and look for solutions. My behaviour demonstrates that I have always wished to support Sianna. Sianna's engagement with me shows her love and dedication to a close relationship. As God as my witness, I have never physically harmed Sianna, not inebriated and definitely not sober. In good conscience, I can never agree to slapping/injuring my child. It isn't true. My love for her is as pure as the light of day. It's evident in the way we communicate. I need support, to feel heard, to know that my voice counts. Sianna and I have always been open with each other.

If Sianna is basing therapy on "false memories" sculpted by society, this is a horrific situation for any parent to endure without support. They are attempting to force supervised visits directly as a result of this allegation. If monitored visits are to take place under the pretext that I injured Sianna, this is truly hard to endure. I wish to have representation in support of family reunification, not the latter. Furthermore, this would be consistent with Josie's child protection and criminal history in Ontario, where she was convicted of assaulting her children. This was part of the reason why they were ordered into the primary care of their father in the courts in Ontario in 2018.

I fought for my innocence and a relationship with my children for eight agonising years. From 2010 to 2012, I was assaulted during my marriage. He used to rage on and abuse me and our finances and drink and drive with our daughters there. His charges were reduced to mischief. In 2013, I was diagnosed with CPTSD.

I suffered a total loss. My health, my career, and my family. 2015 would have seen my admission of guilt if I had mistreated and harmed my girls. I am a sincere Christian, despite what the world may think. I am forgiven for all my past, present and future sins. I do not take my faith and love for God lightly, nor does He. Jesus was persecuted only once. Since 2015, their father has had primary custody. During 2015 and 2016, my access was supervised. After the wrongful and unlawful conviction, I had to serve a 6-month sentence of house arrest. I had endured years of abuse.

My daughters had been brainwashed to despise me. In the wake of the criminal trial, the courts granted their father custody. Ally claims that she previously informed the agency of the abuse she experienced at her father's house. These "facts" were refuted by the courts, judges, and agency, who then unquestioningly returned the children back to their father.

I was hospitalised seven times between 2015 and 2019 due to sporadic, unplanned stenosis attacks, leaving me weak, disabled and paralysed for weeks. In 2018, my severe spinal stenosis was finally diagnosed. In 2020, my medical condition, but primarily my criminal convictions, forced me into an early retirement. Sianna and I spent weeklong summer vacations and weekend getaways together in 2017. In December 2018, their father unlawfully kidnapped the girls to Prince Edward Island. Once again, we went for six months without seeing each other. Their father brought the kids back to Ontario following three court orders and one contempt motion. After dropping them off at the child welfare office, their father returned to the island. Instead of releasing the kids back to me, the agency in Ontario immediately put them into foster care.

In December 2018, her father and I reached an agreement. Ally, almost 15 years old, made the decision that she wanted to stay in foster care, and the judge granted her request.

The judge questioned the father of the girls, "Do you think Mom is harmful to your daughters?" The father responded, "No." Their father stated that he does not think I hurt our daughters to the child protection workers in Ontario and PEI. We spent 15 years together. Sianna and I spent 5 months in 2019 in Quebec. Sianna has fond memories. She was interested in sports, mainly soccer. She had friends. She loved the fair. She loved to swim. We had a good life. There was no harm done. Quebec CAS came knocking as they were informed by Ontario Child Welfare that I was homeschooling. Once again, our time was abruptly interrupted. In 2020, I moved to PEI, where I enjoyed a shared-parenting relationship with their father. Sianna and I generally enjoyed a joyful and peaceful existence. We had our hiccups.

We always managed to cope. When the police arrived in August, I was outside in the camper, cooling off. The situation had already de-escalated. I am again blasted with the newest allegation that I have caused harm to Sianna over the years. Sianna wrote me a letter last summer stating, "You have never harmed me," and rated me a 9/10 as a mother. I hope you believe in me. I have been terrorised by social workers since I was a little girl. I have been judged, abused, and accosted by police and others who believed I was guilty. I have had to run from violence as a result of these false allegations. The threat is real. I have had nightmares for years over mistreatment from the police, the social workers, the lawyers, the unscrupulous judge, the pre-trial, the trial and the after-effects. I am telling the truth. As a child, as a mother, as a woman. I, too, need to feel heard and protected.

Punishment Cycle

Discipline, Damnation, Retribution, Retaliate; the get back or pay back. These areas discussed here, from the police to the courts, are all motivated by motive.

The Borderline, for example, would serve punishment in response to perceived or actual rejection, disappointment, or abandonment. What's referred to as the punishment cycle usually begins with a triggering event. This could range from a minor thing or something more turbulent to the borderline's emotions. A minor dispute or a disagreement, perhaps a comment made that happened to hurt their feelings.

Borderline is accompanied by an intense fear of abandonment; if there is a clue that this will or could occur, it can trigger a wave of rejection. This triggering event will motivate the borderline to unleash the punishment cycle, which can include false allegations and parental alienation.

This is a very emotionally charged time for the individual with borderline personality disorder. They will become impulsive and go to great lengths to attack, which could seem disproportionate to the cause of the actual trigger.

There is a phrase to describe a Borderline's pattern of abuse termed either punishment plan or punishment cycle. It's a conscious strategy to cause great stress and disruption to a loved one. Many reports theorise it's an unconscious behavioural pattern, meaning it's an automatic response. It is like muscle memory, if you will; whether it is an unconscious or a conscious act is not important. What's important is that we recognise what this is and when we are in it. The lesser of the two evils wouldn't need discussion here; what's worse? A person who consciously behaves punishing a close loved one or a person who does it automatically. Either way, this punishment can range for months even years, and the victim can be driven into all sorts of problems. Within such a close relationship, you would be vulnerable to legal issues, possibly prison, from the false allegations. Such a close partner can punish you in terms of homelessness. This punishment involves the usage of Situational Attacks or put simply the unsolicited circumstances purposely brought about by the actions of another. The same way the narcissist is known for given unsolicited advice; to get someone to do something unfavorable that would benefit the narcissist in some way. Using the environment as a weapon, such as courts and prisons. If they have made their victim homeless, it would be weaponising the homeless environment or if living rough, its the usage of the elements. This mirrors narcissistic abuse, and it does get that precise; like a surgeon, they revel in this manufactured suffering.

There is more than one way to skin a cat. These methods are endless; there is parental alienation, there is shame, and there is a burning desire to make the victim of such allegations feel pain. These personality types can be highly creative when it comes to inflicting torture or punishment. The main personality types that adopt this punishment-cycle are Borderline, Narcissistic, Antisocial and Obsessive-compulsive personality disorder.

This systematic abuse aims to cause stress and disruption to the target. This is a consistent and very strategic battle-plan of sorts, and life events or dramas can come at you at angles you could not fathom. This cycle of punishment gives birth to so many of the family court cases we see flooding our court system.

These personality types dish out revenge for seemingly trivial matters at times. Revenge can be disproportionate, and the concepts of what's right and wrong can be skewed. Being triggered is another reason why false allegations are made; splitting and other defence mechanisms within the personality type start to take effect.

Emotional dysregulation has no off button; when a borderline for example, feels like you did something or are about to do something detrimental to how they feel, revenge soon follows. Talionic Impulse is a primal human reaction describing the human motivation of revenge. This can also be lashing out and verbally attacking your partner, for example, and having a punishment obsession with your partner by taking out all your pain on them as if they had caused it. Inflicting misery on others because they feel hurt or have experienced misery.

This is best described by prominent American psychiatrist James Masterson in his classic (The Narcissistic and Borderline Disorders: An Integrated Developmental Approach).

> "Talionic Impulses are the deepest and most ancient of human impulses to exact revenge by taking pleasure and inflicting on others the hurt one has experienced; or as the bible expressed it: an eye for an eye and a tooth for a tooth."(Masterson, J.F,1981)

This punishment cycle is followed by some disappointment and rejection by the individual with the personality disorder. There are multiple reasons why this cycle is evoked; perhaps it's a narcissistic wound. Alternatively, it could have been that the manipulation that was used on the target didn't quite work, and now the answer is to punish them.

It could be from a recent rejection or abandonment or the thoughts of something similar occurring. New supply over recent rejection or just to punish the target. They could be releasing their inner emotional baggage onto you, hoping they'll momentarily feel better. In their delusional thoughts, they find justification to get their loved one to feel how they feel inside. Another possible angle is that they want to ascertain if you try to repair the relationship, which would give them some evidence or closure that they won't be abandoned. The Borderline would execute punitive actions towards others or even themselves, counteracting some of the intense feelings that arise. The negative areas of distressed emotion are the perceived or actual rejection, disappointment and abandonment.

Once the conflict-drama dies down, the person with Borderline personality disorder may actually feel remorse, guilt, or shame for their actions. They could try to convince you to sweep it under the rug by using excessive apologies after displaying such embarrassing behaviour. The next time you trigger the borderline, the cycle starts all over again. Learning to understand these traits helps us to navigate through the bad situations caused and better equip ourselves to react to these complicated issues that would otherwise throw us off. A key so-called protection feature with false allegations is the presumption of innocence.

People are supposed to be considered innocent until proven guilty; unfortunately, concerning false allegations, it's completely flipped around. It's guilty until proven innocent every time, making the system seem like it's designed to create conflict. The Family courts contribute to more violence, suicide, murder and abuse, and the figures keep rising. Wrongful convictions happen too often; they remain unfairly punished based on unfounded accusations. This fight for justice regarding libel and slander is not a fair fight; it's a daunting prospect. Picture this back-and-forth battle in court; with a ruthless person who is prepared to make up any story and try to make it fit within the timeline.

There is too much personal gain out of making false admissions in court; property assets, child custody, leverage on all fronts and also the life-problems brought forth to their opponent. On top of that, the judges don't have time to capture the full story or hear most of the facts.

False accusations can be presented without any fear of consequence, which is why this needs to become a public issue. There should and must be some deterrents, sanctions, and penalties put in place for making false allegations. The distress of family breakdown can lead to mental health problems and even suicide. (Sullivan, 2019)

Chapter 12

Non-Compos Mentis

It's unimaginable to think and visualise, but just for a moment, put yourself in the false accuser's shoes.

The powerful surging feelings one must obtain from manufacturing an attack on a loved one; not only has your importance skyrocketed to insurmountable heights, but you have a mere peasant in the palm of your hand who didn't appreciate you enough.

In a relationship that is going back and forth, what if you could make them pay?

Make them wish they hadn't said or done that thing that you disapproved of.

Make them pitiful, even blameful. To bring about worry and foreboding in their life. Having the responsibility of a God, showing no mercy.

The rush, the impact, the tears, the paperwork- court adjourned...

It's all a form of weaponry, and nobody knows it except you and your prey.

> "These are the people who are so fixated on their Targets that they can't let go,
>
> can't stop themselves, can't change and therefore can ruin lives—including yours."
>
> (Bill Eddy, 2018)

There are several major factors that contribute to the prevalence of false accusations. Personal vendettas are at the top of the list, with or without great cause. Misunderstandings, cruelty and mental health issues bring about allegations, and some people re-offend in terms of falsifying reports.

Attention-seeking, entitlement, relationship issues and societal biases can be reasons too. They all intertwine. It could merely be, and usually is, a form of punishment, placing fear upon the unwitting subject.

Case Study

Anonymous

This next case study was sent in by a mother telling the story on behalf of her son. Like so many, the relationship went sour but quickly led to the wife routinely making false allegations while simultaneously playing the victim. She accused him of raping her, domestic abuse and hitting their daughter, causing bruising to her legs. What followed was a long, strenuous court case of 4 years and counting, including the 2-day fact-finding hearings; all this mixed with some parental alienation,

After a long stint without seeing his daughter, he finally got supervised access every other week for 4 months, each time paying £120 per week to see his daughter.

He does have guardianship, but it didn't do much good as she was allowed to follow the court order for a six-month period and then moved from the district, claiming her extended family, father and mother moved and wanted to be close to them, which they did not move at all; the court allowed it.

It's quite the distance—an 8-hour drive away and a further 8-hour journey back. Their arrangement before the move was just 30 minutes away.

The daughter now talks badly of him; she is only five years old, and it seems she's influenced to slander her dad. He gets indirect contact every fortnight for about 10 minutes on a video call with his daughter. The mother sits right next to their daughter the whole time he is talking to her on the phone, so his daughter doesn't really speak to him much. The court looked at him through the veil of bias, and they believed all her lies with no evidence.

The incidents accusing him of hitting his daughter that were reported to social services, were ultimately dropped, and no further action was required after an investigation. The little five-year-old girl cannot speak words properly. This is a result of too much unnecessary relationship-conflict without any child centred-planning or in other words, simply not taking care of the child.

He loves his little girl and continues to fight a four-plus-year, dead-end battle in court. It has completely spiralled him into a deep depression. He now suffers from his mental and physical health, and he is also on antidepressant medication. The police reports of the allegations she alleged against him were all dropped by the police as no further action was taken but the moral here is the damage is already done.

He becomes very withdrawn now and is utterly depressed and often says, "Life is not worth living."

What can develop and should be noted about personal vendettas is that they can be and often are unprovoked. If you were trapped in a trauma bond relationship and had the privilege of hindsight, you'd soon understand to detach from it and not take anything personally. If it weren't you, it would have been the next person who has fallen victim to the ramifications brought about by the mental illness.

This combative loved one or ex-partner who is Non-Compos Mentis is commonly undiagnosed and unmedicated. Even if it's just specific character traits you notice or a likeness of some disorders, you may never know the complete diagnosis; you may be dealing with a plethora of disorders. Either way, this usage of unethical practices is wicked and should not be tolerated. If you can escape with some dignity intact, you should plan an alternative before becoming another victim.

In fact, the most dangerous of these individuals, in my opinion, is the undiagnosed and unmedicated. Flatout refuses to seek help, knowing full well the implications of their actions. With an inability to take responsibility for being abusive or manipulative. The highly conflicting drama fabrication; these actions will never cease. Leaning into it with glee and joy, unable to empathise or to be remorseful.

In relationships where there has been a history of conflict or animosity between the two people, one may falsely accuse the other as a form of revenge or retaliation. Allegations also arise when nearing the end of a relationship of the coercive kind to further the abusive pattern from afar.

Mental health issues, traits that lack self-reflection or non-accountability exacerbate the plausibility of phoney allegations occurring. People who have acquired a mental illness or have emotional instability may adopt distorted perceptions of reality. Initially, they could be beating the drum of an allegation, so much so that they believe in their own version of events. This causes problems, especially when there is an attraction to the drama on their part; they love drama and constantly display attention-seeking behaviours. No questions are asked on the contrary from others, as the fabricator of such stories begins to garner sympathy and support and becomes revered.

This action of unfairly targeting with false accusations is abuse by proxy; situational abuse.

For whatever reason, the person accusing has a motive, gain and a desire in seeing the victim demonised. Societal stereotypes, bias, self-inflicted wounds, and corroborated stories from flying monkeys can all lead to assumptions of guilt from the get-go, even with incomplete or a lack of evidence. This can have lethal consequences, even with the likelihood of them dropping the case, the victim is changed forever from this situational attack. Once a claim is made, the label sticks, and the social stigma will linger regardless of the outcome of the case; leaving the allegation almost impossible to shake off. Unfortunately, the way life is at present, it is usually far too late to counter or prevent such claims. In a turbulent relationship, even if a person is threatened with a false allegation, it can be easily brushed off and not taken seriously. The reason for this is their partner may always act crazy and say ludicrous things; this is just another weird mood swing, right? Prevention is also tricky because, in a toxic relationship, by default, you can become naive or gullible, and no one can predict what a person can do or say next.

By understanding the motivations and characteristics of a person, reading them like a page in a book, coupled with the understanding of personality disorders, a person can somewhat navigate through the obstacles that are set forth upon them. In the realm of false accusations, there are several different types that can have a detrimental impact on the lives of the targeted real-victim. The most common type of accusation is abuse, which can range from physical abuse to emotional or psychological abuse. These accusations are made by a partner seeking a silver bullet so-to-speak to use against their victim. This is for the person who has had enough of the coercive control and is being punished because of it. The accuser of such allegations may even stay with the quote/unquote abuser, all the while court orders such as protective orders are hanging right over the head of the victim, the real victim. Any false move can result in a call to the police, which will add to another criminal charge. If the choice is to stay together or stay living with the false-accuser, the victim better stay in line.. or else.

These orders are used to intimidate and coerce. There are some people who have claimed they are threatened by the abuser that if they don't stay with them or do as they ask; well then they will be known as an abuser or they will be punished through the legal system by the false allegations that will be said as a result. The abuser shown signs of an itchy trigger finger.

The legalese is enigmatical, leaving the victim feeling trapped with no way to explain such matters; there's too much to go over and explain. The victim becomes a toy thing to gnaw at, simply another life ruined, tarnished and isolated. It's important to realise that fake allegations do not fit any specific criteria; there is no prejudice to race, sex or religion. Everyone is fair game, and this is a worldwide issue with vast numbers of innocent people behind bars for allegations with zero merit. Using the prison system as an environmental attack strategy. It can be uncanny to think of these extremes, but this does happen and can be the demise of a person.

Be on the lookout for characteristics of intent with malice, frequent bearing of unfounded punishment or behavioural aspects like needy and attention seeking. Stay protected, safe and at a reasonable distance from such people. Please don't give them ample opportunity for future allegations or false breaches of an existing order to get you facing a prison sentence. Be cautious when meeting new people, but don't let the actions of one horrible person ruin your social life. Try to rebuild as best you can and get back to living life once more.

We cannot mention Non-Compos Mentis without mentioning the case of twenty-one-year-old Eleanor Williams. She claimed that she was attacked and raped and had the evidence to prove it; it was written all over her face. These injuries were abrasions, bumps, bruises and a nasty swollen eye injury; she was lucky she didn't lose her eye. It all began with her Facebook post of her story along with the pictures of her injuries.

Her story went like this: she was put into the back of a car and taken to an address. There the three Asian men raped her and beat her mercilessly. She claims she was exploited and tortured at the hands of this Asian grooming gang. Apparently, she was in debt to these men, which is why the beating occurred. She did not attend parties for seven weeks due to the coronavirus, alluding to being their prostitute. Her face, body, arms and legs were covered in bruises and scars; she had eight injuries to her head and face. She claimed that three Asian men did this heinous act in May of 2020. The case took place at Preston Crown Court. She denied lying under oath and making this story up. The weapon was passed around the jury in an evidence bag: the extensive blood-stained claw hammer.

Miss Williams inflicted the vicious wounds on herself with a claw hammer. She was a masochist-fantasist, a professional victim, and had a lure for attention. She would derive enjoyment from feeling pain and causing these wounds to herself. A fantasist of rape and being beaten and tortured.

The forensic scientist said the DNA profiles on the hammer matched Miss Williams. The forensic scientist went on to say it would be one in a billion chance that it was anyone else other than Miss Williams. At the time that she was supposedly trafficked, however, there was footage from the hotel in Blackpool where she checked in. There was then more footage of her buying snacks from the shop. Then the most damning piece of evidence there was surfaced; it was footage of her buying groceries along with; a claw hammer.

She was charged with nine counts of perverting the course of justice and sentenced to eight years. If she behaves herself in prison she could be out in two years.

The judge mentioned, "She went to extraordinary lengths to create false allegations including causing herself significant injury".

Mohammed Ramzan, one of the accused, publicly stood by Jorden Tregrove, who did a prison sentence courtesy of Eleanor. Jorden was facing 22 years of prison due to the severity of the allegations.

Ms Williams claimed he raped her, then Jorden was in prison for ten weeks; for nothing. Both Mohammad and Jorden mentioned that they tried to kill themselves as a result of the stress caused by these lies.

Case Study

Dawn

A concerned grandmother, Dawn, contacted us about the story of her son. Her son was the victim of false allegations of rape. Nearly 5 years ago, he was about to start his super senior year of high school as a special education student. He met a girl through a mutual friend, and they had relations at a sleepover. She later made the accusation and had two of her friends lie on her behalf to corroborate the story.

He made the ill decision to try to mediate things, including apologising to her on a pretext call and reaching out online to find out what was going on. Which ultimately was taken as an admission of guilt. He was so embarrassed and ashamed that he didn't tell his family till after he was arrested at school by law enforcement. Dawn had to use her retirement savings to bail him out, hire an attorney and knew a very motivated investigator.

The two witnesses recanted their stories, and an additional witness who had declined a police interview was tracked down. She finally owned up to the false accusations with no consequences for perjury or filing a false police report.

The DA dismissed the charges without prejudice, which means it's dismissed but can be re-opened at any time. The arrest stained the good reputation he'd previously had, and now he has a criminal record forever.

Dawn does some campaign work on the subject and even features on podcasts alongside AFFA, Advocates for the Falsely Accused, with the set goal of exposing the widespread problem of false allegations.

It cost Dawn way over £40K throughout this ordeal, with another $2k to have another attorney look to see if the perpetrator who made these damaging stories can be sued.

He was harassed at school and work and is still trying to move on with his life. Finding it difficult to get work and remains isolated. A far cry from his former life. This attack has led to a deep depression.

The types of personality disorders that are most notable in making false allegations are the cluster B group—that of borderline, narcissistic, antisocial and histrionic personality disorders. If a person shares attributes with one of these disorders, they would feel rejected, let down, used or even invalidated. These people then can alleviate some negative feelings by wanting to place them onto another, continuing to misuse these feelings. They could lay out a plan and bait a victim into a situation unbeknownst to others.

Baiting a victim into doing or saying something to appear as if they are a bad person. To do this would incur the usage of provocation or emotional blackmail. Or any other form of emotional manipulation that would motivate or provoke the victim. If a person becomes vulnerable in a situation or is naturally naive, they could be open to becoming exploited emotionally.

The manipulator could be collecting evidence to use in a future court battle to tarnish their victim, should they not comply with the coercion. A coercive controlling person would plan well in advance of an upcoming attack or method to use against their opposition. Planning with others using triangulation can help add to their vantage point with whatever they plan to do next.

Overwhelming their opponent, leaving them with nothing, confusing the senses with court papers and the constant threat of what may be looming around the corner. Whether you are their significant other or family, friend or stranger, it makes no difference; false allegations can happen.

Without a shred of remorse, the victim will be put on trial for nothing; the constant need for attention or to create an intriguing story is worthwhile in their eyes, not to mention any Gain that a person can get through means of the allegations. There will always be a gain, either a vindictive gain that stems from an unhealthy personal relationship. Or personal gain such as financial or property gain, or even the notoriety of stepping into the victim role.

Killing two birds with one stone can and usually does occur. The satisfaction of watching the person who has really been abused all this time suffer even more. It's a dopamine high, unlike any other, for the person whose central nervous system rewards malicious behaviour and harming others. Restraining orders or similar are used merely as a way to steal the victim's possessions, home, or money. It helps create space to enforce the steal, with real-life court orders getting in the way, all the while making the victim the perpetrator. Their discarded victim suffering is the most important scenario in their eyes, and to do this, nothing is off limits, not even their children (see chapter Inside the Psyche of the Parental Alienator).

Some of the early signs of future false allegations can be seen in the accusation of cheating or being interested in someone else. There could be an ungodly amount of allegations, and this gets pushed aside as just insecurities and eventually forgotten about without any closure. But this constant allegation could be a sign of what's to come if you're getting accused of ridiculous and, at times, improbable instances of cheating; this is an insight into how this person treats their partners. Especially if they've been suspicious of their previous partners at an odd level, this person will accuse and hone in on accusations down the line, and perhaps the accusations may not be as minor as cheating.

Case study anonymous

A young woman reached out, telling her side of an emotionally abusive relationship with her boyfriend—a lengthy relationship of 13 years in total with the continuance of harassment thereafter. The very last year they were together, she was trying to find an escape route out of their toxic relationship. He proceeded to make her life a living hell; The first assault was when I had just given birth. A few days later, he decided to party, and I was extremely disappointed. I wanted to leave, and he pinned me through me to the fridge, and I almost lost consciousness. I reported him soon after, and they did not arrest him until 1 year later, maybe. My mistake was staying in this toxic relationship. I found a message on his phone sent to an ex, stating that he would have rather had my son with her, and he deleted everything that I found. He then proceeded to gaslight me into thinking I was delusional and denied everything. He went on to accuse me of cheating and spread false truths about me to everyone. He never took me anywhere; neither did my kids or his, and we never travelled. He never showed an interest in anything besides drinking and getting high on cocaine every day for 12 years. The relationship was summarised by constant arguments, hate and jealousy. We slept separately for years, and we basically lived our own separate lives. We lost our oldest child, who went to live with his biological mom when he was approximately 13, because of him. I was twice accused of falsely hitting him, and then he claimed the drug use accusation against me. It turned out he was the one positive for drugs, and I was negative, and he almost lost his job at the school district because of it. The accusations were revenge for putting him in jail when he did nothing wrong, according to him.

I know it was purposefully done as when he was in prison, I called, and he said he wouldn't help and I'd never see my son again. I was distanced for years and constantly accused of cheating. He would break doors, follow me and instigate situations with me up to my breaking point, then would say it's all me and that I'm crazy. Prior to the breakup, a year and a half before, I was making up my mind to leave for good. I was working on leaving to get help or support, but he found out about it. He then came to the point of leaving me after having a serious conversation about change and about me being unhappy. He changed for 2 months just to fall back into the same old pattern and then left me at my worst moment as I have debilitating medical issues in which I am partially handicapped. He says the car isn't mine and that I never lived here, and that the problem has been me the whole time, and he has just realised. He bought me the car for my birthday, but it's no longer mine, so he wants me to leave, and I'm not allowed to grieve or to be upset. When I'm stuck in the restroom or I can't move, he leaves me there because he doesn't have to help. He accused me of domestic violence for a slap that happened to defend myself and had my son record only me. I have a restraining order and can't get emergency shelter. My middle son is staying with him; his biological son had to move out to his mom's because he doesn't like him and vice-versa. It was reported at his old school about the incident where he tried putting his hands on his son and my son. I am emotionally messed up dealing with all of this, and yet I'm the criminal while he laughs and sabotages me every chance he gets.

Now, even turning our son against me, who is only 14 years old. I believe he pitted him against me and continues to brainwash him. I'm distraught that he has destroyed every bit of me, and I don't know what to do.

Forgiveness

To forgive at a magnitude of this level is almost not an option. These situations of chaos will test your connection with any form of forgiveness. We should stay guarded and remain at a safe distance where possible. Our entire mindset will naturally be caught up in negativity, either through self-talk or self-deprecating feelings. To go through PTSD, Depression and Suicidal ideation; and when we pass most of the hurdles, how do you forgive? We need to find or look for the best in people; they know what they know, and they do as they do. To not become supply again but to move on without being consumed by hate. People are complex, sure we could isolate ourselves from people and remain safe, never to be hurt again. This only compounds our problems, and disowning negative emotions only worsens the effect they have on us.

> "Many people also know from their own experience how easily and quickly an intimate relationship can turn from a source of pleasure to a source of pain" (Tolle, E,1997)

Toxic relationships can destroy us, but an even better approach would be to become the best version of ourselves. We need to focus and love thy self; this is the only relationship that we have. If we love ourselves enough, we will never tolerate cruelty again.

A toxic individual wouldn't last a second in our lives, and if you're in a horrible relationship, love yourself enough to get out! Get out and talk about your experiences, and help others. Bring awareness about the situation into the public domain. Awareness is currently lacking in this area. Write that blog, make that video and upload that content. Support each other, show your resilience and pivot right by the attacks in any way you can.

If you need to stay in solitude, do so, but do it at a happy, functional pace. Do not cut yourself off from society, thinking everyone is evil or life is against you. If you are on the receiving end of the attack phase at present, stay alert and prepare for battle.

Keep files, documents, evidence or anything that may be of value to your side. If needed, purchase a body cam and conceal it in clothing you wear to catch any threats or manipulation, etc.; if you miss your kids, know that the situation is a vicious tool to make you feel this low. Stay strong for them.

This is a sick game, and the worst thing you can do is get back with a control creep who thinks nothing is worthy of you. Going back into a toxic relationship to see your children could backfire; the same situation, more children, for example.

Be wise, meet new people, attend that class, and follow your instincts.

If you would like to share your story of abuse, coercion and punishment through the Court System or Parental Alienation; used to destroy how you and your children feel;

or anything related to being manipulated and falsely accused, visit www.youvecrossedtheborderline.com

Case Study

Derek

I made the mistake of sleeping with the Devil. The pregnancy went as well as could be expected, but as soon as my son was born, it was like a switch went off. She had her baby and no longer needed a man. When my son was only a few months old, his mother threatened to take him and jump off a bridge. Then she disappeared. For 5 days. I was in panic mode. Called the cops. But when I called the family for help, I was ghosted..Then I knew they were up to something. I've never hit a woman or child in my life, yet this woman played it up. After the 5th day, she finally answered the phone and told me not to come home. I told her I wanted to make sure my son was OK, and I didn't want to go to the police, but that's what I ended up doing. Meanwhile, she's already at the police station, trying to get an emergency restraining order against me, which is always granted. I was kicked out of my house and was not allowed to get any of my belongings. This was Friday night. The hearing was on Monday. Over the weekend, the ex and her cronies took all of my life's possessions, except a few pairs of torn sweatpants, and she put them in a storage unit. Since my name isn't "Evil Narcissist", they wouldn't give me my stuff but encouraged me to bid on them when they came up for auction.

At court, the ex is being consoled by a therapist/court employee.. The judge was a female who clearly, hated men. I raised my hand to ask a question and got SCREAMED at.

Again, I have never hit a woman or child in my life, yet they were painting me as this violent psychopath. I raised my hand to ask another question, and the judge yelled, YOU'RE NOT GOING TO SEE THAT BABY FOR A YEAR!!!! And that was it. She was able to get my son 100% and THEN got herself set up on the ol welfare system, all the benefits.

She lied through her teeth about the earnings she made every year, under the table. She was able to convince the next judge, a year later, that I was this horrible person;

otherwise, why would that first judge order a 1-year no-contact? SOMEHOW, she got my son added to the R.O., and they adjusted it to be a "Forever restraining order". Since there was an existing RO, I would give my child support payments to my lawyer, and he'd get them to her lawyer. I was never late. One day, my lawyer called and said that this was going to be a long, uphill battle. And he knew that I was on a shoestring budget. I was paying him $200 every 2 weeks. He called and said he wanted twice the payment and twice the frequency..I had a contract with him, and never was late or missed a lawyer's payment.

All of my wages went to lawyer's fees and child support. I told the scumbag lawyer that I couldn't and we already had a contract. So, what he did was "forget" to give 2 of my child support payments to the ex's lawyer. I'm being held in contempt, and the Judge didn't give a damn about the dates on the money orders. Out came the cuffs and leg irons.

I went to a maximum security prison for 5 days. 5 days of hell. When I got out, my house had been broken into. What little money I had was gone. Photos and toys I bought for my son were stolen. Tools I needed for work were stolen.
Anytime I went to work, the ex and her cronies would break into my house and steal what little I had. This happened 3 or 4x a week. Cops wouldn't do anything because it was a civil matter.

One time, I wrote a rude FB post about this same issue, and the ex convinced the DA that I violated the Restraining order on 3 different counts. But I hadn't. I never named her. Never contacted her. Never told anyone to contact her, yet again I was hauled off in leg irons for another 5 days in maximum security prison. The hearings went on for more than a year. The stress and anxiety wore me out. They were trying to put me in jail for 5 years..That way the ex could prove her gaslight was true. I beat all of the charges, and she even brought my son to court. He's now 15-16 years old. (It took over a year) She brought him in the hopes that he would see me dragged off in chains.

She's conditioned my son to think that I abandoned him. That I didn't love him. It's all wrong. My son was stolen from me, and the system is designed to screw the fathers. Some mothers get screwed too, but it's mostly fathers. It's been 18 years since I got to hug and kiss my little boy, who's now a young man. She's twisted that poor guy so badly that his Facebook profile even says, "Sometimes I joke about my invisible Dad"..

That's pretty messed up. That poor guy had gone his whole life thinking that I never wanted him. His Mom mentally abused him to the point that he's never going to contact me. He hates me, and he was trained to hate me. Being alienated feels like mourning the death of a child who is still alive. There's a hole in the middle of my chest that will never be filled. No 1st birthday memories. No school shows. No Christmases, no holidays. Nothing. Parental Alienation is child abuse. There's no doubt about it.

Content Creation:

Speak Your Truth

When endeavouring in this field, best of luck; this quick section explains some advice that should be mentioned before you step upon your journey. Don't bring your personal politics or religion into the space you are carving out. This issue of parental alienation, which is tied so much with false allegations, needs a unilateral audience or understanding.

If one sides with a political ideology, it instantly blocks exposure to the other side of the political spectrum. It shouldn't be like that. It may even seem childish, but that's how things seem to be in this disagreeable world. Religion is another big one, there are over 4000 religions, faith groups or denominations. There is no need to cut off the other faiths; everyone that breathes needs to be informed of this message.

Court systems and child organisations around the globe need to reform their approach to sensitive family matters. The nuclear family is under attack; moreover, a separated family dynamic, including parental alienation, is promoted.

I implore you to reach out to people and create your own content. If it's videos that can reach out to the masses, do it that way, either with personal experiences or viral clips of abuse. Welcome your audience into your life and make a difference. Show the effects of false allegations or parental alienation. Write that blog, book, article or story. Help build a team and create a course to educate people on how to divorce or separate amicably. Teach the masses how to co-parent.

Support and share other content; it will take one viral person or post, celebrity or group to help establish this traumatic abuse as a household name. The social groups we have to help victims of abuse aren't enough; the only preventative measure would be a structural change within the legal system and beyond to process data with an audit approach.

A child brought into this life shouldn't be recruited as a puppet to hurt the feelings of another. Guardianship should be reviewed with how we implement it to parents; mental health screenings should be in place if needed for high-priority cases of parental abuse, which is what alienation is.

The perpetrators of false allegations of any kind need to be held accountable and face some penalty. If that's signing on a register at a local police station or a fine, something needs to be put in place. Case officials and staff that deal with such matters need to be up-skilled or retrained in these roles. These are highly powerful roles with dire consequences involved for children and parents alike. All work related to the family should be assessed by two completely different organisations that can develop different points of view, almost checking the work done before them with the ability to rewrite the narrative that is taking place. We need new, up-to-date services that meet alienation head-on, with an understanding of what coercive control is.

The implementation of change has to start. If there's any doubt or evidence contrary to what is current, a thorough evaluation of the case needs to be conducted. Court wait times need to come down; if we have reform of the current structure, it is possible these wait times will naturally dissolve. If a story of abuse is vetted and properly probed, the likelihood of falsified data reaching a courtroom drops significantly.

We need great minds out there to come together and lay the groundwork for alienation awareness. We are currently seeing people who have been that alienated child growing up sharing their stories. However, as of writing, there is no penalty for this or repercussions for such blatant behaviour.

The legal system shouldn't be able to be manipulated or leveraged by any one man or woman. There is a loss of respect for the legal system, this structure is rigged almost in favour of drama and traumatic events to keep fluctuating.

ACKNOWLEDGEMENTS

All stories in this book are painfully real ;

The cover-art (graffiti sentence) used for the cover of this book is also painfully real ;

I took that picture personally from the family courthouse, the address of Dolphin House Essex Street East Temple Bar Family Court, in a cubicle in the men's room. That man was reaching out to other men with a pen in hand, and his life was all but destroyed.

Reading it made my eyes tear as I knew I was walking along the same path as him and many others.

His message was of hopelessness but perseverance, his struggle, his pain, his life!

That message on that wooden cubicle wall as he awaits his fate, a broken man reaching out to others in the same line of fire, that message was the beginning of; you've crossed the borderline

This Book

First and foremost, is dedicated to the shells of the abuse victims across the world who have faced ongoing trauma from loved ones. I want to dedicate this to the people who couldn't remain on this earth and instead took the exit. The people that are gone, Rest In Peace- and the people who continue to persevere.

Whose lives have been shattered by the following;

False Allegations, Parental Alienation, Coercive Control, Police/Courtroom Harassment, Abusive Relationships, Victims of Manipulation and Flying Monkeys.

I also want to dedicate this Book to Sajib Chandra Talukder, who passed away in 2024 from a heart attack in the middle of the Bangladesh riots. Rest In Peace

I want to thank every person who has Cluster B and has been self-aware enough to the point of seeking help. The mental struggle is admirable to go against the paradigm of thinking and refuse to tolerate the disorder. I want to thank my baby for never forgetting me after one and a half years of parental alienation.

I want to thank every person who submitted their case studies for the making of this Book. This Book wouldn't be complete without every one of you. These case studies highlight teachable areas of devastating life situations that regular people can relate to. This can happen to anybody, and we all remain fighting to bring about awareness. I want to thank my family, past friends, and every life event or person who has crossed paths with me. I want to thank my extended family in Ireland and Bangladesh. Thank you for the support; it means everything to me.

I also want to mention the people who wanted to share their stories of false allegations and parental alienation but couldn't.

They couldn't, but they all had the same reason for refusing. It didn't matter what county, race, religion, gender, or ethnicity; they all had the same response.

The response was that they would have to relive this trauma. They would have to bring up all the memories and feelings of old. The thoughts of injustice were too much to relive. They would rather keep it buried, as they would say. Abused and Destroyed, what transpired and happened at the hands of their loved one;

They would rather take it to the grave with them.

This Book is for each and every one of you.

Case Study Ibraheem

I had an epiphany to write a book back in 2015, but I failed to put pen to paper and deeply regret it. I plan to write more books under the Psychology, Self-help or False Allegations banner. I want to bring areas of injustice into the court of public opinion, such as Court Stagnation, Court Incompetence, Parental Alienation, Narcissistic Abuse, False Allegations, Exonerations of the innocent, the inner workings of Personality Disorders and Coercive Control. Including many other areas related to the harassment of people.

This entire experience exposed me to the Family Court mess we currently have; I had never heard the term Parental Alienation before my case. False Allegations were the last thoughts that crossed my mind; now, it is a passion to extract the information and highlight the areas surrounding it to others.

This experience has put me into the fight for challenging current legislation;

This book was partly written in a Dublin city homeless hostel; I grew up with very humble begingings. A Run-down neighbourhood with lower class income. Plenty of drama and issues growing up that most people cannot relate to. Similar to Cluster B, who had hardships growing up of abuse and neglect i too was not exempt from these struggles; That is not to diminish anything that anyone else suffered through, but to highlight the fact I was not perched up on some pedestal- overlooking this group commenting on struggles I know nothing about. I, too, faced challenges more extreme than most while growing up, tolerating abuse in a variety of forms. I lived a journey exposed to mental health issues for as long as I can remember. Fascinated with the limits and motivations of such disorders, I delved into the field of psychology early on. The last year and a half, I have been put through a campaign of harassment. I have faced the suffering of parental alienation while getting harassed by police, arrests and callouts, false allegations and phoney court orders. This campaign of harassment will never end, which put my back against the wall, so to speak, cornered; facing attacks from multiple angles.

The attacks from this campaign of harassment have changed me. In the last couple of years, I have faced enough manipulation to last me for a lifetime. In a coercive controlling relationship, it turned into an assassination attempt after attempt, all using sneaky manipulation tactics such as situational-attacks, all to further this coercion. The trappings of this chaotic drama I found myself in have inspired and propelled me to write this book.

The number of people who have contacted me and have gone through similar or worse experiences inspired me. The corrupt legal system and how these people are getting away with this exploitation and abuse would impel me to expose these areas.

I am currently in multiple cases, I will be as transparent as possible for learnable reasons. For each case or allegation made against me, I have obtained the court transcripts to help in any future court case that should ensue. No names will be mentioned to protect identities, and anything I do mention, I have the legal proof; or it occurred, making this case study legal without any danger of further legal action.

Love Bombing was the manipulation tactic that set up every other manipulation manoeuvre that was used on me. To get to that point I will mention some of the vulnerabilities that this technique exploited within me.

As I was in my early twenties, I fell in love with my long-term girlfriend. This relationship shaped me to become a better person in the long run. We had it all, and it was as though she was my soul mate, and honestly, she was. Ignorant at the time to how life can be chaotic as we seemed untouchable, we seemed to have it all; it brought about an element of ignorance, which is bliss. She was into modelling and won pageants. She was a very humble, loving, beautiful person, the soul of an angel. Eventually, she became pregnant, and with this ignorance of untouchability, I made an error concerning my life choices.

The baby was terminated because of my stupidity. Instant regret surged through me. They seemed to do the procedure at a rapid speed. I recall going for a walk but stopping at a pay phone and calling the clinic to change my mind and keep the baby, but it was too late; the procedure was finished. She didn't want to go through with the procedure in the first place, and I remember her face once it was complete, and we were leaving. It was as if this beautiful angel had her soul ripped out, and it was all my fault.

How could I be so stupid? How could I not see the signs of my surroundings? When we arrived at the abortion clinic, as we were in the reception or waiting around, the atmosphere was wicked. Bloodcurdling screams could be heard from patients' rooms, and sadness and despair coloured the atmosphere. Loud crying, people consoling, and absolute screams of horror, similar to the depictions of hell or burning in the hellfire.

How could I not figure out that this was the reality that I allowed to take over myself and the love of my life? From that moment on, not only has my baby not come into existence, but nothing else good ever came into existence, either. It seemed like everything just went nowhere; it tormented and psychologically damaged us both. The relationship fell apart, as did everything else in my life. From there on, I was haunted by occasional nightmares. Accompanied by visions throughout random days, visions I could see each time I focused or closed my eyes in thought. These were nightmares and visions of a fetus.

This fetus imagery haunted me, and it was the tipping point for me to crack completely. I began to enter more intently into psychology, metaphysics, and the study of the mind and meditation.

All I could do was study constantly to make sense of everything I was going through. Somewhere in my studies, I came across a teaching telling me to bring forth any negative image that I cannot get out of my mind; bring it forth through meditation and be with it, remain with it, and ask it why it's there. So I did; I meditated each night with this fetus. I did not even need to use visualisation; this fetus in my mind's eye was already there waiting for me.

I loved it and apologised to it, giving love to my baby, who isn't here now, over my decision-making. This event traumatised me, and the abortion procedure did not even happen to me; it happened to her. From then on, all I did was study, reading as many self-development books as possible. I studied psychology and the inner workings of the mind and behaviour. Trying desperately not to relive any erroneous beliefs or adopt any fallacy in my thinking going forward. This experience also affected how I see relationships and tarnished any love from then on. No one could live up to my ex. Nobody was genuine like her, so the bar I had raised couldn't be reached. There would never be another, so my standards were always too high. I had a few relationships here and there, but I was always cautious about having another baby, making sure it would never happen. It's almost like I wanted to vet my significant other to see if she was the right woman to settle down with and have a baby.

The duration of this unspoken vetting process was at least a year or over. No sign of a worthy female, I remained away from fatherhood for the following years. Was I being too harsh? Are my standards set too high? Why should I be comparing others to my ex when they can't fill her shoes? It's unfair. Soon, this angst I felt over losing a baby would be used against me.

Fast forward a decade, I began to let my guard down with whom I was meeting. This vetting process no longer applied as I was starting to get old now; perhaps I had to loosen up my grip and give someone a chance. It all started after a complex shift in work. This job was depleting and exhausting and wasn't for me. I was planning to switch roles soon. I took a visit to the local 24/7 petrol station to purchase some cigarettes as a way to cope with the stressful work shifts. I noticed a girl there mid-twenties, very flamboyant and loud. She was also there, to buy cigarettes, waiting in line. This was after the COVID lockdowns, so people have only recently been out of isolation.

Another passerby ahead of me had a dog on a lead, and this girl was behind me in the queue. This unusual girl dressed in shorts and a hoody started crawling in front of me in the direction of the dog, with the dog licking her mouth and face, making a bit of a scene. I made my purchase at the hatch, went around, and sat on the wall outside of the petrol station to light up a cigarette.

This girl walked in the opposite direction across the road, and I could see her glance over at me. She reaches the footpath, and it appears she second-thinks something. She walks directly back towards my direction across the road and sits up on the wall beside me. She began talking, and I saw she had her hoody zipped down slightly, showing cleavage. Talkative, so we talk on the wall, smoking. We must've sat there for about twenty minutes. She told me she's a Muslim and she likes me. I seem nice, not like other white people.

The term white people she would say frequently. I began to notice her flirtatiousness as she offered me to come back to her place. Not even knowing each other's names, I thought, okay, maybe we would gather that information through conversation later.

Once I arrived the flirting was on display again, with her getting quite physical this time. I mentioned for her to come to my place instead, as something didn't seem right with her and her motives. We came to my place, where we had sex almost instantly and spent the night together. The morning came, and I shook her slightly, mentioning that I had to leave for work; she had to go. She didn't want to leave and remained in my bed. She said do you know my name and I had to say I didn't know it.

We talked and exchanged numbers and names, and then I went to work. When I arrived back to the rented apartment, she was still in my bed. This girl lives across the road from where I live, not even a one-minute walk.

I noticed unusual patterns of her not leaving or waiting for me. I don't usually get into a relationship with a fling or a one-night stand, but that's what this developed into. For each work shift, she would ring me and tell me how much she missed me. I would go home from work to shower and relax, and she would want me to go straight to her place. I would say give me an hour or so to get ready, which she would vehemently refuse. Almost unable to wait till I showered, rested my feet, and relaxed as if I had to remain with her constantly. A week or so passed until she wanted me to move in with her. We could live in her one-bedroom apartment, I just have to leave the rented place where I was staying. This means we can settle down and be together more. She would call me her soulmate and tell me how much she loved me. While waiting for a response, she would encourage me to tell her I love her this much and that much with a sort of child-like vocabulary.

This was quite odd for me as I don't usually break the barrier of the vetting process with girls. Something about this barrage of Hiroshimas of Love, that, I was getting bombed with lessened the guard I would usually have held up. We both shared a key to the apartment; this way, we could save a hundred or two each month. Rather than announce that I'm living there to her letting agency. Thinking nothing of this, I was okay with it as I wanted to be as genuine as possible with this person. This action was methodical and would be used to manipulate me later.

We had hopes of moving into a better apartment. She would harass this letting agent guy at the time, and I recall she was calling to try to see if there was any availability. She attempted to call his number; then simply said he's after blocking me; how do you know this? I asked.

She knew what it sounded like, to listen to a blocked tone. This was quite odd, a person who knew the difference between a number blocked, a phone switched off or out of service, on a call, etc, when calling a phone number. People have blocked her so many times that she knew just by a generic tone what it sounded like to be blocked.

She would tell me stories of feeling neglected or isolated. Trouble with her family, especially her father. She spoke sexually or sexualised everything at times and had a run of bad relationships that went nowhere. Men are male chauvinist pigs, treating her terribly with abusive attitudes. Why are people so mean?

One guy she was with kicked her out of his car. Physically kicked her right onto the grass verge on the hard shoulder. This was on the busiest motorway in Ireland, the M50. She told me this and so many other stories either growing up or just unlucky with her circumstances or lovers. Including a BBL Brazilian Butt Lift procedure that they botched in turkey costing 7000 euro. Even worse, they posted her pictures online without consent to advertise the procedure.

Soon, I began to feel sorry for her. What if all her faith in men can be restored? What if all the mistreatment and wrong could be made right? She would be protected and honoured, and we could settle down. She would appreciate it so much, I would make her happy and not use her like the other guys. I had only known her for a couple of weeks, and she kept pestering me for a baby.

Immediately, she wanted a baby, or ten babies, as she put it. Ignoring any red flags, I was completely off guard about this one. Deep down, I, too, yearned for a baby to symbolically restore what I threw away early on in my life. I began to notice some behavioural issues with her, including up-and-down emotions, clinginess, and a child-like way of acting. It was almost as if she was a twenty-five-year-old child; the dishes or cups would never be washed. It was a chore she simply couldn't do.

So I began to do these chores, along with cleaning and washing clothes and practically all the housework. It was as if she was the patient and I was the carer. Over in Ireland, if a person has a mental illness or is physically disabled, it's not uncommon for them to have a carer. A friend or relative who looks after you, does chores, cooks, etc.

We spent every waking hour together, and that dynamic would stay the same. A few weeks after meeting her, she was ecstatic; she was pregnant. Jumping for joy in a shopping centre full of people, she used the ladies' room to take the pregnancy test. She couldn't even wait to get home to use it. I wasn't jumping for joy at all I felt a bit off, but that's expected with the history I had. What could go wrong, right?

Things moved fast; because of her culture, we needed to marry, and I needed to convert and have a name change. I am already a spiritual person, so this didn't bother me. I would be the best husband I can be. So, with her Muslim Bangladesh culture, I would try my best to adopt clothing, wording, diet, lifestyle, etc.

I changed my name to my current pen name, Ibraheem. I began learning the language of Bangla, a complicated language to grasp. I would have notepads and writings full of translations to learn and get used to. Then she threw away all of this work; why would she do this? It was as if she did not want me to know the language huh?

I cared for her, was there for her, and made her pregnancy as fulfilling as possible. She wanted a kitten, and we got one. Then we got some more, and it started to feel like a home. She couldn't cook, and I remember her crying and whimpering because she couldn't cook a meal. I found it adorable and didn't see anything wrong with this behaviour.

Some behaviour did catch my eye, though; in fact, I thought she was bipolar at the beginning. The fluctuating emotions were the most noticeable. Her worst demon was her fierce impulsiveness. She told me a story from a couple of months prior when she would lose control and bang her head against the wall.

Possibly going through struggles in life and retaliating or self-deprecating by smashing her forehead back and forth against a wall. She shaved her whole head off and was really going through it, and then she met me with the hair grown back somewhat. I knew I was dealing with a disorder, and I did not mind. This disorder will only be a challenge, but one we can get past together.

I was naive; I thought I could support her, and we could look out for each other. I was not going to let a disorder change my motivations of care, kindness and love. I will tolerate the outbursts or the suspicion, for example, and I will be her rock, her shoulder to cry on and the support she lacked early on in life.

I didn't think much of it, and in fact, I felt sorry for her and wanted to be there for her even more. I ensured her that she would never bang her head against a wall as long as I was here. She would live a peaceful and loving life, as that's all I want to give. I want to provide the best part of myself to someone and make up for any people I failed in the past. So, time went by; in the second trimester, her symptoms were completely on display, but the pregnancy also covered them up. She was a strange character; everyone around her knew she had something. She couldn't take care of herself. It was either myself or when her family came over to look after her. Her mother called her a Jinn, the Islamic word for a demon.

We spent every waking hour indoors together, joined at the hip. I was studying psychology, and she wouldn't let me physically go to college. She would not let me go to the library to study, which was just across the road. She displayed a weird clinginess.

She would say bizarre things, and strangely, it felt like she meant it, but I would brush them off as banter. For example, if the mailman was at the door, I would run down and get the post. She would say I took too long; what am I up to? When I introduced my older sister to her and had begun regular calls, she would say things such as that we are close and she suspected me and my sister were intimate before or in a relationship. I had a school friend who would call every few days; she would claim we were very close, insinuating something. The kitten liked me more, but she got jealous of that, insinuating something again. A look walking by someone on a street, a clerk in a shop, a phone call I did not answer. Unfortunately, with red flag after flag up about how weird this relationship was, she was pregnant. I couldn't just leave; maybe I could fix this. Perhaps we just need to have this baby and settle down.

It will be a brand-new experience for both of us. The Love Bombing stopped after a couple of months, and it evolved into her demonstrating abusive tendencies, screaming and hollering at the most minute of things. Trying to calm her down was unsuccessful, and she abused people by screaming at them at random. This behaviour would not dissipate, and when she stopped taking her depression tablets, it spiralled and got worse. She was taking Fluzac; her GP prescribed it before I met her. It is for major depressive episodes or obsessive-compulsive disorder. She never got diagnosed or wanted to.

She could not take accountability for anything whatsoever. What followed throughout this weird relationship was no silence or calm, just gaslighting, shifting emotions and coercive control. I never left her side and quit my job at her request just to be confronted with accusations. If somebody were to text me or like my status on social media, then I'm cheating or thinking about cheating. If I am ten minutes late after going to the shops, it would be a considerable investigation. I began to feel smothered. I tolerated much of the abuse, knowing that it wasn't her who was abusing me; rather, it was the condition.

I looked more into borderline personality disorder, and it was like reading her biography. Every single line on the pages of these books sounded just like her. At first, like most cases, bipolar was what it looked like. She has all the hallmarks of Malignant Narcissistic Personality Disorder and has nine out of nine symptoms of Borderline Personality Disorder.

I read borderline book classics such as 'Walking on Eggshells, I Hate You Don't Leave Me, Splitting, Cognitive Behaviour Therapy for BPD, and many others. This was an aspect of psychology I knew somewhat, but in my branch of psychology, the personality disorders were quite different. I used to be an advocate student of sub-personalities, such as the work of Hal Stone and Sidra Winkelman. This work is reminiscent of Gestalt, a branch of psychology founded in the 20th century. Cluster B was fairly new, but the characteristics seemed eye-opening as the symptoms and the behaviour specificity was 100% accurate. This made me wonder to what extent these books will be accurate. Some of these books briefly mentioned false allegations and the borderline's willingness to battle it out in court. Occasionally, I froze, thinking at least I was not there; surely, it would never go there.

The coercive control, dominance, manipulation and tantrums ensued, and now, because of the new baby, there was no exit route. It never did go back to the love bomb days. This was a well-elaborated act to loosen my grip on aspects of life and playoff my innermost vulnerabilities. Using everything against me, including my child. She could see how much happiness the baby had brought me. She planned to break my heart in every way, and the baby was just a tool to execute that.

Then I get threatened by something to the effect of "I'll call the police and pretend you hit me or said this or that, then you'll see" Immediately, I froze once more, reminiscent of the psychology books. She mentioned it one other time, until the following year, just before making her false allegations. I tried brushing it off as more erratic behavior and stayed with her. She has anger issues, throws tantrums every other day, and gets jealous over fictitious things.

I was like her carer, and she was like my patient; with so much time spent together, I became desensitised to her crazy words. Time went by, and she got worse by the day, especially without the medication.

Everything was a manipulation strategy and it was quite evident she was a control freak. She would use homelessness as a constant threat of fear over my head, should things not go her way. She was starting to get aggressive, abusing everything in her path: me, her family, and even the little kittens. She strangled one kitten she mentioned, one time, not to death but for brief intervals. She kicked the other kitten around the place, he used to get it the worst. He always looked so sad, and eventually, she had an idea to sell them all. As sad as it was, I thought it was a great idea. They deserve a good home, and this is far from it.

Her impulsiveness got the worst of her, and she was not able to function and feed the infant child. This child is three years old in May 2025 and he is still fed by breast milk. He cannot eat solid food and these courts don't see any red flags with this. He eats yoghurt and has some breast milk, and that's about it. If something is made it's in puree. I have seen this impulsiveness in action; I have witnessed her shoving spoons down the baby's throat at a fast rate, making him puke and gag, resulting in a complete aversion to the spoon. I have witnessed this woman hold a 2-year-old baby on his back with her knees over his arms, so he is looking up at the ceiling crying while she's scooping food and shoving it down his throat. Force-feeding, till vomits, is the usual meal for my son. He vomits and is sick several times each month.

I had him eating, and he had a great rapport with me. At the time I thought I would stop her and correct her each time I saw this behaviour. Unfortunately, as I think back, I should have just hit the record button. This act of a moral compass I would show probably spooked her into getting rid of me, to further abuse this baby. That is all this personality type knows: abuse to others, nothing else. Pretty soon, my first introduction to parental alienation would arrive. She kicked me out and made me homeless, which became a recurring threat unless I met her unrealistic demands. 2023 in the summer, she kicked me out of the place that we shared. She would have all my money since we met and I thought I could trust her with anything as that's what a relationship is formulated on.

This was during the time she started calling the police every other day, even while I slept. This behaviour was weird, but I just left her and went to the UK, homeless, but I was resourceful. I volunteered for a reception role at a backpackers hostel in Bath, England. I volunteered in exchange for staying in the lively, socially active hostel.

I knew I just had to wait until her anger diminished but I also knew that could be weeks or even months. She would occasionally call me and even start getting jealous of imaginary girls around me, other workers who also volunteered. She then would mention she wanted me back, she was too sick or unwell to take care of the baby. I acted like nothing bothered me, and truly I was enjoying myself in England. Perhaps I was unconsciously using the grey rock method.

I recall her mentioning the baby and how I have not seen him for the past few months, "You don't even care, do you?". I knew what she meant; The parental alienation I had experienced in these couple of months was a mere tactic to get me to start accepting the intolerable behaviour. She knew what she was doing and decided to call it quits, the reason being that maybe another baby would come out of it.

This was my introduction to parental alienation. I missed the baby, I missed his first steps. I thought maybe she realised through this break that her behaviour was out of control. I decided to go back after a week and didn't bring up anything that caused this drama; I acted like nothing ever happened. There would be no point in going back to her just to argue and get to the bottom of who's right and who's wrong. She would occasionally say the phrase that she "was just trying to humble me".

This woman begged me back, but when I got back, my introduction to Flying Monkeys would also be on the horizon. She started making phone calls in front of me, explaining to these flying monkeys that I begged her back and pleaded with her, so she took me back. After the second one of these calls mentioning the same rhetoric ended, I looked at her and explained, "I never said that?". She snarled and proceeded to walk into the other room to continue her phone calls.

We tried getting along, and I was back to the same routine of doing everything for her and the baby. While she stayed in bed and scrolled through social media. This relationship would soon become conditional, she wanted me to buy her another BBL and to have another baby with her. Time went by and we were going about our days as normal, and I was quite apprehensive about the baby idea that she was suggesting.

Then the regular Threats would begin. One threat was to have the baby with her, and there was a time frame. This baby was already named. If it was a girl, which she was keen on, the baby would be named Khawla. The constant threat of homelessness or to make my life a living hell would occur should I not have baby Khawla, with no questions asked. Her behaviour was so obnoxious, intolerable and quite destructive that I did have questions.

This impulsiveness would make her act fast, this anger was explosive. Normal days with no drama were scarce. Days would usually be filled with chaos. This could involve pushing me with the baby in my arms several times; one of these times, I recorded.

These times were tough, and the behaviour was chaotic and dangerous, so I did have a go at negotiating-this baby. I said that we would wait a couple of months to see how things play out. I want another baby myself but under one condition. It has to be a happy home which, by all means, this situation was a melting pot. She couldn't agree to it; she vehemently rejected marriage counselling or seeing a health professional, even to get some antidepressants. In her mind, nothing was wrong, and how dare somebody not tolerate her daily abuse.

There was a time limit in question here; she said a month or two. If she was not pregnant in a month or two, my life would be made hell. At the time, it made me more apprehensive. I have never been in a situation where a Gun is pointed at my temple, metaphorically speaking.

My wait-and-see-if-we-can-have-a-happy-family idea for the children to grow up in was repulsive to her. The ease of the living-hell route would be executed quite easily; remember the flying monkeys have all been set up in advance, months probably over a year of triangulation.

If I had let the coercive control win, it would have led to an alternative narrative to relay to the monkeys. "Oh, I'm pregnant, so I will stay just for the kids", or something along those lines. Or she would probably start pretending woe is her, she is trapped with another baby now.

I was approached by one of her irate tantrums because I had turned the heating off the night prior. Of course, this was just a smoke screen for the real reason, the real reason being she wanted to derail any plans positive whatsoever. I was getting ready to view a place with a two-bedroom for both of us, an alternative living space. We could be landlords and live in one property and have the option to rent out the other. It triggered an abandonment wound within her, and this tantrum was fierce. Five minutes in, she started mentioning ringing the police, and I saw her making up story after story out loud, verbalizing what she would or could say? I start recording the interaction. This was a one-way argument of her screaming and me not responding, just calmly stating words of agreement or saying things to defuse the lopsided argument.

I was quite terrified of what she would say or do. I know that the recording of the interaction irritated her more, but I couldn't pretend I was not concerned by the outcomes of her words and actions. This lasted a half hour; Once I left, thinking maybe she would cool down, she never did. After concluding that another baby with her was not what I wanted, she got a narcissistic injury.

Then it all happened: I was served court papers. She hit me with a protection order, costing me a year and a half and counting of parental alienation. All the police visits to the home for no reason were an attempt to make it look like something had happened. This was a set-up from the start or at least an alternative path should I reject offering her the narcissistic supply, that is in the form of another baby.

For example, she would text me hundreds of texts saying nasty things, wanting me to kill myself, etc, and the one text I reply is isolated and the one hundred before it is blatantly erased. For the entire relationship, after the love bombing phase was over, I was hit with every manipulation tactic possible; my mental health was affected. Mainly, the usage of the elements against me, such as the homeless surroundings and then the threat of jail.

Motivated by nothing more than to send me to prison, she concocted an idiotic story. But any story is good enough to implement parental alienation, and any court would gladly stamp it into approval, even if it stated that I was the real mastermind behind 9/11, which is what it was close to saying.

Nobody cared how absurd the hearsay was. These judges would glance at the court order, if you were lucky. The family court was doing its job, as incompetent as ever. The court order stated that I am a Jihadi Terrorist. I am a beheader, and I am in some terrorist unit or organisation. She was never quizzed on this nor did she have to elaborate any more details. I'm guessing that if pressed, she will say the Islamic State of Iraq and the Levant. The fact that she was not pressed or a simple questioning was conducted inspired the subpart Questioning in the chapter Easily Exploitable Family Courts. This notion was given to the courts that I would behead her over the sink and that I am this dangerous terrorist.

She took all my money each week and even stole a couple thousand euros from me. The money was saved, and also was the money from selling the kittens. She stole all my items without regard or resolve; this was done as a way to bait me into breaching this phoney terrorist protection order. Or as a way to have me coming back, a reason or to try induce me to have a possible change of heart, to go back and fall in line.

This was all purposely driven to hurt feelings or to bring about an intimidation factor. I would get constant calls every other day, usually at 22:30, which I suspected were from the police headquarters. Each evening and night, the calls would surge through. These numbers were missed calls and becoming curious, I decided to ring one of them back. Sure enough, it was the police or Gardaí in Ireland, so I talked to them eventually to see what the hell was going on. They mentioned to come down to the station, "we have a safety order" from your ex, The shock struck me, a whirlwind of emotions.

Never in trouble with the police and completely ignorant of the court order process. I collected this court order from the station, and I soon found out that it was really a parental alienation order. The stuff on it was like a child had penned their imagination down with fantasy fiction. The issue here was that it didn't matter in the eyes of the courts or the police.

The police knew as they were speaking to me that I've never broken any law or breached any order, but it's their job description to follow protocol and make these calls, as they were also subject to receiving calls slandering me. Roughly in the ballpark of twenty-five calls from the police I received, I imagine she called them more. Police visits; around five or six, not counting when they were looking from house to house to find me after the first arrest.

This person is trying as hard as any mere mortal can try to get me locked up in prison, to have me rubbing shoulders with real convicted felons. Just like the constant homeless tactic, it would have me start from scratch and steal everything I own, along with the stealing of my son. This person all of a sudden hates me more than she loves her son, an underweight nearly 3-year-old child. I was the only person who could feed him and had the patience to do so.

I spent every day with him while she was disinterested, and I wouldn't regret a moment. I was haunted many years back by the abortion I should have never had, a dumb move from a younger, ignorant me, which makes me cherish every moment of playing hide and seek or feeding my son rather than scrolling through some junk news feed.

My guess is that she was trying to pander to the probability of white police and court workers, being that we live in Ireland. Maybe they'll hate Islamic terrorists, maybe they'll slam the hammer down and give me ten years in prison. This came to court which they postponed again and again to the point it's a year and a half gone.

With arrangements put as supervised access to see the child, she was present and one time we were at a child's playground. I was going to leave, and mentioned to her the baby needs to see a dietician and he needs to eat solid food. The baby was going on two and a half with a diet of breast milk and yoghurt. I said have a good weekend and did mention I'm here for any help if you need to seek help yourself we will work through it. As I was leaving the child rushes over, not letting me leave, so I carry him and tell him I love him and miss him.

At the other end of the playground I notice my ex with her head tilted as if she was on the phone. Not talking, just listening to some quite whispering.

I approach to give the baby back and leave, and she starts moving away, glaring at me. She then suddenly said, "Stop following me," and I looked and said, "What?". She then just stayed quiet- after looking at her and assessing the situation; I knew this was a weird interaction, even for her. I handed her the baby, remained quiet, waved, and the baby watched me leave. I had the inkling it was the police she was speaking to but was slightly unconcerned as nothing happened. She is a bad actor unlike some other people with cluster B. Whatever she mentioned on the phone was completely liberating for me as we were in public; nothing happened, and to top it off, it was an obvious joke like-call.

There was no arguing or shouting, no nothing, I was heard on this call saying peacefully and in shock, "Here's the baby", while she was trying to make it look like something it wasn't. As I leave, I see police cars coming in and out. I'm on a bus leaving, but surely it's not for me. If it is well, that's great; there are plenty of witnesses, not to mention the CCTV. They can replay the prank-like call and piece things together and use their discernment right?

The answer is no, incompetent police don't care. They knocked on every door associated with me, looking for me for over a week.

More police harassment ensued; I was getting charged, and the charge sheet wasn't even a full sentence. The charge read that I said the baby looked malnourished, and that put her in fear. I was told to hand myself in, which I did; not one police officer bothered to do their job. Treated like a criminal, with my fingerprints and picture taken and a search. Questions such as Do you have tattoos? And do you have any response to the charges? I nearly had a panic attack, my heart was just in shock. I could hardly think straight, staring at nothingness with no response.

Later that same day, this officer would mention my unresponsiveness after being put in a holding cell with real criminals who were waiting to get sentenced for years for their crimes. It was my turn to see the judge. I heard this policeman read out to the judge my so-called charges. He mentions, "Your honour, the accused had no response when I read out the charges". They agreed to punish me and put me on bail, forcing me to sign on at the police station in Store Street Garda Station, Dublin, twice a week, every Monday and Friday.

The times were 9 am to 9 pm, and should the signing-on be missed, there was a warrant out for arrest. Signing on is appearing at that police station on the days and times mentioned to put your signature on a big registry bail book. They purposely leave you waiting around, and the number of people at the stations is ridiculous. They are overloaded with cases granted so many real cases, but in a case like mine, I often wondered how many people were suffering at the hands of a fake case.

She would use the parental alienation tactic for the next few weeks until after court. I moved into my new apartment, I shared imagery of it online briefly before the court case. When a court hearing came, she was piercing through me, staring at me with a demonic stare. It was uncomfortable; minutes and minutes went by, and still this woman was staring like a piece of her soul was snatched. She hated that anything fortunate happened in my life. She spent so much time and energy beating me down, keeping me homeless, keeping me arrested, and throwing everything she could to derail any balance in my life; balance and equilibrium are what these personality disorders cannot bond with.

It is a threat to their existence, in her mind. Unless I'm on skid row, homeless or incarcerated, there is no way I would ever need to take her back. Alternatively, do I need to get what I deserve for causing this narcissistic injury in the first place? As I am the target of blame.

The court date arrived, which I knew in advance was going to be adjourned for another few months. The section 32 report was not done, which is needed for access and guardianship. I was in the pursuit of legal guardianship through the court, even though I was an automatic guardian. In Ireland, if you live with the mother and baby for the first 12 months, you are considered the guardian, which I did. I lived with her since mid-2021, stayed with her throughout the pregnancy, and took care of her and the baby. She lied in court to give me the run-around, claiming I never lived there and it was an on-and-off arrangement.

A quick search online gave her that tactic, and she used everything she possibly could, utilising the head start she had on me when it came to family court.

We all entered the courtroom, both of us, with our lawyers, or solicitors as it is referred to in Ireland. The woman judge, who was in her late fifties, got each request from the parties involved. On one hand, was my guardianship on the other her maintenance or alimony? She wanted one hundred and fifty euros each week for the maintenance but rejected any guardianship. The judge seemed stern and refuted, "I am not refusing his guardianship request and processing her maintenance order". With "what reasoning", the baffled judge put to her solicitor. As I turned to look over my ex was making accusations of drugs without specifying a drug.

The judge then said, "To deny access or guardianship, I need an extreme reason", and then directed everybody to come back in 40 minutes with this extreme reason. I wait in the hallway of the court and return with my solicitor at the 40-minute mark. A few minutes later, my ex and her solicitor arrive, and her solicitor, bright red-faced, begins to speak.

The solicitor mentioned to the judge about me, "Your honour, this is a highly unusual case" about to break the news of this extreme reason which enforces parental alienation. She says "he's a Terrorist member, a Jihadi Islamic extremist".

After hearing this, the judge stated, "You only found this out now, within the last few minutes", talked over her solicitor, and was quite annoyed that her intelligence was insulted. As of now, the judge has a terrorist member on trial here in family court, which is quite ridiculous.

A jihadi terrorist member she was looking to swindle 150 euro each week from; this payment is 50 euro per week per child in Ireland. The judge followed up by saying once or twice, "I find this very peculiar", The case was deliberated for another few months. I couldn't bear to see my son anymore; these past few months petrified me of what my ex might do or say next. The judge didn't look my way once that day, she was fixated on my ex and her solicitor. I was even nodding as she said some liberating things, seemingly seen through the manure she was being spoon-fed.

Unfortunately, I was soon exposed to the inner workings of a clown court. These courts keep delaying cases, and they don't make notes or have the same judges.

I would have preferred to have the same judge or at least had her highlight some of the odd behaviour she just witnessed. She could see through the veil. Why not make a note of it and eradicate innocent people who are going to court for no good reason? I felt liberated coming out of court, and I was more enthusiastic about the case, thinking every case would start to sway in the same direction.

This is not as liberating as one would expect because if I feel like the narrative of this case is swaying, so is my ex. Remember, Borderlines and Narcissists are very good at picking up subtle cues and are in tune with the energy around them. They can be quite ahead in terms of scanning what's going on right now and what may happen. I thought if this woman picks up any bit of emotional feedback that her accusations are starting to fail, she'll soon make a move. She will pretend something was said or fake an incident when I see my son, as a way to bring the focus off the changing narrative. If she can create an event or another allegation, pretend I said something dangerous, and then this will overshadow and cement the previous allegations.

Then, after weeks of supervised access, days in which she would conveniently drop something or get something out of a pram or bag. She would be bending over in front of me in a delayed posture, glancing back at me. This obvious flirting with other types of flirting consisted throughout, such as rubbing up against me or touching my arm or leg briefly, which had me freeze; it made me sick to my stomach. This person is bringing police and judges into my life, and now she's acting like this. I never took the bait or tried to mend things with her. We began to talk more at the visits, keeping things amicable. Then, at the start of one visit, she was saying something about the past, and I mentioned, "Would you have preferred another baby?". As in; with all this mess looking back on it, would you have preferred that outcome, not thinking much of what I just said? She was just quiet.

The word Baby seems to be a trigger to her. Nearly two hours pass, and everything is normal, She is quiet, but it seems normal. We go to a halal restaurant, I get the baby a kid's meal to let him play around with chips and red sauce and teach him how to chew. In hindsight, I probably should have asked her if she wanted anything to eat, but I didn't. I notice two police officers walk by the window and think nothing of it. Then, roughly five minutes later, she is on the phone, speaking low.

She abruptly leaves and is gone for a considerable amount of time, at least twenty-five minutes. I was wondering what the matter was but was enjoying eating chips with my estranged son. Then, she enters the restaurant with two of the police officers. This would be another arrest, now in an embarrassing public place, full of people who can see nothing happened. I went outside with the police officers, they said they would have to place me under arrest. This charge sheet would read that I mentioned the word "Baby". While I was outside, I became argumentative with the police, but in a socially appropriate way; as nothing happened; then she came out. Who runs up to me and hugs me? My son, so I pick him up as he glances at the police officers. He will remember this stupid situation, an unnecessary and unproductive situation that tarnishes his upbringing.

They brought me to the station, and shipped me in the police van to the criminal court. The same rigmarole, pictures, fingerprints and any words. I was more vocal this time, and I mentioned the terrorism case and false allegations. Then they placed me in a filthy cell with other prisoners who are facing lengthy prison sentences; I find myself rubbing elbows again with people that I shouldn't be. Moved to another cell, waiting and waiting with prisoner after prisoner entering the cell.

They could have locked me up for a couple of months for breaching a protection order twice and for uttering the word baby. They then brought me to the criminal courtroom, where I was quite vocal, speaking my truth even though I was supposed to just listen to the judge and not do any talking.

I couldn't help myself; I was being bullied and harassed using this system; I had to be vocal. I mentioned the terrorism and the "baby looks malnourished" charge, and some of what's happening because I know now these solicitors will not speak up for you. These courts don't care about justice or fabricated cases. Then the woman judge gave me another court date to go to, and I was happy to be seeing the back of that criminal court. I have never been in trouble with the law or visited courts in my life, this is the relationship that Cluster B offers.

As I was leaving the criminal court, a solicitor was waiting outside for me. He mentioned I have seen you in there. I want to take this criminal case for you. He gave me his card and was shocked at some of the things I mentioned; it was almost as if he knew it was true, as if he could feel it, or perhaps he is exposed to these types of cases frequently.

I left and immediately got back to writing the book and listening to people's stories. This helped me get through some of my own-latent torment. Helping others is my main goal. I also want to become an advocate for false allegations and parental alienation. The alienation continues; I am being forced not to see my child for fear of more charges. The punishment cycle continues with no sign of it ever ceasing.

All of these court cases are still pending;

This entire drama with her has been the catalyst for this book; I am petrified of her. I know that this intense anger wants to see me dead, in prison or living in a hellish environment. During the making of this book, I have been subject to harassment by the police and by the court system. With ridiculous unfounded false allegations that insinuated I was a terrorist Jihadi member.

I am a loving father and was a loving husband before the BPD got too out of control, and I was punished constantly for existing. I have been left juggling so many police reports, and have visited so many courts, the family court and the criminal court. I have been put in the back of police vans, awaiting a sentence over nothing, just her pretending I breached an erroneous court order. I don't feel safe seeing my child or being around her. It is so intimidating, and on top of that, I am in a box. Nobody cares, not the police or the courts.

I have been harassed for a year and a half; harassed by the police; harassed by each fake court order; and intimidated through these means. Any person who has faced these predicaments will attest to the fact that this life situation is, Creepy.

I am in that much danger, I am boxed into a corner that much, under these unjust circumstances; with the foot never coming off the gas; that I need to be in the public eye.

I need to be a figure in the public domain, I need to be an Author, I need to fight this fight and inspire others and most importantly, I need to inspire change.

I dedicate this book to you, Aayan and promise I will try to make children's books. Preferably mirroring the topics discussed in this book, to make sense of this ineffable situation for parents having trouble explaining why they aren't seeing their children.

I will continue the fight for people around the world who are falsely accused, personally vet their stories and do everything in my power to bring this message to the public stratosphere invoking change and justice. With help from other Creators, Authors, teachers and those who will join this fight in the near future; We will highlight injustice and bring it centre stage into the court of public opinion!

This person needs medication, DBT therapy and a prayer, I could never be comfortable around this person again. It is highly unlikely therapy will ever happen, although I do hope it happens and wish her all the best regarding her mental health.

I work from home. When I am not writing, I work in an insurance job. Every holiday or annual leave days I take off work are spread out, for the multiple family and criminal court dates and adjournments. Once I get paid my salary, I save. Instead of buying the new TV or the new couch, I have to save. The reason for this is that I need backup money for future arrests. I need bail money or money for possible incarceration.

I am being put through a campaign of this harassment that will inevitably never cease.

In my mind, I have seen so many police within the last year and a half, seen so many judges or cells, that it is only a matter of time before I am locked up in prison. The money that I save each month, would be for bills and rent back up to keep in my account. That way, if I do get a six or eight-month sentence, for example, for a false allegation, money will be deducted from my account for the rent each month. This would be to keep the property as I believe that is also one of her triggers. Then, when I get released from prison, I get to go home instead of being homeless again.

These people desire the visual of you incarcerated, as this will result in the loss of so many things. For me, it would be my home, my job, my safety, well-being and so on. She already took my child, which I will fight for the rest of my life for. I will pursue social services and these easily exploitable family courts for years to come.

This epiphany in 2015 to write a book was not followed by Procrastination as such, but rather a lack of desire or an it-can-wait type attitude. It was highly unlikely ever to happen. In hindsight, Now; I get to help people all around the world and challenge areas of much-needed improvement in this day and age. This is the right side of history and I look forward to writing more and advocating against the systematic abuse that is littered throughout this book.

None of this would be possible unless my back was against the wall; Escape is futile, so much so that I have to be in the public eye, I have to be seen or heard. I feel so much safer in the public eye. This situation has scarred me for life. The feeling of being boxed in, surrounded by situational attacks, helpless, defenceless, voiceless; This has inspired me to advocate for this cause, as there are so many others who are trying to make sense of it.

REFERENCES

Alexander L. Chapman, Ph.D. Kim L. Gratz, Ph.D. The Borderline Personality Disorder Survival Guide Everything You Need To Know About Living With BPD, 2007

American Psychiatric Association. Diagnostic and Statistical Manual of Mental Disorders: DSM-5. 5. Washington: American Psychiatric Publishing; 2013.

Ann Johnson, Frank Parlato, et.al,2023 Low Standard of Evidence in Abuse Claims Exploited in "Silver Bullet Divorce" Trend (12th April) available at https://frankreport.com/2023/04/12/low-standard-of-evidence-in-abuse-claims-exploited-in-silver-bullet-divorce-trend/

Baer RA, Sauer SE. Relationships between depressive rumination, anger rumination, and borderline personality features. Personality Disorders: Theory, Research, and Treatment. 2011;2:142–50.

Beyond Borderline True Stories Of Recovery From Borderline Personality Disorder. John G Gundeson , Perry D Hoffman 2016

Bill Eddy, 5 Types of People Who Can Ruin Your Life: Identifying and Dealing with Narcissists, Sociopaths, and Other High-Conflict Personalities, Penguin Publishing Group, ISBN 9780143131366 page 25 (2018)

Bill Eddy, 5 Types of People Who Can Ruin Your Life: Identifying and Dealing with Narcissists, Sociopaths, and Other High-Conflict Personalities, Penguin Publishing Group ISBN 9780143131366 page 14 (2018)

Blackburn R; Psychopathy and personality disorders, in psychopathy; theory, research and implications for society, edited by Cooke DJ, Forth AE, Hare RD. Dordrecht; Kluwer academic publishers, 1998, pp 257-68

British Broadcasting Corporation BBC 28th March 2019 accessed June 2024 source link https://www.bbc.com/news/uk-england-london-47738892

Bursten, B. (1972). The manipulative personality. Archives of General Psychiatry, 26, 318–321

Cafcass, New Domestic Abuse Practice Policy, Published: 9 October 2024 accessed March 2025; https://www.cafcass.gov.uk/cafcass-publishes-new-domestic-abuse-practice-policy.

Candini V, Ghisi M, Bottesi G, Ferrari C, et al. Personality, Schizophrenia, and Violence: A Longitudinal Study. J Pers Disord. 2018 Aug;32(4):465–481. doi: 10.1521/pedi_2017_31_304.

Carole Doré Remove Blockages Qz 02-2 Blockages 2:1-5,03:00

Carole Doré Male/Female Integration Workshop Class 6 part 3 - 24/25 minutes, 2011

Child Well-Being in Single-Parent Families (blog) The Annie E. Casey Foundation 2022 https://www.aecf.org/blog/child-well-being-in-single-parent-families accessed on 15/10/24

Chris Baynes,The Independent 3rd July 2018 accessed June 2024 source https://www.independent.co.uk/news/uk/crime/westminster-pa

edophile-ring-accuser-nick-charged-perverting-course-justice-fraud-chid-sexual-abuse-a8428781.html

Crocq MA. Milestones in the history of personality disorders. Dialogues Clin Neurosci. 2013 June;15(2):147-53.

De Brito SA, Viding E, Kumari V, Blackwood N, Hodgins S. Cool and hot executive function impairments in violent offenders with antisocial personality disorder with and without psychopathy. *PLoS One*. 2013;8(6):e65566. doi:10.1371/journal.pone.0065566

Decleene, C. (2016). Teen Dating Violence in the United States. Encyclopedia of Family Studies. https://doi.org/10.1002/9781119085621.wbefs375

DePaulo, B. M., Kashy, D. A., Kirkendol, S. E., Wyer, M. M., and Epstein, J. A. (1996) 'Lying in Everyday Life', Journal of Personality and Social Psychology, 70(5): 979–95.

Diagram - Selby et al. (2009) J Abnormal PSY J

Dolores Mosquera, Kathy Steele. Complex trauma, dissociation and Borderline Personality Disorder: Working with integration failures 2017

Donald W. Black, M.D.Nathan J. Kolla, M.D., Ph.D., FRCPC , Peter Tyrer, M.D.Alireza Farnam, M.D,Alireza Zahmatkesh, M.D.Rahil Sanatinia, M.D., Ph.D. Classification and Definition of Antisocial Personality Disorder (Textbook Of Antisocial Personality Disorder) World Health Organisation ICD manual chart page 11 (2022)

Dr. Tara J. Palmatier, Narcissists Don't Feel Grief—They Feel Aggrieved—in High-Conflict Divorce; 2024 source https://mail.hostinger.com/?_task=mail&_action=get&_mbox=INBOX&_uid=68&_token=XPk8UxYq94pnzen137rEcTgUZHNvN6dd&_part=8 accessed Sep 2024;

Dr. Tara J. Palmatier, PsyD, Shrink 4 Men, Why Are Narcissists and Borderlines Like Amber Heard Such Convincing Liars? Understanding False Abuse Allegations (2024)

Dr Phil: Family Courts Are Failing America's Children | Dr Phil Primetime 2024 Accessed on july 2024 https://www.youtube.com/watch?v=IsLbeaJ-_O0&t=310s

Duffin, C. (2013) 'Woman Who Made a String of False Rape Allegations Is Jailed', Telegraph, 9 July. Available online at <http://www.telegraph.co.uk/news/uknews/wales/10169257/Woman-who-made-a-string-of-false-rape-allegations-is-jailed.html> accessed May 2024.

Eckhart Tolle The Power of Now: A Guide to Spiritual Enlightenment (1997)

Ekselius L. Personality-disorder; A disease in disguise. Ups J Med Sci (2018); 123(4);194-204

Esbec E, Echeburúa E. Violence and personality disorders: clinical and forensic implications. Actas Esp Psiquiatr. 2010 Sep-Oct;38(5):249–61. English, Spanish.

Esbec E, Echeburúa E. Violence and personality disorders: clinical and forensic implications. Actas Esp Psiquiatr. 2010 Sep-Oct;38(5):249–61. English, Spanish.

Esterberg ML, Goulding SM, Walker EF. Cluster A Personality Disorders: Schizotypal, Schizoid and Paranoid Personality Disorders in Childhood and Adolescence. J Psychopathol Behav Assess. 2010 Dec 01;32(4):515-528.

Felicity Goodyear Smith, why and how false allegations of abuse occur An Overview, page 107, 2016

Frank Parlato, et.al,2023 CT Family Court Uses and Abuses Parental Alienation – Ask Luigi DiRubba, March 16, 2023 Available at
https://frankreport.com/2023/03/16/ct-family-court-uses-and-abuses-parental-alienation-ask-luigi-dirubba/

Gabay, R., Hameiri, B., Rubel-Lifschitz, T., & Nadler, A. (2020). The tendency for interpersonal victimhood: The personality construct and its consequences. Personality and Individual Differences, 165(110134), 1-11.

Gabay, R., Hameiri, B., Rubel-Lifschitz, T., & Nadler, A. (2020). The tendency for interpersonal victimhood: The personality construct and its consequences. Personality and Individual Differences, 165(110134), 1-11.
https://gwern.net/doc/psychology/personality/2020-gabay.pdf

Galit Nahari, Advances in lie detection Limitations and Potential for Investigating Allegations of Abuse chapter 18, (2016)

Grant BF, Chou SP, Goldstein RB, et al. Prevalence, correlates, disability, and comorbidity of DSM-IV borderline personality disorder: Results from the Wave 2 National Epidemiologic Survey on Alcohol and Related Conditions. J Clin Psychiatry. 2008;69(4):533-545. doi:10.4088/JCP.v69n0404

Gunderson JG, Phillips KA. A current view of the interface between borderline personality disorder and depression. Am J Psychiatry. 1991;148:967–75.

Harned, M. S., & Korslund, K. E. (2015). Treating PTSD and borderline personality disorder. In U. Schnyder & M. Cloitre (Eds.), *Evidence-based treatments for trauma-related psychological disorders: A practical guide for clinicians* (pp. 331–346). Springer International Publishing/Springer Nature.
https://doi.org/10.1007/978-3-319-07109-1_17

James F. Masterson MD, The Narcissistic and Borderline Disorders page 12, 9780203776148 1981

J Halliday, B Quinn, J Elgot The Guardian 2015 accessed May 2024 source link
https://www.theguardian.com/society/2015/sep/21/met-admits-mistakes-in-westminster-paedophile-ring-inquiry

Joan Coleman, Attachment, Trauma, and Multiplicity, Working with Dissociative Identity Disorder 2002

Johnson JG, Cohen P, Smailes E, et al. Adolescent personality disorders associated with violence and criminal behaviour during adolescence and early adulthood. Am J Psychiatry 157;1406-12, 2000

Judge Judy Sheindlin, Josh Getlin, Don't Pee On My Leg And Tell Me Its Raining, chapter 6, page 150, 1997

Judge Judy Sheindlin, Josh Getlin, Don't Pee On My Leg And Tell Me Its Raining, chapter 6, page 177, 1997

Judge Judy Sheindlin, Josh Getlin, Don't Pee On My Leg And Tell Me Its Raining, chapter 6, page 178, 1997

Kanin, Eugene J. (February 1994). "False Rape Allegations" (PDF). *Archives of Sexual Behavior*. 23 (1): 81–92. doi:10.1007/bf01541619. PMID 8135653. S2CID 6880191. Archived from the original (PDF) on 3 March 2016.

Ken Alltucker USA TODAY July 17, 2023 (accessed on 20/05/23)
https://www.usatoday.com/story/news/nation/2023/07/17/child-deaths-during-custody-battles/70383774007/

Krista Jordan, PhD
https://www.choosingtherapy.com/bpd-quotes/ 2023 (accessed July 2024)

Lang PJ, Bradley MM. Appetitive and Defensive Motivation: Goal-Directed or Goal-Determined? Emot Rev. 2013 Jul;5(3):230-234.doi:10.1177/1754073913477511. PMID: 24077330; PMCID: PMC3784012.

LeanIn.org/SurveyMonkey,online-poll-February 22-March 1, 2019

Lee YJ, Keum MS, Kim HG, Cheon EJ, Cho YC, Koo BH. Defense Mechanisms and Psychological Characteristics According to Suicide Attempts in Patients with Borderline Personality Disorder. Psychiatry Investig. 2020 Aug;17(8):840-849.

Lenzenweger, M. F., Clarkin, J. F., Fertuck, E. A., & Kernberg, O. F. 2004. Executive neurocognitive functioning and neurobehavioral systems indicators in borderline personality disorder: A preliminary study. Journal of Personality Disorders, 18, 421– 438.

Levine, D., Marziali, E., & Hood, J. 1997. Emotion processing in borderline personality disorders. The Journal of Nervous and Mental Disease, 20, 240–246.

Lewis L, Appleby L. Personality disorder: The patients psychiatrists dislike. Br J Psychiatry. 1988;153:44–9

Linehan, M. M. (1993). Cognitive–behavioural treatment of borderline personality disorder. New York: Guilford Press.

Live 5 Web Staff April 13th 2021 Live5News accessed May 2024 source link https://www.live5news.com/2021/04/13/deputies-arrest-woman-accused-filing-false-report-home-invasion-assault/

Lonsway, K. A., Archambault, J., & Berkowitz, A. (2018). False reports: Moving beyond the issue to successful investigate and prosecute non-stranger sexual assault (Updated September 2018). End Violence Against Women International OnLine Training Institute (OLTI)

Marsha Linehan, NAMI, Understanding Borderline Personality Disorder | NAMI: National Alliance On Mental Illness". *Nami.Org*, 2021, https://www.nami.org/Blogs/NAMI-Blog/June-2017/Understanding-Borderline-Personality-Disorder.

Mason P, Kreger R. Stop walking on eggshells, taking your life back when someone you love has borderline personality disorder- updated third edition 2020

Massaal-van der Ree LY, Eikelenboom M, Hoogendoorn AW, Thomaes K, van Marle HJF. Cluster B versus Cluster C Personality Disorders: A Comparison of Comorbidity, Suicidality, Traumatization and Global Functioning. Behav Sci (Basel). 2022 Apr 12;12(4)

Mateus C, Campis R, Aguaded I, Parody A, Ruiz F. Analysis of personality traits and academic performance in higher education at a Colombian university. Heliyon. 2021 May 11;7(5):e06998. doi: 10.1016/j.heliyon.2021.e06998.

McMillan, L. (2018). Police officers' perceptions of false accusations of rape. Journal of Gender Studies, 27(1),9–21.

Mennin DS. Emotion regulation therapy for generalized anxiety disorder. Clinical Psychology & Psychotherapy. 2004;11(1):17–

Millon, Theodore, Seth Greossman Carrie Millon Sarah Meagher Rowena Ramnath (2004). Personality Disorders in Modern Life. Hoboken, New Jersey: John Wiley & Sons, Inc. ISBN 0-471-23734-5.

Millon, Theodore, Seth Greossman Carrie Millon Sarah Meagher Rowena Ramnath (2004). Personality Disorders in Modern Life. Hoboken, New Jersey: John Wiley & Sons, Inc. ISBN 0-471-23734-5. Diagram page 297

Millon, Theodore, Seth Greossman Carrie Millon Sarah Meagher Rowena Ramnath (2004). Personality Disorders in Modern Life. Hoboken, New Jersey: John Wiley & Sons, Inc. ISBN 0-471-23734-5. Pg 355

Monaghan C, Bizumic B. Dimensional models of personality disorders: Challenges and opportunities. Front Psychiatry. 2023;14:1098452.(cluster a/b/c)

Novais F, Araújo A, Godinho P. Historical roots of histrionic personality disorder. Front Psychol. 2015;6:1463.

Paris J. (The nature of borderline personality disorder: Multiple symptoms, multiple dimensions, but one category. *J Personality Disorders.* In Press.2007)

Pepper CM, Klein DN, Anderson RL, et al. DSM-III-R Axis II comorbidity in dysthymia and major depression. Am J Psychiatry. 1995;152:239–47 9

Peters JR, Eisenlohr-Moul TA, Upton BT, Talavera NA, Folsom JJ, Baer RA. Characteristics of repetitive thought associated with borderline personality features: a multimodal investigation of ruminative content and style. J Psychopathol Behav Assess. 2017;39:456–66.

Quieting the Affective Storm of Borderline Personality Disorder, The American journal of psychiatry. 166. 522-8. 10.1176/2009(Siever,LJ, Antonia N, Goodman,M,Et al,2009)

Quieting the Affective Storm of Borderline Personality Disorder - Scientific Figure on ResearchGate. Available from: https://www.researchgate.net/figure/Subjective-Ratings-of-Unpleasant-Neutral-and-Pleasant-Pictures-a_fig2_24397942 [accessed 5 Aug 2024]

Ramani Durvasula, Should I Stay or Should I Go? surviving a relationship with a narcissist 2015

Ramani Durvasula Should I Stay or Should I Go? surviving a relationship with a narcissist 2015

Robins LN, Regier DA; Psychiatric disorder in America, New York; The free press,1991

Rula Odeh Alsawalqa. Is the sociopath socially intelligent? A new framework for understanding sociopathy Page,7 (2019)

Samuels J, Eaton WW, Bienvenu J, Clayton P, Brown H, Costa PT, et al. Prevalence and correlates of personality disorders in a community sample. Br J Psychiatry 2002;180:536-42.

Sandra Newman (11 May 2017). "What kind of person makes false rape accusations?". *Quartz*. Archived from the original on 5 April 2019. Retrieved 2 December 2024.

Scafidi, B. The Taxpayer Costs of Divorce and Unwed Childbearing First-Ever Estimates for the Nation and All Fifty States,2008

Scafidi, B. The Taxpayer Costs of Divorce and Unwed Childbearing First-Ever Estimates for the Nation and All Fifty States,page9,2008

Selby EA, Anestis MD, Joiner TE. Understanding the relationship between emotional and behavioural dysregulation: Emotional Cascades. Behaviour Research and Therapy. 2008;46:593–611.

Seth Meyers, The Disturbing Link Between Narcissism and Sadism; What drives a troubling narcissistic subtype, and how to recognize it? July 2016, accessed March 2025, source: https://www.psychologytoday.com/ie/blog/insight-is-2020/201607/the-disturbing-link-between-narcissism-and-sadism

Shapiro D. Theoretical reflections on Wilhelm Reich's Character Analysis. Am J Psychother. 2002;56(3):338-46.

Sheryl Sandberg, P&G's Marc Pritchard LeanIn.Org and SurveyMonkey
https://leanin.org/sexual-harassment-backlash-survey-results#endnote1

Shiner, M., Scourfield, J., Fincham, B., & Langer, S. (2009). When things fall apart: Gender and suicide across the life-course. Social Science & Medicine, 69(5), 738-746. https://doi.org/10.1016/j.socscimed.2009.06.014

Skodol AE, Gunderson JG, Pfohl B, Widiger TA, Livesley WJ, Siever LJ. The borderline diagnosis. I: Psychopathology, comorbidity, and personality structure. Biol-Psychiatry 2002;51:936-50

Stepfamily Statistics - Smart Stepfamilies.
https://smartstepfamilies.com/smart-help/marriage-family-stepfamily-statistics

Stern, A. (1938). Borderline group of neuroses. *The Psychoanalytic Quarterly, 7,* 467–489.

Sullivan. (2019). Divorce is a risk factor for suicide, especially for men. Psychology Today. Retrieved from https://www.psychologytoday.com/blog/acquainted-the-night/201906/divorce-is-risk-factor- suicide-especially-me

Tackett JL, Silberschmidt AL, Krueger RF, Sponheim SR. A dimensional model of personality disorder: incorporating DSM Cluster A characteristics. J Abnorm Psychol. 2008 May;117(2):454-9.

Telegraph Reporters (2012) 'Nanny Jailed for Crying Rape after One-night Stand', The Telegraph, 21 November. Available online at <http://www.telegraph.co.uk/news/uknews/ accessed May 2024.

The borderline personality disorder survival guide, Everything You Need to Know about living with BPD, chapter 1 - Alexander Chapman PhD, Kim L Gradz PhD 2021

The Borderline Personality Disorder Survival Guide Everything you need to know about living with BPD, Alexander L. Chapman, PhD. Kim L. Gratz, ph.d. 2007

The Chaos That Borderline Personality Can Generate Borderline personality disorder cuts a wide swath of destruction. Slowly, the condition is yielding to new understanding; provided patients get the correct diagnosis. By Elizabeth Svoboda, published September 2, 2013 - accessed on February 2025
https://www.psychologytoday.com/ie/articles/201309/the-chaos-borderline-personality-disorder-can-cause

The National Registry of Exonerations, website source https://www.law.umich.edu/special/exoneration/Documents/Exonerations_in_2019_Infographic.pdf 2019 accessed 01/06/24

Theodore Millon, Seth Grossman, Carrie Millon, Sarah Meagher, Rowena Ramnath. Personality Disorders in Modern Life, page 478, 2nd edition Ed Theodore Millon

Theodore Millon, Seth Grossman, Carrie Millon, Sarah Meagher, Rowena Ramnath. Personality Disorders in Modern Life, page 478, 2nd edition Ed Theodore Millon

Theodore Millon, Seth Grossman, Carrie Millon, Sarah Meagher, Rowena Ramnath. Personality Disorders in Modern Life, page 498 2nd edition Ed Theodore Millon

Theodore Millon, Seth Grossman, Carrie Millon, Sarah Meagher, Rowena Ramnath. Personality Disorders in Modern Life, page 500 2nd edition Ed Theodore Millon

Time: The Kalief Browder Story 2017 · Documentary · 1 season Netflix
https://www.littlebookofjohn.com/quotes/m/miscarriages-of-justice-browder-kalief

Torgersen S, Kringlen E, Cramer V. The prevalence of personality disorders in a community sample. Arch Gen Psychiatry 2001;58:590-6

True Crime Central, 2024 March 16th, I Am Not A Rapist | Devastating consequences of False Allegations [video] source video youtube https://www.youtube.com/watch?v=5a0-85Wdf_w accessed March 2025

Turner D, Sebastian A, Tüscher O. Impulsivity and Cluster B Personality Disorders. Curr Psychiatry Rep. 2017 Mar;19(3):15.

Vannikov-Lugassi M, Shalev H, Soffer-Dudek N. From brooding to detachment: Rumination longitudinally predicts an increase in depersonalization and derealization. Psychol

Psychother. 2021 Apr;94 Suppl 2:321-338. doi: 10.1111/papt.12279. Epub 2020 Apr 25. PMID: 32333727

Vrij, A., Granhag, P. A., and Porter, S. B. (2010) 'Pitfalls and Opportunities in Nonverbal and Verbal Lie Detection', Psychological Science in the Public Interest, 11(3): 89–121.

Wakefield, H., & Underwager, R. (1990). Personality Characteristics of Parents Making False Accusations of Sexual Abuse in Custody Disputes. Issues In Child Abuse Accusations, 2(3), 121-136.

Whitbourne, S K, Why People with Borderline Personality Can be So Hard to Please -Psychology Today 2018)

Zanarini, M. C., Frankenburg, F. R., DeLuca, C. J., Hennen, J., Khera, G. S., & Gunderson, J. ~1998!. The pain of being borderline: Dysphoric states specific to borderline personality disorder. Harvard Review of Psychiatry, 6, 201–207.

Zanarini, M.C., Ruser, T., Frankenburg, F.R., & Hennen, J. (2000). The dissociative experiences of borderline patients. Comprehensive Psychiatry, 41(3), 223–227. doi: 10.1016/S0010-440X(00)90051-8

Zepezauer, F. S. Believe her! The woman never lies myth. (1994)

Zimmerman M, Mattia JI. Differences between clinical and research practices in diagnosing borderline personality disorder. Am J Psychiatry. 1999;156:1570–4

Collaborate with Due Process

Are you a writer? Do you have a passion for writing?

Do you have a background in law, psychology, psychiatry or exonerating victims of crimes they did not commit?

Are you a content creator, or do you run a website or blog?

Are you a Narcissistic abuse survivor, or are you a self-aware Cluster B content creator?

Has family life led to being a Parental Alienation/Exploitable Family-Court Speaker?

Are you an Alienated Child content creator?

Books, Seminars, Talks, Exonerations: Due Process would like to reach out an invite to any group, company or individual for possible future work, collaborations on projects, or even just to keep in touch regarding these issues; We share a common goal. Here, we believe there is no competition. Not in this field. This is right and wrong, good and evil, victim and abuser.

We support other creators; we extend the olive branch, so feel free to write to us and stay in our line of contact. This could be future work together or sharing stories back and forth or policies, legislation etc. Help bring deceit, deception and incompetence into the court of public opinion.

admin@dueprocess.icu

Protected with www.protectmywork.com

Reference Number: 27824010425S028

© Copyright 2025 Ibraheem

All Rights Reserved.

www.ingramcontent.com/pod-product-compliance
Lightning Source LLC
LaVergne TN
LVHW091652070526
838199LV00050B/2152